STANLEY CAVELL'S
AMERICAN DREAM

Cary Grant and Eva Marie Saint in Alfred Hitchcock's *North by Northwest*.

LAWRENCE F. RHU

STANLEY CAVELL'S

American Dream

SHAKESPEARE, PHILOSOPHY,
AND HOLLYWOOD MOVIES

FORDHAM UNIVERSITY PRESS
New York / 2006

Copyright © 2006 by Fordham University Press

Library of Congress Cataloging-in-Publication Data

Rhu, Lawrence
    Stanley Cavell's American Dream: Shakespeare, Philosophy, and Hollywood Movies / by Lawrence Rhu.—1st ed.
        p.   cm.
    Includes bibliographical references.
    ISBN-13: 978-0-8232-2596-5 (hardcover : alk. paper)
    ISBN-10: 0-8232-2596-8 (hardcover : alk. paper)   1. Cavell, Stanley, 1926–   2. Shakespeare, William, 1564–1616.   3. Philosophy.   4. Motion pictures.   I. Title.
B945.C274R48   2006
191—dc22   2006007880

Printed in the United States of America
08 07 06   5 4 3 2 1
First edition

FOR SARAH AND DANNY

It is impossible to say why he is here. Is it part and parcel of the complex business of coming up in the world? Or is it because he believes that God himself is present here at the corner of Elysian Fields and Bons Enfants? Or is he here for both reasons: through some dim dazzling trick of grace: coming for the one and receiving the other as God's own importunate bonus?

It is impossible to say.

Walker Percy, *The Moviegoer*

Our words need not haunt us. If we learn how to entrust our meaning to a word, the weight it carries through all its computations will yet prove to be just the weight we will find we wish to give it.

Stanley Cavell, *The Senses of Walden*

CONTENTS

Acknowledgments   **xi**

Foreword   **xv**
   Stanley Cavell

Introduction: Beyond Adaptation   **1**

1. **Meeting Places**   **24**

2. **On Bloom and Cavell on Shakespeare**   **60**

3. **From Skepticism to Perfectionism**   **83**

4. **From Cyprus to Rushmore**   **105**

5. **Reading Cavell Reading *The Winter's Tale***   **136**

6. **Cavell's Rome**   **172**

Notes   **211**

Index   **241**

ACKNOWLEDGMENTS

*W*riting this book has been a journey with many pleasant surprises. My enthusiasm for Stanley Cavell's work proved impossible to resist despite what seemed the dictates of prudence and professionalism. One day I found myself writing an essay about Ariosto as a source in *Much Ado about Nothing,* where honesty required me to acknowledge in the footnotes repeated debts to Cavell's writings about Hollywood movies. What is going on here? I wondered to myself, and I was pretty much lost after that, overcome by skepticism and desire, both of which required an unavoidable reckoning. This book is my response to that moment and many others enough like it for me finally to learn how to acknowledge at least their family resemblance, the cycles of lostness and recovery that have moved me to think and write about Stanley Cavell.

I needed a lot of help in this effort, and help has come in abundance, often from unforeseeable sources. I met Stanley Cavell by playing hooky from my dissertation on Torquato Tasso and sitting in on his seminar about Hollywood melodrama. As he has helped me appreciate more deeply, thinking and thanking often go hand in hand; so, thanks again, Stanley Cavell. Institutions may or may not be the lengthened shadow of one man, as Emerson tells us, but you think for thousands and are a beacon of light. You prompt us to think for ourselves.

At my home institution Tom Brown, David Cowart, Martin Donougho, Scott Forster, George Geckle, Nina Levine, Steve Lynn, John McMichaels, David Miller, Mark Sibley-Jones, Meili Steele, Hans von Rautenfeld, and Laura Walls have all helped me move ahead with this project. Meili Steele, in particular, made me see it decisively as a book and kept me at the labor of realizing that vision with timely urging and warm intellectual friendship.

Christy Desmet and Robert Sawyer published an abbreviated version of Chapter Two in *Harold Bloom's Shakespeare,* and Robert Coles welcomed my suggestion of a piece on Cavell for *DoubleTake.*

Among Shakespeareans and Renaissance scholars, Daniel Javitch, Robert Knapp, Gail Paster, Richard Strier, and Richard Wheeler all helped me find or create occasions to share my work. Raphael Falco provided a salutary blast of constructive criticism.

Abraham Anderson, Sarah Beckwith, James Bense, Ralph Berry, Ron Hall, David Justin Hodge, John Lysaker, David Mikics, Toril Moi, William Rothman, and Charles Warren have all heard, or read, and commented upon either parts of this book in various stages of its creation or the whole of it in nearly final form. Ralph Berry's thoroughness, perspicuity, and candor have illuminated otherwise shady corners of my thinking. William Rothman and Charles Warren have frequently sped me along my way with understanding and good will always pertinent to my efforts. David Mikics has given so generously and intelligently of his attention that I am tempted to drift beyond gratitude into wonder at his willingness to help. It has been invaluable.

The NEH Emerson Institute at St. John's College in 2003, organized by Russell Goodman and Steven Affeldt, put me into many fruitful conversations not only about Emerson and Cavell but about Montaigne as well. John Tobin's invitation to edit *The Winter's Tale* for the Riverside Press made me enter the archive on that play more deeply and fruitfully than I would have otherwise.

While I was a Fulbright Lecturer in Lisbon, José Gonzalez, Rui Romão, Ana Soares, and Mirian Tavares all gave me Iberian opportunities to share my work, as did the Associação Portuguesa de Professores de Inglês. António Feijó and Miguel Tamen were my generous hosts at the University of Lisbon, as was João Bénard da Costa at the Cinemateca Portuguesa. The Cinemateca's two-week cycle of films, "Stanley Cavell e o Cinema Clássico Americano," memorably kicked off my seminar, The Availability of Philosophy in Film and Literature, in the Program in Literary Theory at the university. Among my students in that seminar, Teresa Bairos, Humberto Brito, and Maria Mendes created welcome opportunities for me to make some things clearer than I had previously managed, as did Steve Baarendse, Ellen Brightwell, and Graham Culbertson among my students at the University of South Carolina.

I revised this book pervasively during my semester in Lisbon. The challenges of Portuguese freshly heightened my awareness of both the limits and resources of intelligibility available through language. I also wondered anew at the idea of language as private property, which Steven Greenblatt feels he must warn us against entertaining. At times in Portugal, language seemed to belong to everybody but me, and that was not because I just happened to have my own private version, a chosen code that others could not crack. My inexpressiveness made my words sound less idiomatic than idiotic, but coming to grips with this recurrent challenge was a provocation to rediscover the felicity of the most everyday resources of speech in English and Portuguese, in body language and silence. How did philology and historicism, or text and context, ever come to seem at odds with one another for scholarly attention?

The *sine qua non* of this project, Karen Murphy, has made this writing possible for me by the pleasure of her company and the provision of circumstances conducive to such work. Our children, Sarah and Danny, have been the central care and delight of our lives during the last dozen years. I dedicate this book to them in hopes that they will have such teachers as I have been blessed to have. William Alfred and Robert Coles come instantly to mind in this regard, as does Stanley Cavell.

For our twenty-fifth reunion, my college classmates decided not to invite any of our teachers to address us. Rather, we would talk to each other via panels on such topics as Vietnam, Women's Liberation, Civil Rights, and Gay Liberation. These were interesting occasions, worthwhile in their way, and it was a pleasure to enjoy them with my friends and classmates. But over the past decades I have often had other things irresistibly in mind that such conversations can make inaudible. They are not merely private concerns nor do they require a private language, but the din of polemics can drown them out or so drain them of immediately apparent meaning as to produce illusions of their inconsequence. Disillusion is a good thing because it prepares us for reality; but, lest we should fall for the exclusive claims of any such bill of goods, I am grateful for Cavell's addendum to that maxim of his: we first need to know what our illusions are.

São João do Estoril, Portugal
May 2005

FOREWORD

*I*t is my impression that Lawrence Rhu is right in describing the bulk of writing that has been published about my work as tending to consider one or another of its fields or chapters (Austin, Wittgenstein, skepticism, Shakespeare, Emerson, film, etc.) in separation from the others, and so misses a bet (anyway, does not assess my own wager) that there is an impulse to integration or development (neither is the same thing as unity) in my work that is essential to its value, or to lines of thinking along which I have supposed its value might principally lie, and I am most grateful for his remarkable effort to venture a different course. He does, however, note that I myself have encouraged a certain idea of separation as fundamental to what I do when I insist that in tracing something I find to be philosophically pressing in, say, Shakespeare or film or Emerson, I mean to gain no philosophical advantage that is not rooted in, hence is often in competition with, a critical reading of texts (including films as instances) represented in, say, a selection from the past two centuries of Shakespeare criticism. At the same time, as Rhu also notes, I perhaps just as often feel free, having for some reason found myself stopped by a text (for example, by the thought that since Cordelia's initial words in *Lear* are twice an aside, hence not heard in her world and as if therefore overheard in ours, we are being prompted to ask what kind of hearing Shakespeare's singular texture invites; or by the thought that Austin's quoting Euripides' Greek near the opening of *How to Do Things with Words* is a signal that he senses his superb work on excuses to bear on the idea of tragedy) to follow my own lead in speculating further along the trail of such implications, or of what seem to me to constitute implications. Efforts to integrate a body of thought run the risk of reducing it to a settled, repetitive frame of concern. I am happy to report that I find no such result here, that on the contrary Rhu's sympathetic intelligence and his body of learning seem to me to introduce expansions or extensions of my texts of a most welcome kind, ones that lead him to further, surprising thoughts of his own, compliments to us both.

Rhu suggests on occasion that my turning somewhat from producing reasonably uncontroversial philosophical texts, which characteristically requires responding to other uncontroversially philosophical texts, and instead taking up philosophical hints in literature or in film, which I find to allow, perhaps to require, some amplification of what I want to call philosophy either in those texts or in my own, is caused by a wish to make my philosophizing more accessible to an audience beyond professional philosophy. I found that this idea took me by surprise, not as an aspiration but as an explanation. Much as I recognize myself to aspire to a further audience, and to a further understanding of what an audience for philosophy is, I had, I think, rather thought of myself as wanting to make philosophy more accessible to ranges of experience that the protocols of analytical philosophy, philosophy as I had mostly encountered it in my education, whether by accident or by necessity, and whether gladly or reluctantly, tended to rule out of order. But I think Rhu is right to put these aspirations for philosophy and for an audience for philosophy together. In coming to think of my desire for an opening to experience lost as calling for a further responsiveness from philosophy, I have also found myself proposing responsiveness to be the first virtue of philosophy. (Whatever dissatisfactions I sometimes express with John Dewey's philosophizing, I recognize my emphasis on philosophy's responsiveness as a direct and continuing effect of my early absorption in his writing.) Certainly the dispensation of Anglo-American philosophy has markedly extended and deepened its range of concerns since the days of my schooling in the subject, as the names, for example, of Hilary Putnam and John Rawls and Richard Rorty attest and as the array of interests among gifted younger philosophers, intersecting various forms of cultural studies, have gone on to prove. But the task, once known to be philosophy, of integrating human existence with human reflection on its existence is essentially unending, I would say essentially restless.

Such a task is in effect recalled in Rhu's connecting what I write with events and interests and conditions of my more extended life, most consistently with my life as a teacher. This is I suppose an unfashionable intellectual gesture at present but one I find congenial, indeed one that I

treasure, especially in relation to teaching. The gesture takes a certain
tact—there are modes of philosophizing in which to know the life of the
philosopher seems at a glance, however interesting certain details may
have become, more or less inessential to understanding the work (Aristotle, Saint Thomas, Leibniz, Hobbes, Locke, Hume, Kant, Carnap),
and modes in which at least curiosity about it is soon unavoidable, if
controversial (Plato, Saint Augustine, Montaigne, Pascal, Descartes,
Thoreau, Nietzsche, Heidegger, Wittgenstein). (With exceptions, those
whose lives seem most to impinge on their thinking are those whose
claim to philosophy can seem most questionable.) I think it is, as Rhu
finds, granted a certain interest in what I do, worth knowing, for example, that my fascination with Emerson and, differently, with Austin has in
each case probably been intensified by having been born to an immigrant
family. (Emerson because of his unassailable Americanness combined
with his insistence on change, on expanding the self's circle of experience; Austin because of his enviable sureness in and of English.) Rhu
establishes the decorum of such connections by introducing moments of
his own intellectual autobiography—for example, by taking turns and
juxtapositions of mine to prompt paths through his admirable expertise
in the history of literature, as in a small spectacle that I find particularly
heartening, when, having broached my conjunction of Milton and film,
Rhu cites the formidable Milton recommending the use, for the education of novices, of "arts most easy."

Inevitably, another's descriptions of one's life, as would likely be obvious in the case of another's descriptions or criticisms of one's parents or
one's children, can sometimes tend to make one defensive. I think of
Rhu's taking up the decisively important crisis it was for me in "giving
up" music and turning to a search for philosophy. He speaks of my discovering myself to be a "failed musician," a brief phrase summarizing
what was for me a multitude of doubts. What the brevity leaves out most
particularly is an undoubted talent that I came to feel was taking me, in
its very reality, in directions that came to seem incompatible with the
time I was spending reading and writing something I called philosophy.
That the history of a talent, as of a passion, real enough but perhaps
no longer consuming might play tricks with one's life is an idea whose
importance it was hard for me to see, and it is one I do not want to lose.

Rhu's book comes at a time in my life when I seem to have found
the means, for which I had for some years sought in vain, to compose a
kind of autobiography, a book of self-portraits with others. It is a distinct
similarity between our enterprises that what makes it worth taking my

life as a subject, even momentarily and intermittently, is a function of placing some value on the writing I have done. A difference between the enterprises begins with the fact that I cannot take it as given that there is value in this writing, beyond I mean my sense of how valuable the experience has been to me in working at it. No one but I can write my confessions. What I cannot do is to address myself about the events of such confessions in such a way as to reassure myself of the comprehensibility and usefulness of my writing, hence in that way of the reality of the effects I have wished it to achieve. Austin might point out that "to reassure" is not a performative verb—that is, to say "I reassure you" is not as such to reassure you; in recently returning to Austin's theory of the performative I have followed out the consequences of the thought that in such a case you are a better judge of the soundness of the utterance than I am. If I am meant to be reassured by a response, that response must find its way to convey reassurance by, for example, showing something I have written to be prompting and useful, worth taking on for some distance in another voice. This is not the fate of all modes of philosophizing, say those where pertinent forms of criticism are recognized in advance. It is rather a mode necessarily exposed to various forms of rejection. But in the present case I have the pleasure of simply repeating my gratitude for the richness and care that Lawrence Rhu has brought to the work before us.

Stanley Cavell
January 21, 2006

STANLEY CAVELL'S
AMERICAN DREAM

INTRODUCTION:
BEYOND ADAPTATION

*T*his book centers upon the convergence and elaboration of three major subjects in the philosophy of Stanley Cavell: Shakespeare, Emerson, and Hollywood movies. Links among these three topics often make Cavell's thought more accessible to a wider audience than would typically take an interest in the writings of professional philosophers. Cavell's concern about his readers has characterized his work from the outset, and the grace of his writing has won him a wide readership in an exceptional diversity of fields from early on.[1] However, his commitment to sustained study of these mainstream subjects has enabled his thought to achieve pertinence in areas usually out of bounds for his disciplinary colleagues. It has made his words matter in worlds where everyday moral reflection remains consequential despite the esotericism of academic expertise in many such contexts.

Cavell finds unprecedented connections between Shakespearean drama and classic Hollywood films from the thirties and forties. When challenged, Cavell appeals to Emerson's openness to such unorthodox possibilities. Emerson's readiness to characterize such an insight as merely a whim does not deter him from following it out and seeing where it will take him. He hopes "it is somewhat better than whim at last, but we cannot spend the day in explanation." Taking his cue from Emerson's active shunning of family ties, Cavell links this turning away with another passage from "Self-Reliance," where Emerson defines his essay's title and theme self-reflexively as the "aversion" of conformity.[2] Moreover, such a turning suggests to Cavell an experience quite different from simply willful avoidance. "Aversive thinking," as Cavell characterizes this

Emersonian response to inspiration, calls up the idea of conversion. It entails nothing less than the transformation of the self.

The writings of Thoreau also encourage Cavell in this sort of advancement of learning. As Emerson's truest inheritor, he thus serves as another American exemplar for Cavell's endeavor. Thoreau calls his sojourn at Walden Pond an "experiment" in much the same spirit as one of Shakespeare's favorite philosophers, Michel de Montaigne, refers to his writings as "essays," trials whose results are unforeseeable. Thoreau is not the sort of thinker who already knows where his thoughts will lead and comes to the task of reflection with a ready-made theory whose cogency he seeks to demonstrate. Rather, Thoreau promises "a success unexpected in common hours . . . if one advances in the direction of his dreams, and endeavors to live the life he has imagined."[3]

Thus, Cavell is an American dreamer of a recognizable kind despite occasional interludes of mistaken identification. Moreover, his elective affinity for the American dream factory that goes by the name of Hollywood makes a similar sort of sense. Over a quarter of a century ago, when Cavell began advancing such claims about Shakespeare and romantic comedies like *The Philadelphia Story,* the interplay between serious literary scholarship, or professional philosophy, and popular culture seemed more novel, if not blatantly indecorous. Cavell felt obliged to defend himself against charges of "hysterical impropriety" or to anticipate, and try to dispel, the appearance of "courting outrageousness." A younger generation of critics has grown accustomed to easier passage between popular and elite culture, or they have found readier support in defying conventions that once segregated mass culture from canonical texts. They can also find in Cavell a precursor of their own thought's yearning to trace kindred and illuminating ideas beyond the bounds of disciplinary protocols in a manner that allows them to affirm the intellectual and emotional validity of their own experience.

Cavell's dedication to the writings of Emerson and Thoreau makes his affinity with American Transcendentalism undeniable, but he also reveals a demonstrable kinship with such American novelists as Saul Bellow, Ralph Ellison, and Walker Percy. In Bellow's novel *Herzog,* the epistolary compulsion that drives the title character, Moses Herzog, to address letters of civic concern and political exasperation to President Eisenhower, among others, looks a lot like the spirit in which Cavell writes his "love letters of nightmare" to his native land during the escalating conflict in Vietnam.[4] Likewise, the high aspirations of Cavell's assimilation of the best products of the Hollywood studio system to the works of no lesser a dramatist than William Shakespeare bespeaks the lofty ambitions entertained by Ralph Waldo Ellison and his boyhood friends in Oklahoma City. In that modest outpost of American progress during the first quarter of the twentieth century, these African American youths dreamed of becoming nothing less than Renaissance men. Ellison's engagement of Emersonian thought is undeniably more critical than Cavell's readings of Emerson, and perhaps it was thrust upon him in part by the name his parents gave him. Still, both Cavell and Ellison indicate a shared awareness of the nineteenth-century essayist as a literary ancestor who requires a reckoning in their own efforts to achieve audibly American voices.[5] Similarly, the wonder to which Binx Bolling awakens and responds in *The Moviegoer* by Walker Percy looks precisely like what Cavell calls thinking in both its active and passive modes of reception and synthesis. Moreover, the wonder that dawns upon Binx often leads him to the movie theaters in New Orleans, where he cultivates moods frequently akin to those in which Cavell responds to Hollywood movies of various kinds. For that reason I single out Percy for special emphasis among this group of near contemporaries with whom Cavell reveals telling affinities. In the post–World War II era, movies served each of these writers as occasions for memorable reflections about the dreams and disappointments that Americans shared in their experience of the world as they found it in the decades after that cataclysmic conflict.

In recent years numerous studies of Cavell's writings have appeared. Because of the range of interests explored in those writings, such studies have tended to be topical, isolating Shakespeare in one chapter and film in another and Transcendentalism in a third. They have also tended to be developmental, concentrating on the origins of Cavell's thought in the ordinary language philosophy of J. L. Austin and the later Wittgenstein and recounting its evolution toward Emersonian perfectionism.[6] Though I have profited considerably from reading such books, my interest in Cavell's work has always centered upon moments of convergence where traditionally disparate elements—such as Shakespeare, film, and Transcendentalism—come together and illuminate one another in the expression of Cavell's thought. Such a moment becomes particularly visible in the late seventies and early eighties. Cavell's essay on *Othello*, his earliest essays on Emerson, and his book on the Hollywood comedy of remarriage belong to these years, as the Introduction to *Pursuits of Happiness* and its chapter on *The Philadelphia Story* vividly demonstrate.

These convergences bespeak Cavell's ambition to make his thought more widely available than academic philosophy customarily manages to be. Lecturing to undergraduates at Harvard in the Program in General Education and in the Core Curriculum provided Cavell with a forum in which he could address the sort of audience that his work often seeks: serious-minded non-specialists with an appetite for moral reflection inspired by masterworks of our shareable, if not common, culture. Cavell auditioned his earliest writing on Shakespeare, "The Avoidance of Love: A Reading of *King Lear,*" in a course called "Ideas of Man and the World in Western Thought." Subsequently, that course morphed into a course called "Moral Perfectionism," which was directly inspired by Emerson's philosophy.[7] Cavell first aired his most recent writing on Shakespeare, "Shakespeare and Rohmer: Two Tales of Winter," in the latter course, which featured weekly screenings of mainly classic Hollywood movies.[8] The earlier course had experimented with viewing one of these films, *The Philadelphia Story,* in its last year (1979), by which time the Shakespeare reading also had changed from *King Lear* to *Othello* and *The Winter's Tale.* Given those changes, the course had become by then an occasion for experimenting with the types of convergences this book seeks to explore.[9] Within a few years Cavell would also publish a collection of essays whose playful title, *Themes out of School* (1984), indicates more generally his debt to opportunities that the academy offered him for doing his kind of writing. Like tales told out of school, such themes—or the essays that explore them—may transgress conventional boundaries of genre, style, and occasion. They may test the dictates of decorum that reign in the institutions that sponsor the events that enable them to come into existence at all. Democracy thrives on precisely this sort of daring from a loyal opposition, and moral perfectionism is an attitude especially suited to motivate such criticism from within. For, while the genius it seeks to cultivate is equally distributed, the desire for such cultivation depends upon the willingness of the individual.

Geographically speaking, the America that Cavell has dreamed up, or discovered, lies in the land where these diverse worlds of intellectual and artistic endeavor—Shakespeare, philosophy, and Hollywood movies—become intelligible to one another. They are prominent neighborhoods in his city of words. This book explores precisely these areas of Cavell's thought and demonstrates how the connections that Cavell makes among them render his philosophy invitingly available despite the neglect or resistance it has encountered in the discrete fields which attend to one or another of Cavell's central concerns. Other books have treated Cavell topically and developmentally in their efforts to elucidate his thought and thereby make it more widely available, but they have neglected the very means by which he has sought a broader audience. This book seeks to use those means that Cavell himself chose to achieve this central goal of his work and to illuminate them and that work in the process.

This opening chapter aims to demonstrate the availability of Cavell's way of doing philosophy first by examining together his reading of *Macbeth* and his reading of *Gaslight*. On these discrete occasions Cavell makes kindred claims that bespeak recurrent concerns of his thought despite the ostensibly distinct contexts in which they appear, an essay on a Shakespearean tragedy and an interpretation of a film melodrama. This chapter demonstrates further the availability of Cavell's philosophy by showing the affinities between Walker Percy's first published novel, *The Moviegoer,* and Stanley Cavell's way of doing philosophy via the reading of literary texts and films.

Not only do their literary vocations lead both of these writers to deploy artful prose in the service of philosophical reflection. Their mutual interest in film and their shared struggles with skepticism and the malaise of everydayness also reveal their spiritual kinship. Those struggles represent their equal reluctance to adopt particular responses to our being in this world, such as Stoicism and dogmatic skepticism, and thus to adapt to those versions of our world expressed by such philosophies. Inasmuch as they emphasize our experience of consciousness and our capacities beyond adaptation, Cavell and Percy are both transcendentalists of a sort. They acknowledge the constraints of determining conditions while insisting upon the decisive role of the spirit in which we respond to the world as we find it. Indeed, those conditions and our response to them are an inseparable whole that constitutes our experience, and its evanescence issues a wake-up call that we ignore at our peril. Self-loss and the loss of felt connection to others are the high, if not tragic, price we may pay for disowning such knowledge.

Lost in Space or Right at Home?

Cavell's writings on Shakespeare and on film defy easy classification. To some they seem to come from another planet, whereas they make others feel more at home on this one in areas of study that have become increasingly focused upon a limited range of issues. Harry Berger dubbed Cavell's reading of *King Lear* the essay from outer space, whereas Richard Wheeler took comfort and encouragement from that same piece.[10] Wheeler found in it an affirmation of issues in Shakespeare studies that greatly mattered to him though few others were noticeably attending to them. Even when Cavell's observations have a considerable impact on writing within a given field, such as Shakespeare studies, those who follow their lead often give no indication of an awareness of the context in which they arise. For Stephen Orgel and David Miller, Cavell's preoccupation with how readily the death of Mamillius seems forgotten in *The Winter's Tale* decisively influences their individual responses to the play, but neither notes the lines of romanticism that Cavell is following out in making this observation nor Wordsworth as its immediate provocation.[11] Such tunnel vision in recent years has moved Cavell to refuse standard requests to reprint his essay on *King Lear* because editors usually cut it in such a way as to leave the philosophy out.[12]

However, despite occasional shortsightedness, Shakespeare scholars have welcomed Cavell's work in their field far more hospitably than film scholars. John Joughin invited Cavell to write the foreword to *Philosophical Shakespeares,* the volume he edited in the Routledge series Accents on Shakespeare. He also featured discussion of Cavell's work prominently in his Introduction, though none of the Shakespeare scholars who contribute to the book mentions Cavell even once in his or her essay.[13] Stephen Greenblatt provided a flattering blurb for the cover of Cavell's *Disowning Knowledge in Six Plays of Shakespeare,* and it survives sixteen years later on the updated edition of that book, but Greenblatt has never engaged Cavell's thought in anything he has written about Shakespeare.[14] This benign neglect differs significantly from the attack upon Cavell that the film scholar Tania Modleski launched in *Critical Inquiry,* where Cavell comes off as a sort of poacher (Shakespeare could identify with that!) who comments upon issues and films central to film study without engagement, or even acknowledgment, of feminist scholarship that has amply addressed these matters heretofore.[15] Though obviously a headstrong gambit in the gender wars of its moment, Modleski's charge points to an important concern about Cavell's writings: their occasional failure to observe professional protocols that characterize scholarly conduct of argument and interpretation in particular fields.

Cavell's genteel description of his Shakespeare criticism as "amateur forays" into that field of study awakened Richard Halpern's skepticism, for Cavell's reputation as a philosopher affords him a serious hearing that belies such modest disclaimers.[16] Yet, as a philosopher, Cavell's mode of operation challenges the whole notion of philosophy as a profession while it seeks to recover what that field of study loses—or, as Cavell likes to say, what it *represses*—by its compulsion to turn a calling into a profession in its bid for respectability. Cavell finds in Emerson and Thoreau crucial precursors, whom he sees as willfully overlooked within the American professionalization of philosophy and simply ignored within the European dispensation of that discipline.[17] For their part, Cavell's professional colleagues describe his writings as self-indulgent.[18] Whether they intend that critique to indicate a lack of rigor or a guilty pleasure remains an open question. Perhaps his writings remind them of what professional philosophy has often failed to claim or felt it necessary to sacrifice, and such a critique bespeaks the resentment of a painful loss whose memory is stirred by Cavell's work. The liberties it takes and the success it often enjoys rub a sore spot.

In a way, if Cavell is not simply guilty of violating several current taboos, he flirts with doing so dangerously enough to make himself strongly suspect among more conventional critics of our moment. He seems to believe that human nature is *constitutionally*—to borrow a fraught term from Emerson—susceptible to skepticism, and this conviction makes him vulnerable to the charge of essentialist humanism leveled at him by Richard Rorty.[19] He also believes in transcendence, not as a human ambition, but as a human resource in circumstances that sometimes make our full inhabitation of the world virtually impossible in its present dispensation. Both of these convictions run counter to dogmas of the dominant historical materialism that have governed literary study for over a quarter of a century.

If we consider Cavell's most recent reading of a Shakespeare play, we can see where he parts company with such current isms as new historicism and feminism. Moreover, if we appreciate how Cavell's Shakespeare studies address issues that he often raises in his interpretation of film and how Emerson's philosophy now pervades his work in all areas, we can see how his essays and books become points of convergence for these main lines of thought that help him to articulate his own reflections.

Macbeth and *Gaslight:* New Historicism and Feminism

Cavell's essay on *Macbeth* explicitly questions the idea of history that informs much recent Shakespeare criticism because, in its quest for understanding of the past, it too often abandons the present as the moment in which the past can take on new life in immediate meaningfulness as an inspiration for fresh understanding and action. He cites passages from Emerson's "History" to exemplify a different idea of the past, one in which time's sway yields to the responsiveness of a present reading and, to paraphrase Robert Frost, we possess what before had possessed us via the inertia of ignorance or of a kind of knowing that insists on otherness and resists transformation.[20]

Discussing the final sentence of the opening chapter of Stephen Greenblatt's *Shakespearean Negotiations,* Cavell expresses his sense of frustration in being asked to affirm things he never denied. Greenblatt writes, "The speech of the dead, like my own speech, is not private property," and Cavell, whose early philosophical engagement with Wittgenstein's so-called "private language argument" appears in "Knowing and Acknowledging," a virtual companion piece to his essay on *King Lear,* feels understandably put in a false position.[21] He wants promptly, if not impatiently, to retort, "Who ever said it was?" Indeed he spends some time in this essay rehearsing basic arguments from ordinary language philosophy that fundamental premises in new historicist writings like this piece of Greenblatt's and an essay on *Macbeth* by Steven Mullaney mystify by positioning the reader in opposition to them. However, the passage from which Cavell excerpts Greenblatt's sentence deserves fuller citation to indicate both where Cavell and new historicism part company and some features they share: "I had dreamed of speaking with the dead, and even now I do not abandon this dream. But the mistake was to imagine that I would hear a single voice, the voice of the other. If I wanted to hear one, I had to hear the many voices of the dead. And if I wanted to hear the voice of the other, I had to hear my own voice. The speech of the dead, like my own, is not private property."[22]

Like other ordinary language philosophers, Cavell stresses the inevitably shared quality of language and meaning. Thus, he cannot help hearing many voices in the words of any single voice, and in such a representative one as that of Shakespeare, he hears it "thinking for thousands," as Emerson puts it. Perhaps as a literary historian Greenblatt feels obliged to emphasize the pastness of the past by stressing the deadness of those with whom he yearns to speak. Cavell stresses instead the vitality of the past texts that he seeks to read, which are admittedly a select canonical few as opposed to Greenblatt's manifold archival discoveries. Indeed, for Cavell, those texts have the capacity to read us, who, in this transaction, may be the dead parties in need of revival. As Cavell tartly puts this point in his essay on *Macbeth,* perhaps those critics who suggest there may be a scene missing from this play are simply failing to respond to what is there, and "speculation about a missing scene is a cover for the speculator's missing response to the scenes that *are* present."[23]

But Greenblatt's verve as a writer belies any such characterization, and his own curiosity and wonder about the texts he surveys make a palpably vital impression on any attentive reader of Greenblatt's own texts. The passage above is a case in point, however much a mystification of common sense may produce part of its evocativeness. Indeed, once we suspend that charge, we can see a great deal that it shares with Cavell's approaches to Shakespeare. Cavell finds in Shakespeare an Emersonian representative man whose capacity to "think for thousands" derives from his indebtedness to a language shaped and transmitted by many thousands more. Susceptibility and attunement to this collective effort accounts for Shakespeare's expressive power, not Shakespeare's singularity as an exception to all the rules.[24] Emerson may celebrate self-reliance and condemn conformity, but this line of his thought leads to the goal of recovering the ordinary in all of its freshness and commonality. It is this aspect of Emerson's project that reveals his affinity with those ordinary language philosophers in whom Cavell first discovered a way of doing philosophy that he wished to pursue.

In the Greenblatt passage, however, there is an apparent stability in the difference between self and other that distinguishes his approach from Cavell's. When he writes that "if [he] wanted to hear the voice of the other, [he] had to hear [his own] voice," he stops a step short of the key emphasis in Cavell's way of reading before he turns more emphatically outward with his assertion about the collective nature of human speech—his, ours, and theirs. When Emerson reads a work of genius, he encounters his own words in their alienated majesty, as when he read Montaigne and felt he had written Montaigne's words himself;[25] and Cavell finds decisive instruction in this aspect of Emerson. The perfectionist moment in Cavell's way of reading occurs when we see ourselves as another and respond by beginning to recover from that estrangement by taking its cue and becoming ourselves. This vital connection does not entail denial of difference; it simply affirms our capacity for productively overcoming such differences as impair the onwardness of the self, its taking the next step.

Other features of Cavell's essay on *Macbeth* reveal his aversion to the insistence upon difference at the expense of common ties of humanity in feminist approaches to this play exemplified by Marjorie Garber and Janet Adelman. Cavell wants to emphasize the distinction between what we might call human kind*ness* (emphasis added) and monstrosity as more to the point than an absolute difference between masculinity and femininity, as though human nature was gendered irretrievably all the way down.[26] Indeed, if we trace our humanity as it is represented in Lady Macbeth's phrase, "the milk of human kindness," it will lead us directly to a gendered trait, sucked from the mother's breast in infancy; but this need not preclude aspects of our selves that transcend such sharp distinctions, as for example Macduff's claimed need to feel the death of his family "like a man," that is, to cry, because without that womanly response, he would not be a man at all. He would be inhuman—a destination at which Macbeth ultimately arrives just as his wife goes mad due to the progress she makes in that direction. Lady Macbeth without doubt taunts her husband with disparagement of his masculinity, but the boundary they both dread to cross comes between their humanity and the monstrous deeds that ambition moves them to commit.

Cavell reads their marriage as a perfectionist relationship gone as wrong as possible: it brings out the worst in both of them. That reading shows its links to Cavell's work on the genres of classical Hollywood movies, where Cavell follows Milton in defining marriage as "meet and happy conversation," a concept that links such relations between the sexes to the tradition of philosophical dialogue as a means of education and an agent of transformation. The intimacy between the Macbeths seems almost telepathic. Yet its morbidity and the wickedness that it promotes require a darker characterization, and Cavell settles upon the term vampirism to meet this challenge.[27] In the Hollywood melodramas he studies Cavell characterizes the negation of conversation as irony that pervades and empties exchanges of immediate resonance for their interlocutors, and Cavell's preoccupation with film melodrama becomes relevant in the *Macbeth* essay because he sees this play as Shakespearean melodrama in the "contest over interpretations" that it dramatizes in the responses of its characters to the events that unfold in the play.[28]

In *Gaslight,* the first melodrama that Cavell reads in *Contesting Tears,* he describes the relationship between Gregor Anton (Charles Boyer) and his wife Paula (Ingrid Bergman) as one of vampirism—"one life the sapping of another's"—and he turns to Emerson's "Fate" for a portrayal of this condition.[29] Later, in *Cities of Words,* Cavell modifies this description to emphasize Gregor's possessiveness, but the link between *Macbeth* and *Gaslight* remains clear and reveals lines of thought that Cavell is pursuing in tandem, so to speak, in Shakespeare and in film.[30] In the *Macbeth* essay, for example, Cavell draws upon "Fate" to explore what he calls our "fatedness to significance," a concept that clearly contradicts the assumption that language is, in any way, "private property." In the introduction to *Contesting Tears* Cavell acknowledges directly that his "immersion in these structures"—i.e., the four melodramas to which he dedicates the four chapters in that book—opened an avenue for him to think through

"Macbeth's murderous questioning of his wife's knowledge of herself,"
which he then identifies as "a way of putting the subject of [his] 'Macbeth Appalled.' "[31] That subject emphatically diverts attention from Lady
Macbeth as a "sexual terrorist," as Greenblatt describes her in a phrase
redolent of the impact of feminist readings of the play such as Garber's
and Adelman's.[32] Subsequently, in "Naughty Orators: Negation of Voice
in *Gaslight*" Cavell detects an "apparent allusion to Macbeth's halluci-
nated dagger" in the penultimate scene, where Paula denies her husband's appeal that she cut him loose with the knife she brandishes while
questioning its very existence—a moment that echoes, in its way, Gregor's denial of the existence of a letter that Paula has just discovered
hidden in a desk drawer a few scenes before.[33]

Examples such as these abound and illustrate the interconnection between Cavell's reflections on Shakespeare and on film, as well as the ways
in which those thoughts frequently achieve expression in Emersonian
formulations. But the mere compilation of such examples serves no purpose without an understanding of Cavell's guiding principles as a writer
and reader of texts. He is, by design, a devotee of the particular case and
insists that his readings of Shakespeare and of film should stand or fall on
their own terms as exercises in practical criticism of individual works. He
is also deeply inquisitive about the relations between philosophy and
literature, and especially concerned about the role of examples in philosophical argument. Philosophy should not merely seek in the arts instances of the points it aims to convey. Different arts have their own ways
of making their points, and translation of artistic expression into argument reductively coerces it into a pale reflection, if not a gross distortion,
of itself. Besides, different art forms also have their own ways of thinking
about themselves and their purposes in the process of achieving them.
They are both philosophical and philosophically self-conscious. As Cavell puts it about the latest of those arts that he engages critically, "To my
way of thinking the creation of film was as if meant for philosophy—
meant to reorient everything philosophy has said about reality and its
representation, about art and imitation, about greatness and conventionality, about judgment and pleasure, about skepticism and transcendence,
about language and expression."[34]

Cavell writes of "two myths of philosophizing" that account for philosophy's current disposition.[35] In one the philosopher must have read
everything, and Heidegger serves as the exemplar of this way of doing
philosophy by retelling the history of philosophy as a way of receiving
its legacy. In the other the philosopher needs to have read nothing; indeed, this is the desirable condition in which to proceed with thinking,

and Wittgenstein is its exemplar. Cavell follows a third path in which the role of argument is played by taking complete responsibility for one's own discourse, although this keen sense of discursive accountability implies no private ownership of the language one employs. Emerson and Thoreau exemplify this approach, and their work has little or no importance among professional philosophers in Cavell's experience. All of these philosophers—Heidegger, Wittgenstein, Emerson, and Thoreau—have decisively shaped Cavell's philosophical practice, in which the reading of texts figures as the central activity, and both movies and Shakespeare's plays are considered as texts. But when we take the measure of Cavell's work from within the fields he frequents to conduct his business, we should give him no special dispensation that he does not fully earn. Rather, we should assess his writing by both the criteria that he has articulated and those of the field in question. Perhaps he will just be doing something different, or perhaps he will be doing something that shows the unnecessary limits that some fields have imposed upon themselves and those who venture into them.

For example, Cavell's insistence on the significance of human identity in *Macbeth* runs counter not only to the emphasis on difference in current criticism but to antihumanist campaigns that often see any appeal to a common identity as a cover for injustice and ongoing discrimination.[36] Cavell finds in skepticism an inevitable human inheritance, a common predicament that goes with our condition as users of language fated both to expression and to disappointment in our expressive powers. Cavell's reading of *Gaslight* echoes this feature of his Shakespeare criticism in its exploration of the abyss of doubt into which Paula seems to have irrevocably descended. Her inability to discern the pattern of her husband's deceit leads Cavell to formulate a playfully Cartesian description of her cluelessness, which he dubs (*not* unsympathetically) "hyperbolic stupidity."[37] However, he sounds frankly Shakespearean when he asserts that even a dog could read the signs that indicate what Gregor is up to, for the boundary between the human and the animal in Shakespeare often defines the sort of difference that Cavell seeks to emphasize in distinguishing between the human and the monstrous. "You know, don't you?" exclaims Paula's rescuer, Cameron (Joseph Cotton), in sympathetic astonishment at Paula's benightedness. She simply cannot *not* know. Rather, she must, in Cavell's phrase about the skepticism he finds throughout Shakespearean tragedy, disown her knowledge in this regard. This penchant for holding back and refusing to acknowledge our insights about ourselves and others becomes for Cavell a feature of our human condition, a proneness to skepticism that we all share. And it makes Shakespearean tragedy, on Cavell's reading, deeply relevant to our self-understanding.

Well, who ever said that it wasn't? Literary historians who read Shakespeare from the margins of his culture have taught us a great deal indirectly about our neglect of those on the margins of our own present-day culture. Such instruction, at its best, can help us overcome divisions and misrecognitions of self and other that keep us apart. It is a way of opening up Shakespeare's texts to include an array of concerns more diverse than the aesthetic, moral, and political concerns of humanist criticism have traditionally entailed. Cavell's turn to Hollywood movies as objects of interpretation involved a kindred shift from elite to popular culture, and Shakespeare often became a means of legitimation in making this turn. He served Cavell as a touchstone by which to affirm the excellence of Hollywood film at its best.[38] But despite his insistence upon particular cases, Cavell also finds in these works examples that transcend in their humanity the confines of an isolated instance, even though it often is their specificity (sometimes to the point of idiosyncrasy) that reveals the humanity of stars who perform on screen. Among other things, they can become, paradoxically, examples of the isolated instance that each of us can sometimes feel himself or herself to be. As Cavell writes of Felicie in *Conte d'hiver,* a descendent of Perdita in *The Winter's Tale,* "She's the girl they can never find. Who is not?"[39]

By finding such examples on screen, Cavell has frequently prompted, among film scholars, the charge of naïveté, of standing in an unexamined relationship to the figures he views on screen. Those who have read his film criticism know that, if not "everything," at least a great deal, that "philosophy has said about reality and its representation" figures centrally in his "reflections on the ontology of film," as he subtitles *The World Viewed.* Moreover, he links this problem directly to the skeptical crisis in early modern thought expressed most definitively in Descartes's *Meditations on First Philosophy* and Shakespeare's proleptic articulation of version after version of that crisis in his tragedies and tragicomedies. Film, however, enables Cavell to bring the experience of this crisis closer to home, so to speak, and to make the recognition of human limitation harder to resist and yet more honestly inhabitable. "I understand Buster Keaton, say in *The General,*" Cavell writes,

> to exemplify an acceptance of the enormity of this realization of
> human limitation, denying neither the abyss that may open at any

time before our plans, nor the possibility, despite that open possibility, of living honorably, with good if resigned spirits, and with eternal hope. His capacity for love does not avoid this knowledge, but
lives in full view of it. Is he dashing? He is something rarer; he is
undashable. He incorporates both the necessity of wariness in an
uncertain world, and also the necessary limits of human awareness;
gaze as *we* may, there is always something behind *our* backs, room
for doubt (emphases added).[40]

Cavell ends this passage by putting us in Keaton's place, as though we
could have a full share in what he stands for, and this sense of his "reality"
(for us) exemplifies the kind of response that Cavell's critics target as his
chief shortcoming. Cavell insists that the value of art resides in its formative power, a power released by our response to its shaping influence;
and his critics indict him for ingenuously connecting with a make-be-
lieve world and its denizens as though it were a real one and they were
real people in it.[41] Cavell has regularly shown a willingness to run the
risk that he may be wrong in this regard about characters in plays and
movies. "Let us treat the men and women well: treat them as if they
were real," he seems to say with an Emersonian readiness to call the bluff
of those who demur. "Perhaps they are."[42]

If we call to mind the conclusion of *Gaslight,* we can see how this
film addresses this problem; and we can also use it as an occasion to
invoke a novel, *The Moviegoer,* by a writer of Cavell's generation, Walker
Percy, who explores the challenges of skepticism and belief with a degree
of depth and nuance missing in the assessment of Cavell's work by contemporary film scholars yet present in that work itself, as the above passage demonstrates. Once Paula has been released from the spell of
Gregor's manipulation and he has been taken away by the police, she
emerges from the attic onto the balcony. Cameron emerges behind Paula
with consoling words about the dawn that comes after even the darkest
of times, and an appropriate skyscape complements the melodramatic
excesses of this occasion. It is a moment fraught with enough sentiment
to induce a naïve viewer into imagining a romantic future for Cameron
and Paula, as they stand in apparent isolation against the backdrop of the
heavens.

Indeed the film promptly includes such a viewer, Miss Thwaites
(Dame May Whitty), who, coming upon the two alone, gives a cry of
surprise that could easily be read as suggesting that the intimacy of this
moment signals the promise of love between them. Miss Thwaites has

already been introduced to us as a glutton for the emotional extremes of murder mysteries, and we have come to know her as a snoopy neighbor with a vivid imagination. Thus, her overreaction here, if we are mindful, should serve to dismiss the idea of romance as this moment's meaning; for she readily inspires disagreement, as does our memory of Paula's vulnerable condition throughout this film. Cameron then makes a sensible appeal that puts this finale into perspective when he expresses a desire simply to visit Paula and talk with her. Conversation in a context where words signify something we can agree upon, as Cavell puts it, in our attunement can begin to heal the shattering disappointments of betrayal and the skepticism they inevitably inspire.

This moment expresses the way in which language can provide access to a shareable world, "a world," in Auden's words, "where promises [are] kept/And one [can] weep because another wept."[43] Speech there is not only public property; it is trustworthy, due to our tenable belief in the good faith of others. Intersubjectivity has a basis, though by no means an unshakable one, in the honestly used language we can share. We can have one another in mind, which is an apt way of describing the reassurance that Binx offers his wife Kate at the end of *The Moviegoer,* when she has been badly shaken by the death of Lonnie, her husband's teenaged stepbrother. This utopian vision of such a world is expressed via marriage as conversation in Cavell's reading of the Hollywood comedy of remarriage. It is public enough in its intelligibility to moviegoers to stand as a rebuke to the actual world we inhabit. There the inevitable ambiguities and misunderstandings of verbal communication become opportunities for malefaction, both by design and by accident; and marriage can become, in Milton's words, "economical [i.e., domestic] misfortune" and "household unhappiness."[44]

Beyond Adaptation: Walker Percy and Stanley Cavell

Among film scholars the relative neglect of Cavell's remarkable writings has not gone unnoticed. William Rothman and Marian Keane have recently made a commendable effort to remedy this situation in their careful study of the first of Cavell's four books about film, *Reading Cavell's* The World Viewed: *A Philosophical Perspective on Film.* In introducing their monograph, these co-authors observe the almost total divergence from mainstream thinking that distinguishes Cavell's film criticism. Then they add their hopeful anticipation of productive challenges that may arise from the expanded awareness of alternative approaches made possible by an acquaintance with Cavell's thought. "Almost invariably," Rothman and Keane aver, "Cavell's intuitions run counter to views generally accepted . . . . In providing meaningful alternatives to views that are so often accepted without question within the field of film study, *The World Viewed* is capable of challenging the field to question the unquestionable, to check its theories against the test of experience, thereby opening for exploration regions that have remained closed."[45]

This claim justly characterizes the value of Cavell's other books on film as well, though suspicious readers, viewing his work through the lenses of feminist and Marxist approaches, have characterized Cavell's responses to Hollywood movies as naïve and mystifying.[46] Given Cavell's insistence upon art's fundamental value in helping to realize the wish for selfhood, perhaps such suspicions are unavoidable. The process of reading requires belief before it can confer understanding, as Cavell sees it, and we are thus vulnerable to mistaken identification. But standing coolly apart has its hazards as well. Though fools rush in where angels fear to tread, we do not have wings, so we may need to make the most of our folly. Taking instruction from our mistakes can turn our errors into a truer direction, but we must first take the steps necessary to test our intuitions. No theory, however grand, can protect us from fallibility.

There is a prostitute in Flannery O'Connor's *Wise Blood* who receives this memorable characterization: "[S]he was so well adjusted that she didn't have to think any more."[47] At this juncture O'Connor's sharp satire takes its cue from the secular religion of mental health that widely prevailed when her novel first appeared in 1952. Celebration of the ability to adjust, regardless of circumstances, often seemed prized above any other accomplishment. No matter what question of value was at stake, emotionalism betokened trouble. Though lack of affect could occasion concern, the passions appeared bleached of all color in the clinical discourse of popular psychology at midcentury. This discourse set standards for the assessment of character by social scientists, and society at large widely accepted their authority. Professional jargon of this sort thus became the frequent target of mordant satire such as O'Connor's.

The reasonable sort of accommodation commended by detached analysis became even easier to dismiss when cries of injustice were heard in the series of political struggles that soon emerged over civil rights, Vietnam, and the status of women during the early decades of Cavell's academic career, the sixties and seventies. Dispassionate reason in the interest of human advancement, the Enlightenment project if you will, lost credibility in strife over matters of race, gender, class, and empire. Detached analysis of one's own psychological condition and that of others became similarly liable to characterization as an empty gesture. Likewise, an even older model of such equanimity, the stoic ideal of the will's masterful transcendence of the passions, had long ago fallen into disfavor. Yet its hierarchical partitioning of the self into reason and passion, and its affirmation of the will's capacity to rise above storms of emotion, retained a surprising allure. This claim of individual sovereignty despite the most adverse of circumstances remained a compelling alternative even in the triumphant Christian culture that supposedly put such rival pagan philosophies into decisive eclipse.[48]

In his explorations of the film genre that he labels the Hollywood melodrama of the unknown woman, Stanley Cavell discusses his protagonists' capacity to judge the world at certain junctures where one could mistakenly claim that they simply rise above it, mystically taking their leave of the human realm altogether.[49] For example, Charlotte Vale (Bette Davis) decisively transcends the understanding of her circumstances expressed by Jerry Durrance (Paul Henreid) at the end of *Now, Voyager*. Yet she remains very much a worldling, a resident of this earth who consciously selects a course of life that Jerry fails to comprehend. Indeed, he construes her situation in such conventional and sanctimonious terms that Charlotte directly chastens him for what finally seems his dim-witted misprision of her self-understanding in this film's closing moment.

But Charlotte's painful unknownness to Jerry does not make her completely unintelligible, for the film does not confine us to Jerry's perspective. Likewise, according to Cavell, Stella Dallas (Barbara Stanwyck) makes recognizable choices that determine her fortunes at the end of the 1936 film named after her. She is not merely a victim of others' class prejudice or her own envy of their privileges. She makes choices that indicate her distaste for their world, which she once aspired to join but now decisively rejects. Stella Dallas exercises her capacity to judge *their* world and, finding it wanting, she walks ecstatically away from a life she no longer desires. But such ecstasy is not simply "blissing out." As Thoreau puts it, "With thinking we may be beside ourselves in a sane sense."[50]

Almost three decades earlier Cavell makes a kindred point about Shakespeare's *King Lear*. Cavell confronts the unbearability of this tragedy, registered most notoriously by Dr. Johnson's reaction to the death of Cordelia;[51] and he directly counters the despair that such a moment can awaken. "There is hope in this play," Cavell opines; and he pointedly adds that "it is not in heaven." This obvious echo of a resonant biblical claim from the Book of Deuteronomy 30.12 directly counters the presumption that such hope is escapism in the same way that the transcendence Cavell attributes to Stella Dallas and Charlotte Vale, in their unknownness, need not be at all otherworldly or despairing. Where then does Cavell find this hope in *King Lear?* He answers this question in the following manner:

> In the realm of the spirit, Kierkegaard says, there is absolute justice. Fortunately, because if all we had to go on were the way the world goes, we would lose the concept of justice altogether, and then human life would become unbearable. Kant banked the immortality of the soul on the fact that in *this* world goodness and happiness are unaligned—a condition which, if never righted, is incompatible with moral sanity, and hence the existence of God [Cavell's emphasis]. But immortality is not necessary for the soul's satisfaction. What is necessary is its own coherence, its ability to judge a world in which evil is successful and the good are doomed; and in particular its knowledge that while injustice may flourish, it cannot rest content.[52]

The argument that Cavell advances in *Contesting Tears* defines melodrama as a genre that purposefully trades in emotional excess. Its hyperbolic gestures aim to open hearts otherwise inclined to lose touch with currents of feeling whose expression convention constrains. By "figuring our hidden screams, and then understanding us despite ourselves, despite our inexpressiveness," melodrama represents the realm of the spirit in such a way that passion can inform reason and animate judgment.[53]

Passion, of course, is conventionally assigned a gender, and that is female. Cavell challenges this customary attribution most memorably when he describes Adam Bonner, Spencer Tracy's character in *Adam's Rib,* as "something of an unknown woman himself."[54] Of course, Adam just pretends to cry in the scene that earns him this characterization, and he subsequently calls this performance a "little trick." But the very theatricality of his gesture indicates that neither sex holds exclusive title to certain regions of feeling. Rather, behavioral styles and the conformity that they tend to enforce arbitrarily link maleness to stoical impassivity and femaleness to emotional expressiveness. Granted that Adam's timely improvisation of tears may express genuine feeling despite his avowal that it was merely a ploy, still the surprise it produces in Adam's wife,

Amanda (Katharine Hepburn), also indicates the arbitrariness of certain social roles, what we commonly call their constructedness.

One of the most memorable representations of stoic resignation in modern fiction appears in *The Moviegoer* by Walker Percy. It is Emily Cutrer, the formidable great-aunt of that novel's alert narrator and questing protagonist, Binx Bolling. This generally uneventful novel tells the story of a week in the life of a New Orleans stockbroker who quietly makes some changes in his way of life and suffers a few others as well. Besides attending to financial matters, Binx habitually goes to the movies and tries to enjoy the company of attractive young women whenever occasion allows. Movies fascinate him precisely because of their seductive allure and their power to enthrall our imaginations. Though Binx usually stands securely aloof from this power, he revealingly succumbs to it and becomes their thrall at a decisive turn in the novel, its deceptively undramatic climax. Mediated exclusively through Binx's perspective, the novel's main subject is human attachment, or what you might call love, if you qualify that claim with a healthy dose of irony about romance in reduced circumstances.

The stoic Aunt Emily herself amounts to something of an unknown man inasmuch as William Alexander Percy, the novelist's second cousin and beloved "Uncle Will," served as the model for this figure.[55] She quotes Marcus Aurelius and keeps the stiff upper lip required of such types when they face what they deem the deterioration of cherished values and modes of conduct.[56] As the old order passes and is replaced by questionable upstarts who neither esteem nor embody the noble codes that allegedly guided their precursors, a studied detachment offers such stoics refuge. Aunt Emily bears unmistakable marks of this view of the world, which Percy himself no longer considered an option for his generation of Southerners despite his high regard for William Alexander Percy.[57] Aunt Emily even compounds her recourse to detachment by identifying herself as "spiritually a Buddhist."[58] The anodyne of indifference commended in that Eastern tradition bears a recognizable affinity with the equanimity achieved via stoic detachment.

The ultimate legacy of stoic high-mindedness that haunted Walker Percy was the suicide of his father. He would reckon more directly with this traumatic inheritance in his second novel, *The Last Gentleman;* but Binx Bolling's fiancée, Kate Cutrer, confronts him with a comparable challenge in *The Moviegoer.* Her self-destructive behavior, however, manifests itself in mood swings that represent precisely the opposite of stoic impassivity. Indeed, her instability and the desperation that goes with her consequent inability to find peace ironically enable her to take Binx's measure with disarming candor. This philosophical charmer can get very cozy with the reader, who is mainly confined to his perspective as narrator except for occasions of dialogue. But then Kate can take on a life of her own, prodding Binx, even "figuring [his] hidden screams," to borrow Cavell's phrases about melodrama, "and then understanding [him] despite [himself]."[59] Or, at the very least, Kate can make Binx confront his own coldness and detachment in their frank conversations.

Ironically, film of no kind has this effect on Binx. His moviegoing habit entails, almost as a fundamental principle, a pervasive, even absolute, distrust of the stories he sees on screen, despite the fascination they stir in him. Their characters and, in a way, the actors who play them do not impress Binx at all as real people. Cavell's alleged gullibility seems the last kind of weakness Binx would display. He views movies with dogmatically skeptical detachment: "The movies are onto the search, but they screw it up. The search always ends in despair. They like to show a fellow coming to himself in a strange place—but what does he do? He takes up with the local librarian, sets about proving to the local children what a nice fellow he is, and settles down with a vengeance. In two weeks' time he is so sunk in everydayness that he might just as well be dead."[60]

Binx's own story takes the form of an avowed search, which, ultimately, has no specific object and remains conspicuously inconclusive at the novel's close. Still, if it were not for Binx's resolute anti-romanticism, the title of one of Cavell's books, *In Quest of the Ordinary,* would capture a good bit of Binx's search. For Binx, however, the ordinary remains elusive, when it is not simply dispiriting. There are, in Wallace Stevens's wonderful phrase, no "tootings at the weddings of the soul" for Binx.[61] Yet the philosophy of Kierkegaard that resonates most deeply with the ambitions of Binx's search and permeates Percy's fiction appears in the description of the knight of faith in *Fear and Trembling,* and Cavell explicitly notes its congruence with the Emersonian quest to recover the ordinary that he invokes as a prime provocation for his study of Hollywood comedies of remarriage.[62]

Cavell's responsiveness to Hollywood at its best differs significantly from the foregone conclusion at which Binx has arrived: "The search *always* ends in despair" (emphasis added). Binx's knowing anticipation of hackneyed routines reveals an understandable impatience with formulaic products of the studio system, whose happy endings arrive on schedule like a timely fix. However, it also preempts other possibilities. As Cavell argues, the excesses of melodrama aim to open these options up precisely because of the everydayness into which we too readily sink without recourse to such extreme measures. These emotional extravaganzas mean to break the trances into which ordinary routines all too often lull us. They aim to awaken our hearts and thus make us think with more passion than usual and with greater consequences.

The Moviegoer is also a story about what Cavell calls thinking, as he discerns it in Emerson, for whom passion, or what Kant calls inclination, requires no apology. It is told from a point of view whose changes of mood are at least as important as the events of the plot, if it is even possible to distinguish between these two elements in this text. Percy himself would have balked at such a distinction, as his response to suggested revisions from his editor, Stanley Kaufmann, reveals. Kaufmann urged Percy to tighten the plot of *The Moviegoer,* and he replied: "Your calling attention to dropped characters and interrupted story-strands is certainly valid novelistic criticism, but it does not seem applicable here—at least it does not strike a chord with me. *Passage to India* is a much better constructed novel than [Jean-Paul Sartre's] *Nausea,* but *Nausea* would be wrecked by a revision along these lines. I suppose I am trying to say that the fragmented alienated consciousness, which is Mr. Binx Bolling, cannot be done up in a *novel* [Percy's emphasis] in the usual sense of the word."[63]

At the beginning of *The Moviegoer,* Binx becomes, you might say, an American scholar: he wakes up and starts thinking about the predicament in which he discovers himself. He thus becomes not merely a thinker but man thinking, as Emerson defines the scholar, a man who brings active reflection to bear upon the world as he finds it. He ceases to haunt his life and begins to live it because of no more than a change of mood, a funny feeling he has one morning as he contemplates his "personal effects"—the wallet and keys, change and cards strewn on top of his dresser. Somehow he sees them differently after he wakes up and is getting ready to go out for the day. It dawns upon him that his personal effects could easily turn into his "last remains." Thus, he becomes a philosopher in one of the oldest senses of that term, which claims that to philosophize is to learn how to die. At an odd moment Binx is graced with an awareness of his own mortality. That awareness sticks, and it starts to change his everyday approach to his passage through life. As Emerson remarks, "We must be very suspicious of the deceptions of the element of time. It takes a good deal of time to eat or to sleep, or to earn a hundred dollars, and a very little time to entertain a hope and an insight which becomes the light of our life."[64]

21

Walker Percy's favorite philosopher, Søren Kierkegaard, distinguishes between being and existence in a way that enables us to appreciate the change that Binx begins to undergo: "A human being can forget to exist," the Danish philosopher declares.[65] Binx's casually glimpsed insight into his own finitude helps to save him from becoming a casualty of his own obliviousness. What happens to Binx is that he starts to remember to exist and thus ceases to be a mere thinker; or, in Percy's way of making this process clear, Binx abandons mere spectatorship and idle moviegoing, and he becomes more responsive and engaged in his life as it passes. The epigraph of *The Moviegoer* offers another version of this same perception from Søren Kierkegaard: "The specific character of despair is precisely this: it is unaware of being despair." Binx becomes conscious of the despair in which he has been living. That consciousness dawns upon Binx in the way Emerson characterizes as intuition. One day it just happens to happen that Binx sees himself in a new light, and that fresh perspective makes him wonder enough to pay much steadier attention than usual to life as it passes thereafter.

Furthermore, Binx is responding in an Emersonian fashion to his unforeseen insight inasmuch as "Self-Reliance" insists that every intuition requires a tuition, a follow-up that seeks to discover where such intuitions will lead. Binx calls his response, with merciful restraint, a search; and, ultimately, it leads him nowhere, if you are expecting revelations of the sort that the idea of a quest can melodramatically make us anticipate. He gets married, becomes a medical student, and sees his beloved through a painful loss—no more, nor less, than these ordinary events sum up where he is bound when we leave him at the novel's end. But if we listen to his words and his voice, and if we trust our own intuition, we may know what Emerson says we can know instantly—whose words are loaded with life and whose are not.[66] Those of Walker Percy undeniably abound in their capacity to make that impression upon us.

The hazards of moviegoing in Percy's novel coincide with those of reading in "The American Scholar." In distinguishing between a mere thinker and man thinking, Emerson wants to give books no more than their due and to warn the scholar away from the dangers of becoming a bookworm. "Books are for the scholar's idle times," he writes; and he expresses his wariness of their over-influence when he declares, "I had better never see a book than to be warped clean out of my own orbit and made a satellite instead of a system."[67] Star-gazing and the fixations of cultish celebrity are versions of this hazard that Walker Percy investigates in his novel, and it stands in a long and distinguished line of literary works that explore this kind of idolatry and its manifold complexities.

Forgetting that figures in fiction are creatures of the imagination is the sort of mental lapse that creators of fiction have often taken as their central theme. In *The Moviegoer,* Walker Percy offers us an account of exactly what this sort of obliviousness might look like at the movies. As such a story, this novel deserves an estimable place in the tradition of exploring the fortunes of gullible readers like Don Quixote and Emma Bovary in the works named after them. Like Binx, those devotees of the fashionable narratives of their times were too emotionally responsive to discern the difference between, on one hand, their own lives' options and circumstances and, on the other, the fictional realm inhabited by the figures of whom they read in romances and novels. They became, for better or worse, unwitting victims of the imaginary lives to which they unguardedly opened their hearts.

Binx Bolling, however, seems nothing if not guarded about his susceptibilities to film narratives. As we have seen, his knowingness leads him to the dogmatic dismissal of their routines when he speaks of how they "screw up" the search that preoccupies him. Binx's ironic detachment about movies will not go unpunished, if that is the right word. During a crisis at the novel's climax, a helpless relapse into despair will expose Binx's own vulnerability to these film narratives that he deems so predictable and feels he can view with such impenetrable skepticism about their power. Still, despite the dogmatism of this particular view, Binx's capacity for rational supervision of his own conduct and that of others also becomes a resource for stability in both his professional and private lives, rather than merely a temptation to absent himself from felt connection with others. In the novel's epilogue, he helps his new wife, Kate Cutrer, face the death of his step-brother Lonnie, one of the novel's two other characters who is explicitly labeled a moviegoer.[68] We may take the occasion of that moviegoer's death as a hopeful sign, inasmuch as it also becomes a moment when the other moviegoer, Binx, seems to have decisively returned to a world not merely viewed but inhabited.

1

MEETING PLACES

. . . to confront the culture with itself, along the lines in which it meets in me. This seems to me a task that warrants the name of philosophy. It is also the description of something we might call education.[1]

In *Disowning Knowledge,* Stanley Cavell indicates the radical potential that he attributes to the words of William Shakespeare and the high stakes at risk in efforts to realize that potential. According to Cavell, those words can serve as meeting places in an otherwise groundless world. But, thus conceived, they also suggest images of our lost conviction in shared understandings; they show that our mutual participation in common cultures such as those words might constitute is always in jeopardy. "After such words, in their occasions," Cavell writes, "there is no standing ground of redemption. Nothing but the ability to be spoken for by these words, to meet upon them, will weigh in the balance against these visions of groundlessness."[2]

The urgency of this challenge to our reading of Shakespeare signals the serious project that Cavell's essays on the plays seek to advance. But our effort to understand that project should not proceed in isolation from the contexts in which it began and has moved forward and continues on its way. Other meeting places besides Shakespeare's words have offered Cavell decisive opportunities to pursue the concerns that draw him to the study of Shakespeare. Moreover, they have not only enabled him to find companionship while peering into the abyss sometimes opened by "such words, in their occasions." They have also helped him to share moments when the abyss disappears.

The Green World and General Education

Undergraduate teaching and moviegoing, for example, have repeatedly provided opportunities for Cavell to formulate his thoughts and give them intelligible, engaging expression. Such meeting places as classrooms and movie theatres have enabled Cavell to reach beyond the audience for philosophy as it is often conceived by professional practitioners of that discipline. Indeed, my acquaintance with such settings decisively helped me to appreciate the powerful pull that his thought can exert.

Though I was never a student of Cavell's, I took courses, as an undergraduate at Harvard, in the Program in General Education. Cavell initially presented his lectures on *King Lear* that became the first part of "The Avoidance of Love" in his course in that program, Ideas of Man and the World in Western Thought. Appearing in 1969, that essay made an unforgettable impression upon Shakespeareans. As we have seen, one of them (Harry Berger) dubbed it "the essay from outer space," and it remains a favorite of anthologists who seek to collect significant work of our era on that play of Shakespeare's. It also contains a long second part on the nature of tragedy that wonders about our present ability to experience such works of art. Cavell has described parts of these pages as love letters of nightmare to his native land.[3] He was prompted to write them as much by the agony of America's involvement in Vietnam as by the challenges of reading Shakespearean tragedy.

The response of the young to that conflict frequently made teaching, in any conventional sense of that word, impossible on many campuses in the late sixties, when I was an undergraduate. Therefore, as our country emerged from that traumatic era, Cavell was looking for ways to connect with his students by offering them something of their own culture that he considered both delightful and profound, something worth studying and worth celebrating as part of a useable past they could profitably inherit. This search led him back to the favorite movies of his own youth, which he had enjoyed seeing with his parents when he was a boy. Their accessibility and ordinariness could make them as much the basis for conversations as for lectures. Also, thanks to French New Wave Cinema of the fifties and sixties, these films had gained a new lease on life in American intellectual and academic circles. French directors especially admired their directors, who were deemed masters of the art of cinema—*auteurs* worthy of emulation. The idea that these films are merely products of the Hollywood studio system captures none of the esteem that they then enjoyed among French cinephiles and their American counterparts.

STANLEY CAVELL'S AMERICAN DREAM

During my summer break from teaching high school in 1981, I encountered *Pursuits of Happiness: The Hollywood Comedy of Remarriage* for the first time. The exigencies of that particular moment can clarify the ecstasies that I enjoyed in reading that book. I was then, as the saying goes, "ABD," or "all but dissertation," in Comparative Literature at Harvard and still entertained ambitions of completing my dissertation during whatever stretches of time offered themselves for concentrated effort. Summer break for high school teachers is long enough to reanimate intellectual enthusiasms abandoned in the daily press of duties during the academic year. But it is, unfortunately, too short for such enthusiasms to bear fruit in completed projects of any depth or complexity. Moreover, it is a vacation, a time to replenish spent energy and recover lost strength for the challenge of the year to come. So, during such all-too-brief interludes, I had keenly felt the expense of spirit wasted upon an unfinished project that was coming to seem interminable.

During the previous summer I had struggled to revive the dissertation that teaching had forced me to abandon, but whatever momentum I gathered quickly dwindled away when the new school year forcibly drew my attention to more immediate obligations. By the summer of 1981, the year when *Pursuits of Happiness* initially appeared, I had decided to give myself a break by forgoing the frustration of demands that a shortage of time simply made it impossible to satisfy. Instead of working on my dissertation, I would read some of the books that I'd be teaching for the first time in the coming fall, make notes about them, and compile vocabulary lists that would help me meet the challenges of the approaching semester. I would also relax and enjoy myself back in Cambridge, Massachusetts, where a friend's invitation to house-sit enabled me to return for the first time since I had started a job teaching high school in New Orleans.

It took some conscious commitment to enjoy my vacation despite a nagging conscience about the unfinished business of my dissertation. I was reluctant to admit that my life included such a lengthy false start. It took considerable effort for me to accept the undeniability of that obvious fact: given the unavoidable constraints of my present situation, I could never complete my dissertation. If failure was the right word for that fact, or just how it felt to me, you could say I was feeling downright un-American when I first encountered *Pursuits of Happiness*. Even modest success had eluded me despite allegedly abundant opportunities. Still, I was determined to make the most of what seemed reduced circumstances, though, it now seems, I was simply coming to more honest terms with my actual options.

Pursuits of Happiness was hard to miss in bookstores around Harvard Square that summer. Given Cavell's local reputation, they tended to feature his book prominently on display. Moreover, repertory theatres like the Brattle in Cambridge and the Coolidge Corner in Brookline, as well as the Harvard Film Archive, ran series of films that centrally included those comedies of the thirties and forties that Cavell examined in his new book. Before 1981, I believe, I had never seen any of those films, though this conviction now strikes me as quite remarkable, even impossible. How could I have missed them? They arrived, nonetheless, like utter newcomers whose prepossessing energy and intelligence simply astonished me.

I cycled back and forth between Cambridge and Brookline to see *The Philadelphia Story, Adam's Rib,* and other such comedies. In tandem with multiple viewings of the films he discusses, I read Cavell's book on what he calls the Hollywood comedy of remarriage. *Pursuits of Happiness* fully deserves Carolyn Heilbrun's guarded superlative in characterizing the book as "perhaps the best marriage manual ever published," and I welcomed the wisdom it offers on relations between the sexes.[4] The failure of my first marriage had made me wary, though undespairing, of coming to agreeable terms in a relationship that might fit that description: a marriage. I had not abandoned that hope so, it's fair to say, I began reading Cavell and watching old movies as though my life—or, should I say, my happiness?—might depend on them.

I was also having a good time and learning things too. "Things," of course, is a vague way of putting an experience for which I knew a much more accurate description, and one for which, almost two decades earlier, my parents had begun paying what now seems the rather modest sum of $1,700.00. That was the tuition at Harvard College when I first had matriculated there almost two decades earlier. What I recognized in Cavell's book were ideas that he must have consolidated, and found clear and resonant means of expressing, in the process of teaching his course in the Humanities Division of Harvard's Program in General Education. Cavell's manner of thought and expression bore undeniable marks of such scenes of instruction, and they also announced clearly their connection to his reflections on Shakespeare and Emerson.

For example, the unremittingly dark world in which Rosalind Russell and Cary Grant play out their comedy of remarriage in *His Girl Friday* defies one of Cavell's central premises about the structure of that movie genre. According to Cavell, Hollywood comedies of remarriage revive a Shakespearean pattern that Northrop Frye observed and influentially formulated in his discussion of the Green World in such comedies as *A Midsummer Night's Dream, The Merchant of Venice, As You Like It,* and *The Winter's Tale.*[5] In Shakespeare this world offers a retreat from concerns of the city and court that impede the course of young love. Desires that encounter obstacles of law and society in courtly and urban settings can proceed unimpaired toward their goals in alternative spaces such as the woods around Athens in *A Midsummer Night's Dream* or pastoral Bohemia in *The Winter's Tale.* In remarriage comedy, however, unhappy lovers take their marital squabbles to Connecticut. There they enjoy the same sort of release from otherwise insurmountable problems as their Shakespearean antecedents experience in their idyllic escapades.

In *His Girl Friday,* however, there is no countryside into which to retreat. This film offers no relief from the grim Gotham of its setting, which exposes murderous corruption among politicians and chronic cynicism among hardened observers in the press corps. Success in this urban combat zone seems only a more advanced symptom of an epidemic social pathology. Walter Burns (Cary Grant) is the *genius loci,* if not the hero, of this dark world. Through brazen ploys he achieves triumphs so compromised by this depraved context that the wit of his machinations threatens to inspire nothing more than guilty pleasure. Anyone would be hard put to redeem Walter and turn him into something more than a sociopath unless we can get a clear idea of the world in which he moves and has his being.

In an exemplary gesture, Cavell turns to Hobbes and Locke and performs what one might too jazzily call a sort of canonical riff. He invokes two big-timers and a common theme in the Western intellectual tradition to gloss a moral issue raised by a Hollywood comedy. Their reflections on the state of nature thus provide a perspective on Walter's world as he describes it to Hildy (Rosalind Russell) in these terms: "This is war, Hildy." Cavell's move from mass culture in the form of *His Girl Friday* to the Western canon in the form of John Locke's *Second Treatise of Government* perhaps seems unremarkable nowadays when critics more frequently, and less surprisingly, shift from popular to elite arenas of culture. However, Cavell's gestures of this sort openly went against the grain of academic fashion by courting an outrageousness now *à la mode* and thus rendered invisible without clear-eyed hindsight or some sense of history in this regard.

But this turn to Hobbes and Locke is exemplary not only because it offers an instance of Cavell in action as a thinker and the "undisciplined" connections he is likely to make between mass culture and high culture.

It also offers a model of how to use Hobbes and Locke in what we might fairly call everyday life and thus represents a deep ambition of democratic thought. Such vital exchange between high and low does not simply demote the former and elevate the latter in a zero-sum game of profit and loss. It imparts energy and confers dignity while opening common ground where ostensibly remote affinities become mutually recognizable and strengthen one another.

By using a famous phrase from the Declaration of Independence in his book's title, Cavell clearly indicates the inevitably political nature of his interest in these films. Yet in *Pursuits of Happiness,* he still engages the question of marriage in Hollywood romantic comedy with a keen sense of its irreducibility to institutional terms, whether those of church or of state. In *It Happened One Night,* when Peter Warne (Clark Gable) and Ellie Andrews (Claudette Colbert) attempt to elude detectives at an auto camp, they impersonate a young married couple by pretending to argue boisterously. The detectives readily construe their shouting as the sort of exchange one expects in a marriage and decide to look elsewhere for the fugitive heiress they seek. The film ends in another auto camp with the ceremonial tumbling down of the "walls of Jericho," as Peter famously dubs the blanket he strings up between Ellie's single bed and his own. The audience easily recognizes this event as a sign of this couple's consummation of their union, but it completely perplexes the proprietor of the auto camp and his wife. Indeed, as the world goes, this puzzled pair is a married couple if there ever was one, "so sunk in everydayness that [they] might just as well be dead"—to quote Binx Bolling, the protagonist of Walker Percy's novel *The Moviegoer.* Significantly, Ellie has fled what the world obviously deems a marriage ceremony to reach this destination. Her flight from this utterly intelligible rite helps to create the conditions by which the film can represent an alternative to marriage that retains a worthy claim to that name.

Perhaps the light-heartedness of the comic mood makes such movies easier to dismiss than somber melodrama, but Cavell takes the happiness achieved in this final moment with utmost seriousness. Peter and Ellie, on this occasion, represent a utopian accomplishment, which can stand not only as an ideal toward which to aspire, but also as a rebuke of our present shortcomings. Indeed, like John Milton, Cavell sees the "meet and happy conversation" of this couple's remarriage as an analogue to political systems whose legitimacy is tested by the contentment of all parties to the arrangement. Though Cavell admits he may be courting outrageousness, he even claims for Peter and Ellie in this movie the capacity to stand for a democratic version of what Immanuel Kant calls the "realm of ends," an eventual community worthy of our highest aspirations, where people are treated as an end in themselves and not as a means to some other end. Cavell's trespass of conventional boundaries between high and low culture, between Kant and Capra, provocatively signals the inclusiveness of the vision he means to convey.[6]

By fleeing the altar in full bridal array, Ellie offers proof that neither church nor state maintains its official capacity in such affairs. We witness the cameras rolling as she takes flight, just as the newspapers have sought to cover her previous escapade, but this rejection of the authorized version of marriage has become news worth recording on film. If we want to write it up as a story, its headline might read: COUPLE FINDS HAPPINESS IN AMERICA. Like the marriage of Dexter Haven and Tracy Lord in *The Philadelphia Story,* this flight from what the world calls marriage is an event of national importance. Later, when the walls of Jericho tumble and the screen darkens, we all know what's not being shown, though its ultimate import must remain unexpressed.

Or do we know? What the Production Code kept off screen does *not* include those instances of meet and happy conversation that we have already witnessed. It's just that no official code calls them a marriage, so that knowledge must remain secret or, rather, private—as private as a popular movie can claim to be once it becomes a subject of such an interpretation! Or as private as the subjectivity of an interpreter can remain once he has offered a reading of any film.

Subject and Object

Put philosophically, this sort of political distinction between public and private sounds a little different from the distinction between subject and object but runs parallel to it. In a memorable phrase, Cavell characterizes Ralph Waldo Emerson as an epistemologist of moods. In other words, his theory of knowledge includes how we feel about what we know. Reason is *not* a flight from emotion but inevitably compounded with it. The attraction of what interests us is what gets us thinking to begin with. Indeed, it was the appeal of movies that made Cavell start thinking in more depth about them, and he wanted to use the energy of that attraction to motivate philosophical writing. As an epistemologist of moods, Emerson serves as a model for Cavell's refusal to split the difference between subject and object. Simply put, this means that there is no pre-established boundary between the self and the world, where we end and it begins, though personally I would be wary of offering my own young children such instruction in so unqualified a way.

Students of Renaissance culture and classical languages are especially well prepared to understand this point in grammatical terms because they are likely to appreciate the ambiguities of the genitive or possessive case in Latin and Greek. Erasmus memorably exploits the resources of these grammatical conditions of speech by calling his most famous book *The Praise of Folly,* a title designed to raise repeated questions about who's praising whom or what and, thus, what is praiseworthy to begin with. But the grammar I refer to here is not only linguistic. It is the condition of our relation to the world we inhabit inasmuch as language, at its most effective, enables us to express that relation more intelligibly and thus to inhabit our world more intimately or less remotely. Our ordinary words can thus become a revelation of our being in the world just as our everyday experience can dawn upon us in ways fraught with significance that can transform us, though we often miss their capacity to influence us so profoundly.

Cavell's most prominent declaration of this refusal of the difference between subject and object appears in the title of his earliest essay on Emerson, "Thinking of Emerson," and it can be heard in the title of a later essay, "The Thought of Movies," in which he uses Emerson to defend himself from a particular reviewer of *Pursuits of Happiness.* Such expressions play upon the ambivalence of the genitive or possessive case, which can be either subjective or objective or, of course, both. Take the title "Thinking of Emerson," for example. Does it declare that this essay's topic will be Emerson or Cavell on Emerson? Or does it declare the intention—or, should we say, inevitability—of having it both ways? Cavell's alertness to the manifold meanings that our words bring with them enables him implicitly to answer his own famous question, "Must We Mean What We Say?" (the title of his first book) by turning the constraints of language into choices, and our discoveries of its rules and conventions and peculiarities into possibilities of invention or creativity, into the resources of expressive power. Moreover, "thinking," the other word in his first Emerson essay's title, only increases the multiplicity of meanings here brought into play, for it may be a participle (as in the way we sign off in a letter, "thinking of you") or a gerund, a verbal adjective or a verbal noun. And this word gains further resonance by precisely echoing Emerson's famous characterization of the American scholar *not* as a thinker but as "man thinking." Thus, in "Thinking of Emerson,"

31

Cavell refers unequivocally to Emerson's 1837 address at Harvard College, "The American Scholar," in a phrase fraught with multiple meanings.

These are grammatical remarks such as Holofernes in *Love's Labors Lost* or Polonius in *Hamlet* or some other Elizabethan pedant might readily make in parsing the inflections that reveal how Latin words in a phrase or a sentence fit together. But they are also expressions of grammatical relations in the way that such a philosopher as Ludwig Wittgenstein uses that term. They are called transcendental relations in Kant's way of speaking, which Emerson borrows from him in labeling the kind of American thinking that he and his younger friend Henry David Thoreau most memorably represent, Transcendentalism. Such phrases express the conditions of possibility for what Emerson calls thinking by including both subject and object at the same time. Thus, the relation between them remains present to our minds, and we do not let our attention to one obscure the simultaneous presence of the other.

By comparing him with Walker Percy, I mean to put Cavell in the company of a novelist who, among other things, is highly esteemed as a master of his craft, a *literary* talent of exceptional stature. In recent years, as Cavell has begun to consolidate his identity as a perfectionist philosopher, he has acknowledged that such thinkers entertain poetic ambitions for their prose, hoping it will, like poetry, "[make] things happen to the soul."[7] But signs of such aspirations appear earlier in Cavell's writings. His major work as a philosopher, *The Claim of Reason,* begins with a sentence over two hundred words long. It thus poses implicitly, in what some would readily consider the stylistic impropriety of its first sentence, the question explicitly asked in its last: "[C]an philosophy become literature and still know itself?"[8] Though philosophers such as Anthony Kenny and Mary Mothersill have complained about the "self-indulgence" revealed by Cavell's distinctive style, creative writers, like the poets John Hollander and Charles Bernstein and the novelist Jay Cantor, have paid Cavell the sort of tribute that affirms his literary powers.[9] But this divergence of opinion does not divide exclusively along professional lines, pitting the ostensibly critical (and reflective) calling against the nominally creative. Cavell's question thus remains provocatively open and challenges us further to sustain this interrogative mood.

Another key question that recurs in Cavell's reflections upon the relations between literature and philosophy addresses the role of examples. Does a literary work, with its resources of narrative and dramatization, merely serve the philosopher as an illustration of some line of thought?

Cavell emphatically rejects this approach to literary texts in an effort to grant them more autonomous capacities as works of art.[10] Ironically, at certain turns in *The Moviegoer,* Percy or, rather, Binx, seems unambivalently inclined to the practice of philosophical exemplification. Binx recounts certain events to illustrate particular ideas such as certification and repetition (which is straight out of Kierkegaard's book of that name), and a personal anecdote enables him to distinguish between the vertical and horizontal dimensions of his search.

But Percy's main method derives from existentialist writers like Jean-Paul Sartre and Albert Camus. It was, simply stated, to put a certain person in a particular situation and see how he'd make out.[11] Importantly, it was not the sequence of events but the consciousness of the individual that prevailed in Percy's concern. This attention to consciousness, not only as the filter of events, but as the main event itself, the heart of the matter, bespeaks the influence of phenomenology upon the philosopher-novelists with whom Percy acknowledges a kinship, such as Jean-Paul Sartre and Albert Camus. Charles Taylor has aptly characterized phenomenology's ambition as "overcoming epistemology," that is, recovering from the attitudes of the new science that emerged in the seventeenth century, the era of Bacon, Descartes, and Locke. Taylor first identifies the continental philosophers Martin Heidegger and Maurice Merleau-Ponty as the primary challengers, in their generation, to the epistemological tradition, though he subsequently includes the later Wittgenstein in this project. "[T]hose who have followed him," Taylor continues, "have shown a certain affinity for the critique of disengagement, instrumental reason, and atomism."[12]

Just as Percy inherits the continental tradition through his debts to Camus and Sartre (among others), Cavell readily qualifies as such a follower of the later Wittgenstein or, rather, as a persuasive inheritor. He transforms that legacy as he transmits it in such contexts as his readings of Shakespeare, Transcendentalism, and Hollywood movies. Moreover, the three objects of critique—disengagement, instrumental reason, and atomism—which Taylor specifies above and which reappear as the "Three Malaises" of modernity in the variously titled expansion of Taylor's 1991 Massey Lectures, *The Ethics of Authenticity* or *The Malaise of Modernity,*[13] aptly thematize key elements of the transition in intellectual history that Cavell seeks to convey by his suggestive, though cautious, linking of Shakespearean tragedy's demise with the rise of the new science. "Nietzsche," Cavell writes,

33

thought the metaphysical consolation of tragedy was lost when Socrates set *knowing* as the crown of human activity. And it is a little alarming, from within the conviction that the medium of drama which Shakespeare perfected also ended with him, to think that Bacon and Galileo and Descartes were contemporary with those events. We will hardly say that it was *because* of the development of the new science and the establishing of epistemology as the monitor of philosophical inquiry that Shakespeare's mode of tragedy disappeared [Cavell's emphasis]. But it may well be that the loss of presentness—which is what the disappearance of that mode of tragedy means—is what works us into the idea that we can save our lives by knowing them. This seems to be the message both of the new epistemology and of Shakespeare's tragedy themselves.[14]

When Cavell makes this connection between the new epistemology and Shakespearean tragedy, he appends a footnote that reveals a decisive moment in his own development as a thinker. To gloss "the loss of presentness" that he attributes to "the unbroken tradition of epistemology from Descartes and Locke to the present," Cavell records the fact of his initial studying and teaching of Heidegger's *Being and Time* in 1967 as a hopeful challenge to this tradition. Elsewhere Cavell characterizes skepticism and our susceptibility to doubt and despair with a similar phrase when he speaks of our lost "intimacy" with existence,[15] a condition comparable to being so sunk in everydayness that we might as well be dead, according to Binx. For Cavell, tragedy and melodrama, each in its historical moment, are means to rouse us from such a stupor; but Percy, though he sees such resources in reading fiction,[16] communicates, through Binx, skepticism about their availability in Hollywood movies.

Now, Voyager

Cavell's reading of *Now, Voyager* contains an effusive paean to movie stars that sharply distinguishes his perspective from that of Binx Bolling. Cavell develops his celebration of stars by glossing a line of dialogue from Charlotte Vale after she has rebuked Jerry for his self-righteous conventionality:

> Let us take "We have the stars"—since it is beyond the security of shared idiom—allegorically, that is, as an interpretation of what stars (literally) are. Then we have them as examples and guides. So to begin with, we have the stars as Bette Davis is a star, hence we

have images of independence to aspire to, individuality to the point, if necessary, of undeciphered idiosyncrasy. Further, we have stars as Emerson and Thoreau had them, as signs of a romance with the universe, a mutual confidence with it, taking one's productive habitation on earth; signs of possibility, a world to think. Is this not enough?[17]

Thus, Cavell wholeheartedly celebrates the beneficent powers of awakening that such a star as Bette Davis can exercise upon a receptive audience, her capacity both to signify possibilities of selfhood that we tend to overlook and to inspire us to their realization. Cavell drops his critical guard and shows his admiration in an expression of unreserved praise that complements an earlier, more defensive moment in his essay on *Now, Voyager*. On this previous occasion, Cavell briefly apologizes for his felt need sometimes to speak on behalf of the unknown women in the films he has selected for study. This apology follows hard upon a moment of daring ventriloquism or, if you will, complete identification with Charlotte Vale and with her tears in particular. Cavell readily acknowledges that his assumption of Charlotte's voice could be contested. It could be construed as a depriving, a takeover that usurps the place of another. But Cavell sees it otherwise. He sees himself, on this and other similar occasions, as giving voice to selves unnoticed and unaccounted for.[18]

The words that Cavell makes this special effort to elucidate have been characterized (and misquoted) by Slavoj Žižek as "one of the purest and therefore one of the most efficient nonsenses in the history of cinema."[19] Fortunately, Žižek tends exuberantly to embrace such nonsense rather than arbitrarily to dismiss it, though the illustrative uses to which he puts movies much more resemble the practice of Binx Bolling than that of Stanley Cavell. However, Žižek's interest in fateful repetition aligns his somewhat cursory and inaccurate reading of the conclusion of *Now, Voyager* more with Cavell's thoroughgoing effort to rescue this moment from perfunctory misprision as a tale of noble self-sacrifice. For the central woman's disappointment in her relations with the male protagonist in the melodramas that Cavell studies as a genre also leaves open the option of revenge. The emotional attraction of revenge exerts a powerful appeal, not only upon the unknown women portrayed by the stars in these films, but also upon the audience, whose sympathy they fully arouse. This magnetism, however, is not irresistible. They are free, as are we, to forgo vindictiveness (in full awareness of its emotional appeal) and choose some more magnanimous response such as acceptance or forgiveness of another's disappointing limitations. Thus, when Žižek speaks of "the price of . . . freedom" exacted by Charlotte's decision to devote herself to Jerry's daughter, his mention of freedom marks his entry into the region of Cavell's reading of this film's finale. Likewise, Žižek speaks of Charlotte's choice in terms that reckon intelligently with the question of sacrifice central to Cavell's reading. "Charlotte does not 'sacrifice herself for the other's happiness,'" Žižek avers; "by sacrificing herself, she honors her debt to *herself.*"[20]

Cavell emphasizes Charlotte's transcendence of Jerry in the film's final scene, and he gives voice to her mind in a way that reveals her magnanimity or, as Cavell puts it, her gallantry. At this juncture, Jerry's limitations cost Charlotte his conscious companionship in matters of the heart, but they do not erase her mindfulness of his role in her transformation into the person she has become. By taking the risk of speaking Charlotte's mind, Cavell offers us a persuasive version of her otherwise unknown inwardness at this movie's end. It is an understanding of her inner self, as Bette Davis conveys it, that can indeed stand as a "[sign] of possibility, a world to think."[21]

Now, Voyager concludes with a reprise of earlier moments when Charlotte and Jerry enjoyed a mutual understanding that has now vanished. If we take it from the perspective of Cavell's impersonation of Charlotte on this occasion, the previously definitive gesture of their intimate mutuality here recurs ironically emptied of its former significance. "Shall we just have a cigarette on it?" Jerry asks, and then he holds a pair of cigarettes in his mouth to light them both at the same time, one for her and one for himself. The campiness of this emotional moment has attained enough notoriety to justify an exercise in female impersonation. But the impact of this finale resides in its overcoming of any such subversive possibilities, as does the force of Cavell's response to Charlotte's closing line: "Oh, Jerry, don't let's ask for the moon. We have the stars." Taken at its worst, such a conclusion is "*efficient* nonsense," in Žižek's phrase (with emphasis added); but Cavell makes a much stronger case for its aesthetic power.

Charlotte's transcendence of Jerry costs her what she describes to her uncomprehending companion as "an old maid's tears of gratitude." This mild note of gracious acceptance sounds suspiciously resigned, coming, as it does, from a woman who has attained an expressive power of selfhood too strong to sign off so meekly. Charlotte's release from her mother's oppressive influence has enabled her to acquire an erotic presence that threatens promptly to undermine any idea of her tranquil acceptance of sexual isolation and thus invites further speculation. Cavell suggests a "homosexual possibility" for Charlotte, and Teresa de Lauretis elaborates interestingly on some of the complexities that such a reading entails. Although de Lauretis resists what she calls Cavell's "universalizing claim that Charlotte represents 'the irony of human identity itself,'" she registers her esteem for his reading by employing such terms of praise as "singular" and "personal" to characterize Cavell's response to *Now, Voyager*. A "sophisticated, nuanced, and compelling response to the film," she affirms, "can only come from a particular spectatorial position, one sustained by a very personal set of identifications."[22]

Cavell's manner of writing has been called "personal" before, and he has notably balked at this label, which he characterizes as "a hasty, and to [his] way of thinking, misguided description."[23] Cavell shares with Emerson the conviction that the self is the critic's prime resource and that it offers him the means of pertinent communication with others. As Emerson puts it, such a scholar "learns that in going down into the secrets of his own mind he has descended into the secrets of all minds."[24] Of course, such an attitude can lead to "universalizing claim[s]" that warrant interrogation. But a limited range of particular "subject positions" does coercive violence to subjectivity, just as the demand for personal identification can force the false intimacy of a pseudo-confessional mode upon a critic's responsiveness. The gallantry and aplomb with which Davis's Charlotte Vale transcends the limited options for intimacy that her male companions present her requires clear acknowledgement. Whither such reduced circumstances may prompt her to turn is harder to say. Limitations of this sort remain widely recognizable, just as Charlotte's grace and courage in facing them can offer inspiration beyond the elements of camp in the situation where she comports herself with such exemplary independence of spirit.

Stoicism tempts one to withdraw into what Walker Percy aptly describes as "the wintry kingdom of the self," and it thus offers an inadequate account of Charlotte's transcendence of her limited options.[25] The resignation that motivates stoic detachment can isolate a person, not only from felt connections with others, but also from a vital awareness of his or her own feelings. This hazard always shadows the commitment to reason's absolute precedence over emotion. In Cavell's reading of Charlotte's predicament in the movie's last scene, however, her unknownness reveals Jerry's benightedness, not her own. We can hear passion in her rebuke of his conventionality and realize that she simply occupies a ground different from his, a higher one, if you will. But there is no need for such images of ascent. Nor does she deny him access to the place she now inhabits. It is simply unapproachable from where he stands, like that "new and excellent region of life" that Emerson calls "this new yet unapproachable America [he] has found in the West."[26]

Temporary Idolatry

Cavell's remarkable paean to movie stars pays them tribute because they can become inspiring models. They can elicit decisive responses from those who receptively witness their portrayal of compelling examples worthy of incorporation into our guiding ideals of conduct.[27] The very slippage that the camera effects between star and character—between Stanwyck and Stella or Davis and Charlotte—can powerfully bring home the reality of the impact such fictional experience can have upon receptive viewers.

In elucidating the psychoanalytic process of transference, Adam Phillips aptly suggests that a facet of this dynamic exchange might best be described as temporary idolatry. Thus, he gives the lie to the superstitious dimension of a therapeutic mode of relating that aspires to the status of purely scientific practice.[28] Perhaps healing exchange depends momentarily upon mistaken identity or, rather, mistaken identification, which can, by the very energy of such a deeply felt connection, transfigure determining conditions into welcome challenges. As Cavell appositely remarks in his *Lear* essay, "Reason seems to be able to overthrow the deification of everything but itself."[29] The enabling power of an emotional response is thus frozen and awaits release by forces beyond the purview of mundane perspectives and familiar rationales.

Cavell has previously written about how access to texts that we would interpret requires transference.[30] More recently, he has borrowed from the lexicon of religious discourse to describe the sort of response upon which his film criticism depends: "The problem here is of requiring belief before achieving understanding—a dangerous demand from philosophy, a necessary demand (if dangerous still) from religion. But I think commitment of this sort is required of what we used to think of as the humanities. Commitment gets formed long before one has arrived at an understanding sufficient to justify the commitment."[31]

Remarkably, this account of a moviegoer's response reprises the language of Martin Luther in his characterization of a sacrament or mystery as "a secret thing described by words, but seized by faith in the heart."

At this juncture, Luther speaks of "those preachers who preach Christ and proclaim Him as the power and the wisdom of God, and this in such a way that, *unless you believe, you will not understand*" (emphasis added).[32]

The strength of the response that Cavell describes and the reality that he attributes to the stars who occasion that response have led to some rather reductive accounts of his critical procedure. It strikes Ann Kaplan almost as though Cavell failed to remember that he was at the movies when she distinguishes his approach from that of feminist film critics: "Cavell treats characters as if they were existing people whom Cavell might know in real life; film scholars—especially feminists—have rather been interested in understanding the characters as constructions of a particular historical era and as bearing the burden of prevailing discourses of that era."[33]

In *The Moviegoer,* as we have noted, Walker Percy explores the challenges of credulousness and skepticism from within his main character. Despite the wonder that animates him, Binx Bolling manages to keep his critical distance most of the time, unlike Cavell, according to Kaplan. His ironic detachment even enables him consciously to employ attitudes and mannerisms derived from movie stars in hopes of advancing his designs upon women. He initially keeps a "Gregory Peckish sort of distance" to enhance his own powers of seduction in the play he is making to turn his new secretary, Sharon Kincaid, into the latest of his girl Fridays to stay for the weekend.[34] Though Binx admits without prompting that these would-be romantic conquests lead precisely nowhere and end in increasingly awkward silences, this pastime meets new complications when his attachment to Kate Cutrer becomes more serious. Binx's irresponsible behavior greatly alarms his Aunt Emily because it now seems to threaten her stepdaughter, Kate.

Emily dresses Binx down for what she deems unconscionable carelessness in his treatment of Kate, whose precarious condition requires due consideration. Though Emily remains poised and alert, she calmly exercises the privilege of anger to which her disdainful withdrawal from a world in decline entitles her from the stoical perspective that she articulates. Granted, the world is going downhill; but to behold her young confidant, Binx, not only yielding to that momentum, but even taking Kate down with him, seems fully to justify Emily's reproach of him. Binx, at least, is unable to reply to her forthright queries. He palters his way through the scornful measure that Emily takes of him, or he simply remains mute: " 'What do you live by? What do you love?' I am silent."[35]

When Binx emerges from this humiliating exchange, Kate arranges to meet him soon, and she acknowledges that she overheard Binx's conversation with Emily: "I heard it all, you poor stupid bastard."[36]

While Binx waits for Kate, he enters a passionate sort of suspense that is impossible for him to sustain. Cavell might describe his condition as living one's skepticism, a feat Binx has been attempting throughout the week-long course of the novel; but now its impossibility becomes undeniable. Though it produces a remarkable denunciation of midcentury American everydayness on this occasion, such an effort is doomed to fail.

> [O]n this my thirtieth birthday, I know nothing and there is nothing to do but fall prey to desire.
>   Nothing remains but desire, and desire comes howling down Elysian Fields like a mistral. My search has been abandoned; it is no match for my aunt, her rightness and her despair, her despairing of me and her despairing of herself. Whenever I take leave of my aunt after one of her serious talks, I have to find a girl.[37]

As the apt evocation of the Greek underworld signals here, via the name of a New Orleans street, this is a dead man walking and, soon enough, talking. Percy's deft exploitation of what used to be called local color, together with what used to be called universal aspects of human experience, indicates how much we stand to lose in appreciation of both the particularity and resonance of a work of art when we insist so resolutely as Kaplan does on confining our attention to its historical dimensions as the only appropriate objects of study. Jay Tolson has demonstrated that precisely this combination of groundedness in local detail with broader philosophical concerns accounts for much of Percy's achievement in *The Moviegoer*.[38]

But what becomes of Binx in this predicament demonstrates the very alternative that Kaplan imagines to be Cavell's approach to film criticism, as she proceeds to narrow the range of concerns for other film scholars and "especially feminists." Binx, who is ostensibly the hardened skeptic in such matters, begins to act as though movie characters, as they are portrayed by certain stars, "were rounded existing people whom [he] might know in real life," of whom indeed he might become a local incarnation. Desperate for a girl, any girl, Binx addresses Rory Calhoun as though he were somehow there and might understand the urgency of his need. He has thus apostrophized this star before; but, on this occasion, he succumbs to illusion and involuntarily becomes something other than himself. When he tries to reach Sharon and has to settle for her room-mate, Joyce, the voice of "[o]ld confederate Marlon Brando" actually usurps Binx's own, and he eavesdrops on himself in a moment of surprising inauthenticity.[39] What he overhears is not conscious impersonation but automatic ventriloquism. To paraphrase Thoreau, without thinking one can be beside oneself in a mindless sense! We may be driven to distraction by our failure to acknowledge our susceptibility to powers of art to which others more readily, or openly, succumb. In the process, we may not only lose sympathy for such others; we may also lose touch with that other in our selves.

This is the Binx whose ironic detachment at the start of the novel enabled him calmly to savor the impact of sighting a star, William Holden, slipping out of Pirate's Alley in the French Quarter. He notes the shock of recognition among the unsuspecting, who are taken completely by surprise on this occasion. He relishes their emotion from the secure perch of disinterestedness, a mere observer of the human scene.[40] Should he dream that he can tranquilly persist in this condition, we might fairly deem him an "*idiot,*" which is precisely what Kate calls him in the aftermath of his climactic talk with Aunt Emily. Though Kate's mood allows Binx to disregard the possibility of any harsh censure in her light-hearted name-calling, we have just seen the depth of Binx's despair. Indeed, Binx complacently assumes that Kate thinks he has "carried off a grand stoic gesture, like a magazine hero."[41] Perhaps that is what she thinks, for his paltering silence in the face of Aunt Emily's severe criticism could be so construed. But we have long known that Emily's stoicism is untenable for Binx, just like "the wintry kingdom of the self" that Walker Percy rejected in the stoicism of William Alexander Percy and his like-minded compatriots.[42]

The Sublime and the Pedestrian

During the time Stanley Cavell was a self-confessed moviegoer in Berkeley and Cambridge, and braving the headier pursuits of intellectual life in the modern university, Walker Percy, you might say, took Søren Kierkegaard to the movies in New Orleans.[43] That melancholy Dane's spirit pervades *The Moviegoer* from its epigraph to its epilogue, where Binx Bolling thus signs off from his narratorial duties: "As for my search, I have not the inclination to say much on the subject. For one thing, I have not the authority, as the great Danish philosopher declared, to speak much of such matters in any way other than the edifying, since the time is later than his, much too late to edify or do much of anything except plant a foot in the right place as the opportunity presents itself—if indeed asskicking is properly distinguished from edification."[44] The aggressive irony on this occasion of summing-up and leave-taking recalls Binx's impatience with American religiosity. Its routine affirmations of faith had induced him to compose his own testimonial for the radio program, "This I Believe." His credo simply claimed, "Here are the beliefs of John Bickerson Bolling, a moviegoer living in New Orleans" . . . "I believe in a good kick in the ass. This—I believe."[45]

Binx, however, is a searcher afflicted with the malaise of everydayness that settles like noxious spirits upon what Emerson calls the common, the familiar, the low.[46] Popular piety, like other habitual dispositions of Binx's fellow Americans, stops him before he can even get started because complacent certainties of this sort refuse to acknowledge, or even leave room for, a search such as his and the doubts that provoke it. Cavell's "inquest" of the ordinary bears telling similarities to both the moods and ambitions of Percy's novel. When he explains his motivation for meditating upon classic American movies as he introduces his readings of remarriage comedies, Cavell cites Emerson's exhortation to scholars to show "the sublime presence" in phenomena that, because of their everydayness, are too easily taken for granted. He links this Emersonian imperative with the projects of ordinary language philosophy exemplified by his early mentors, J. L. Austin and Ludwig Wittgenstein. But no sooner has he established the concerns shared by these European thinkers and nineteenth-century American transcendentalists than he widens this fellowship of philosophers to include Søren Kierkegaard and, especially, what this Danish writer calls "the perception of the sublime in the everyday."[47] Precisely this dimension of Kierkegaard's thought preoccupies Binx, whose "search" begins in a moment of wonder that he experiences while beholding commonplace, if not negligible, aspects of existence that somehow take him by surprise in odd moments.

These projects also share the writerly challenge of linking high and low without the embarrassment (or should I say crime?) of what we have come to call elitism. Highbrow pretension or, rather, dominance justly deserves the guffaws or censure it sometimes awakens; but they should not be allowed to supply fashionable masks for the inverted snobbery of willful ignorance. That is just laughter in the dark. Taking Kierkegaard to the movies in New Orleans—or Kant and Wittgenstein to repertory houses in Cambridge or Berkeley—entailed risks for Percy and Cavell that are all but invisible in a book like Slavoj Žižek's *Enjoy Your Symptom!*

Jaques Lacan in Hollywood and Out (1992). That book's easier intellectualism bespeaks our academic culture's present absorption in French theory and its postmodern comfort both with boundary-crossing and with gaps without bridges or, as it is often put, incommensurability. The American film critic David Denby strikes a very different note when he sets out upon his *Adventures with Homer, Rousseau, Woolf, and Other Indestructible Writers of the Western World,* as he subtitles *Great Books* (1996). In opening this account of his return to Columbia College for a reprise of his undergraduate experience in the introductory courses Literature Humanities and Contemporary Civilization, Denby sounds somewhat as though he's taking a retreat from the exhausting duty of paying daily attention to movies. He wants to cross a bridge and draw it up, though, of course, that proves impossible.

In Kate Cutrer, Binx Bolling's cousin (and, ultimately, his wife), his philosophical exercises at the movies acquire a foil that exposes the occasional risibility in such speculations and their potential evasiveness. Certain films, or the occasions of their viewing, can provide metaphysical solace for the spiritual drifter, and Binx cultivates such experiences with a somewhat categorical mindset. For example, he dutifully pigeonholes such events with Kierkegaardian labels: "Tonight, Thursday night, I carry out a successful experiment in repetition. . . . What is a repetition? A repetition is the re-enactment of past experience toward the end of isolating the time segment which has lapsed in order that it, the lapsed time, can be savored of itself and without the usual adulteration of events that clog time like peanuts in brittle."[48] This beautiful passage reveals Binx at his worst, yet such preoccupations do not lack a certain appeal when we see they are not merely willful avoidance. As mortal beings, we all know the desire to preserve time in amber, the wish to keep the fly out of the ointment. Kate forbears in bemused patience and gives Binx a chance to get this particular quirk out of his system. There is nothing inherently wrong or bad about this search for order, for *system,* in our understanding of experience. Inasmuch as this turn of mind in Binx represents such a search, Kate would (and will) profit from this disposition in her future husband, especially given the habits of her heart, which are prone to excesses of feeling. Binx, however, cultivates this mindset to the diminishment, if not exclusion, of his own presence and availability in his relations with others, and that is a shortcoming for which he will receive his comeuppance.

It is as though Descartes actually thought he didn't exist because he couldn't prove it, or that a good proof would be all that it takes to solve such a problem. How could you *not* know that you exist? What does that mean or, better yet, what does it feel like? If you hit upon a proof that gives you a claim to the missing knowledge and even gives you criteria by which to test other claims to knowledge, have you solved the problem you initially faced? Indeed, is it a problem of the sort that requires a solution, and does such a solution allow you to move ahead? Actually, it is not hard to imagine a mood in which a conviction of one's non-existence could gain serious credit, but it is well described as hyperbolic, a metaphysical bewitchment from which we require release into the ordinary. Would it not be more worth our time to elaborate what such a predicament feels like? But that is a literary challenge from which philosophy, at least as proposition and argument, shrinks. Cavell finds a "grammatical response" to Descartes in Emerson and a cinematic response to him in the face of the camera when it projects Mr. Deeds (Gary Cooper) as both the object and subject of the camera's gaze. [49] Both Emerson's prose and Capra's movie, *Mr. Deeds Goes to Town,* address us from beyond epistemology and remind us of everyday conditions where habitation and experience become present possibilities rather than research agendas.

In Binx's New Orleans, however, it is the ordinary that oppresses him with its everydayness, and movies sometimes offer relief if the world we view and the world we inhabit significantly coincide. For example,

> *Panic in the Streets* is playing on Tchoupitoulas Street. The movie was filmed in New Orleans. . . . Kate understands my moviegoing but in her own antic fashion. There is a scene which shows the very neighborhood of the theater. Kate gives me a look—it is understood that we do not speak during the movie.
>
> Afterwards in the street, she looks around the neighborhood. "Yes, it is certified now."
>
> She refers to a phenomenon of moviegoing which I call certification. Nowadays when a person lives somewhere, in a neighborhood, the place is not certified for him. More than likely he will live there sadly and the emptiness which is inside him will expand until it evacuates the entire neighborhood. But if he sees a movie which shows his very neighborhood, it becomes possible for him to live, for a time at least, as a person who is Somewhere and not Anywhere. [50]

Percy's novel stands in a line that leads back to *Don Quixote* and its investigations of fictionality and reader response. In this regard Cervantes's debt to Ariosto is considerable, and he drew significantly upon Renaissance debates over the status of history and imagination (or should I simply say lying?) in Italian narrative poetry.[51] But the modern inheritor of that legacy whose work bears the deepest affinity to *The Moviegoer* is Gustave Flaubert, who details the seductions and betrayals of the indiscriminate consumption of popular art in *Madame Bovary*. Binx's moviegoing, however, cannot just seduce and betray him. It can also provide occasions for companionability, and it can even supply moral guidance, say, in helping Binx to assess his feelings about a possible intimacy. For example, when Binx visits his step-brothers and sisters on the Gulf Coast and introduces them to Sharon, his latest girlfriend, he happily notes that "she is natural with the children." Marcia, an earlier companion, "made too much over them, squatting down and hugging her knees like Joan Fontaine visiting an orphanage."[52] Of course, this judgment uses film negatively: it is a sign of inauthenticity, when behavior in life corresponds to that on screen. Indeed, Percy's anti-romanticism is strong; Binx's moviegoing, like Emma Bovary's novel-reading, threatens to lead him dangerously astray. It can undermine his sense of reality and lead him into self-delusion. Both characters thus become incapacitated in everyday contexts that require a more grounded sense of the ways of the world. Fortunately, Binx recovers and makes a Kierkegaardian turn from the aesthetic to the ethical and ultimately (perhaps) to the religious. Binx decides to go to medical school, and he marries Kate—to summarize the sequence of events adumbrated at the novel's close. The conclusion is full of peril and promise, and fully alive to both prospects.

Percy's anti-romanticism sharply distinguishes him from Cavell, especially with regard to Hollywood movies. Percy also lacks Cavell's commitment to serious sustained interpretation of such films. However, as a writer of a philosophical novel such as *The Moviegoer,* Percy struggled to find ways for philosophy and film hospitably to cohabit the same field of discourse, ways that allowed them mutually to illuminate one another and to welcome readers into the play of mind they can promote. Despite important differences between these two works, that account of Percy's struggle strikes me as an equally fair description of a key aspect of Cavell's project in *Pursuits of Happiness.* Moreover, it is important to find ways to advance such a claim. For the level of achievement in both of these books is exceptionally high, but it is also easy to misrecognize Percy's novel or Cavell's philosophy by taking their measure with false standards. Both cogently bring together aspects of popular and elite culture in ways that deeply tap into resources from each realm of experience. We deny their distinction if we deem them anomalies that make lucky leaps across unbridgeable gaps or pretend that the cultural differences among which they so skillfully mediate simply didn't pose immense challenges to the writing of each book.

Percy articulates the challenges of such a project in a manner that shows how the high seriousness of intellectual ascents can leave the aspirant breathless. Without mediation between high and low, one can simply come down with a thud and an empty sense of disconnection. Here is Binx's account of how such an experience changed his approach to the search upon which he has ventured:

> Until recent years, I read only "fundamental" books, that is, key books on key subjects, such as *War and Peace,* the novel of novels; *A Study of History,* the solution to the problem of time; Schroedinger's *What Is Life?,* Einstein's *The Universe as I See It,* and such. During those years I stood outside the universe and sought to understand it. I lived in my room as Anyone living Anywhere and read fundamental books and only for diversion took walks around the neighborhood and saw an occasional movie. Certainly it did not matter to me where I was when I read such a book as *The Expanding Universe.* The greatest success of this enterprise, which I call my vertical search, came one night when I sat in a hotel room in Birmingham and read a book called *The Chemistry of Life.* When I finished it, it seemed to me that the main goals of my search were reached or were in principle reachable, whereupon I went out and saw a movie called *It Happened One Night* which was itself very good. A memorable night. The only difficulty was that though the universe had been disposed of, I myself was left over. There I lay in my hotel room with my search over yet still obliged to draw one breath and then the next. But now I have undertaken a different kind of a search, a horizontal search. As a consequence, what takes place in my room is less important. What is important is what I shall find when I leave my room and wander in the neighborhood. Before I wandered as a diversion. Now I wander seriously and sit and read as a diversion.[53]

Binx's transition from the vertical search to the horizontal could serve as an allegory for the major change in Renaissance studies in recent decades, the emergence of the new historicism (which would also christen that field anew as early modern studies). This shift toward reading works within their immediate historical contexts amounts to an effort at getting to know the neighborhood in which literary "products" of one sort or another had their first airing. Thus, we can better understand not only the convergence of forces that went into their making but also the social meanings that ramified in various directions at the time of their appearance. To speak of works that have "stood the test of time" as though they exist outside of time and entirely transcend the particularity of the cultural moment of their original production denies their initial (and ongoing) contingency and promotes an idealist illusion of their transhistorical values.

Indeed, Walker Percy's fidelity to the world as his narrator finds it—Percy's realism, as it is filtered through the consciousness of his protagonist—could raise some questions about the credibility of Binx's viewing *It Happened One Night* in Birmingham, Alabama, over a quarter of a century after its initial release in 1934. Where would such a Hollywood classic have received a public screening in that place at that time? Late-night TV seems a likelier occasion for seeing such a film as that in the fifties, and suburban domestication and placelessness both define the context of such an experience. We can thus become Anyone Anywhere, which Binx dreads, right in the comfort of our own homes. Or perhaps Percy saw it earlier and elsewhere, in New York in the forties, when he was a medical student there and found moviegoing irresistible in the same way that Cavell did during his stint as a student of composition at Julliard only a few years later? Perhaps the movie's title itself suggests the very experience Percy aims to express with bewitching vagueness and willful mystification? What, after all, is "it" but this would-be spell of indefiniteness, "the view from nowhere," as Thomas Nagel memorably formulates "it" several decades later? Is this what Emerson means by "the moral sentiment" or "virtue is height"? Does one thus become not only Anybody Anywhere, but Mr. Nowhere Man himself? Or can one learn that the spirit's furthest ranges need not be only an obstacle to inhabiting the immediate neighborhood. They are part of the gamut we are destined to run and may indeed be a resource to relieve the occasional pressures of settings too near, too hard upon us. The view from nowhere need not be the view of no one. It can be a place of perspective, a "green world" that refreshes our take on the potentially illusory confines of the present, when we fixate upon them.

In Shakespeare studies this paradigm shift from a focus on canonical texts and authors to a concern for the margins of early modern culture has intensified the dialectic of bardolatry and bardicide, a phenomenon Cavell recently began to address by exposing the iconoclastic impulse in certain modes of skepticism that has made itself felt in Shakespeare criticism.[54] He proceeded further along this path in taking up the problem of praise more fully in his Spinoza Lectures presented in Amsterdam in the fall of 1998. But his engagement in promoting conversation between high and low culture, between film and philosophy, prepared him especially well for this later phase in his writing on Shakespeare. Moreover, since his work on film and his work on Shakespeare have evolved in tandem and reveal obviously deep connections, they are complementary parts of a pervasive effort to overcome false limitations in the pursuit of a shareable, if not common, culture.

Shame and the Origins of a Calling

As a forty-something recidivist at Columbia College, David Denby's adventures with great books in the Western canon bear telling relations to Cavell's effort. For example, although Denby temporarily retires from his active life as a movie critic to the contemplative groves of academe, he brings with him a way of writing that allows certain liberties few scholars would presume to take. It could perhaps go without saying that Denby's account of his adventures does not observe the protocols of scholarly research, though each of these pursuits, professional scholarship and critical freelancing, deeply derives from the mode of the quest. Rather, Denby offers a personal story.

When he reads *King Lear,* he diverges into recollections of the decline of his elderly mother, Ida Denby, into a sort of madness that sorely tested the strong filial bond between them. This chapter of *Great Books* originally appeared in *The New Yorker* under the title "Queen Lear," which made it sound like a trendy intervention into the feminist discussion of this most patriarchal of Shakespearean tragedies. Denby writes of Edward Tayler's unusually passionate exposition of this play one day when Denby's wife, the novelist Cathleen Shine, had accompanied him to class. The pedagogical melodrama prompts her to look at her husband oddly, "as if to say, 'Who is this guy?' "[55] She thus strikes a note reminiscent of Kate Cutrer's occasional angle of vision upon Binx Bolling's preoccupation with his search in *The Moviegoer.*

Tayler nearly breaks down in tears while earnestly expounding the deep motives of shame that advance the tragic action in *Lear.* To support this claim he justly summons arguments from Stanley Cavell's "The

Avoidance of Love," which memorably elaborates precisely this line of thought. However, Denby's evocation of this scene of instruction brings to mind another such occasion that Cavell recounts in his affectionate sketch of J. L. Austin, by far the most influential teacher in Cavell's philosophical training. Austin's William James Lectures at Harvard in 1955 caused Cavell to scrap completely his original dissertation project and proceed along fresh paths opened for him by this Oxford philosopher of ordinary language.

In Harold Bloom's quest for priorities in discovering the deep causes of memorable writing, the Scene of Teaching hits bedrock, enabling Bloom to shuffle off Freud's Primal Scene and Derrida's Scene of Writing.[56] Though the element of one-upmanship in this aggressive mode of inquiry recalls what Erik Erikson characterized, with ironically mimetic clumsiness, as the psychoanalytic practice of "originology," it does take us to a depth where fundamental motives become more evident. Moreover, Cavell himself traces his attraction to Austin's kind of philosophizing back to such dynamics, which crystallize decisively (though by no means exclusively) in a moment of shame.

Austin's teaching excited Cavell because he was, in his own words, *prepared* for it by his own father's strengths and limitations: "[M]y affinity for ordinary language philosophy and Austin's practice of it was prepared by my father's reaching, say, the point of my birth with no language ordinary or natural to him (the old gone or frozen, the new broken from the beginning); and he was nevertheless famous in our small circle as I was growing up for his ability to tell stories full of leavening pleasure in a life on the move, and of argumentative pertinence."[57] Given the central thematics of shame that focus and drive Cavell's argument about *King Lear* in "The Avoidance of Love," it is important to register an experience of this sort that Cavell records in an account of his interaction with Austin over lunch in a circle of students. Cavell aims to distinguish between what some may have mistaken as personal coldness in Austin and what Cavell describes as "reserve or even strictness"—favoring the second of these latter terms. It is to strictness that Cavell attributes the succinct correction he received from Austin on that occasion. "I felt an utter, quite impersonal, shame," Cavell notes, "shame, and a kind of terror, as if before the sacred task of philosophy, for having been faithless to its calling."[58]

Perhaps this moment fits Bloom's description of a Primal Scene of Instruction. Obviously, it registered deeply enough to linger in Cavell's memory and elicit a subsequent profession of the strength of the lesson imparted. Since so much of Cavell's power as a thinker derives from his writing's "companionability," its demand for the reader's friendship, it is unavoidable to note his insistence here on the "impersonality" of the shame he recalls experiencing as the recipient of Austin's correction.[59] Moreover, likening that shame to terror in the face of a sacred calling further assimilates Cavell's experience to models from biblical tradition such as Bloom adduces in elaborating his paradigm for the Primal Scene of Instruction. Cavell himself summons such models from prophetic call narratives in his argument for the "scriptural" status Thoreau asserts for *Walden*. That text, like those of Emerson's to which Cavell subsequently dedicates essays of interpretation, will become the legacy of American philosophy that he increasingly seeks to rescue from what he calls "repression" within the professional practice of that discipline. They are also the texts that he increasingly seeks to receive as his own inheritance.

Protestations of unworthiness are a recurrent feature of call narratives in the Hebrew Bible. The finger of fate seems fickle indeed when God so regularly singles out reluctant, if not merely unwilling, leaders and spokespersons. Moses, Gideon, and Samuel, for example, all in some way balk at the divine summons. Evasive, incredulous, or simply ignorant in the midst of such a moment, destiny's call, they change the topic, dismiss the possibility, or simply don't get it. Later, once the era of prophecy and kingship has fully arrived in biblical Israel, Isaiah, Jeremiah, and Ezekiel, for example, all enact similar scenes of vacillation that express their feelings of unworthiness for the role to which God is assigning them. They do not volunteer for the momentous parts they are to play; they are chosen. That is the chief lesson we can draw from such occasions when we observe this recurrent pattern underlying them all.[60]

To demonstrate the scriptural status that Thoreau claims for *Walden*, Cavell has recourse to episodes from Jeremiah and Ezekiel that exemplify the conferral of divine authority upon a speaker's words. But Cavell seeks to articulate the fate of writing when the word was no longer lively in Israel. After the institution of prophecy had declined and virtually disappeared, the Bible became the repository of God's word; it became scripture, or in Thoreau's terms, "the father tongue." This formulation leads Cavell to raise a series of questions, which he then seeks to answer:

> Why is the isolation of the written word from the spoken word his understanding of the father tongue? Why is it his realization of the faith of the prophets? That is, how does his understanding of his

position . . . take him beyond the knowledge prophets have always had of the ineffectiveness of God's words in their mouths; or take him to a different resolution of his ordainment?

I understand his strategy as an absolute acceptance of Saint Paul's interpretation of Christ's giving "gifts to men" (Ephesians 4): "I therefore, the prisoner of the Lord, beseech you that ye walk worthy of the vocation wherewith ye are called." . . . For the writer of *Walden*, in declaring writing to be such a gift, in such a service, the problem of walking worthy of it is different from, anyway later than, Milton's view of his talent: he must learn not merely what to write, in order that his trust be not buried; he must undertake to write absolutely, to exercise his faith in the very act of marking the word. He puts his hand upon his own mouth.[61]

Cavell's final sentence evokes the call of Isaiah, whose protestation of "unclean lips" dramatizes his sense of unsuitability for a divine summons. The penultimate sentence not only echoes the Pauline passage cited immediately beforehand; it also alludes to Jesus' parable of the talents, with "talent" translated into "trust," a word that can bear the weight of that faith whose exercise the very act of such writing—Thoreau's, Cavell's—exemplifies. Thus, before he raises a couple of questions that lead into his second chapter, Cavell closes the first chapter of his book on *Walden* with a sort of credo: "[O]ur words need not haunt us. If we learn how to entrust our meaning to a word, the weight it carries through all its computations will yet prove to be just the weight we will find we wish to give it."[62]

Such claims require action; faith of this sort, without works, is deader than dead, hyperdead. Fortunately, what Cavell sometimes calls his "little book" on Thoreau now stands early in a sequence of volumes that testifies to the validity of this profession of faith. Cavell's words did not fall dead to the ground; rather, they kept finding new places to stand: Emerson's essays, different genres of Hollywood film, plays by Shakespeare that Cavell had not yet examined at length. But none of his books ventured more deeply in the American grain than *Pursuits of Happiness,* nor did any other produce a harvest richer than the companion to that volume, *Contesting Tears.* Thus, an appreciation of the nature of this particular accomplishment can open up revealing vistas on many facets of Cavell's career overall. Attaining such perspectives, however, requires clearing our jaundiced eyes and locating this book in proper contexts.

Milton at the Movies

In 1991, ten years after Cavell's *Pursuits of Happiness,* when David Denby was interrupting his career as a movie critic for *New York* magazine to study once again what he calls "great books" in the two basic courses required of all Columbia College undergraduates, he encountered among the classics of Western thought no work that more challenged his competence as a reader than Immanuel Kant's *Foundations of the Metaphysics of Morals.* "I was a student of Kant," he writes, "and the struggle with the text was fierce, close, exhausting, and not always successful." However, he does claim ultimately to have experienced "great satisfaction . . . once [he] got the hang of . . . [t]hat hapless difficulty of style, the awkward, cranky, hammerheaded obstinacy and rhythmless rectitude."[63]

Perhaps an acquaintance with Cavell's approach to Kantian concerns via one of the Hollywood films that he labels "comedies of remarriage" would have given Denby some friendly assistance and spared him unnecessary struggle. It would have returned Denby to a familiar medium, one seemingly less formidable in the challenges it poses for critical understanding, and it could have thus cleared the way for him to address metaphysical topics such as Kant expounds in his prohibitive prose style. Finding readier access through the ingratiating appeal of ordeals undergone on screen by the likes of Clark Gable and Claudette Colbert in *It Happened One Night* can add a charge of delight to such a daunting intellectual challenge as fathoming Kantian deontology. Moreover, it can lead to further links between realms of culture that otherwise seem to keep a wary distance from one another.

As we have seen, Cavell's conception of Thoreau's vocation as a writer makes him significantly "different from, anyway later than [Milton]" in his "view of his talent." In Cavell's metaphorical transformation of the call of Isaiah, Thoreau must touch his own lips. Still, the prophetic conviction that underwrites Milton's sublime egotism does not alone impose enough of an obstacle to make his work inaccessible to American thought of the sort Cavell pursues, in grateful imitation of Thoreau and Emerson, at many turns in his readings of remarriage comedy.

Moreover, Cavell's skillful mediation between popular and elite culture entails applying the pleasure principle to pedagogy in a manner John Milton might well have appreciated. Though the Puritan poet's idea of fun would necessarily have precluded moviegoing, the Epicurean deployment of pleasure as a stimulus to otherwise reluctant learners has its place in Milton's philosophy of teaching. For example, in *Of Education,*

Milton expresses the following sentiments about traditional curricula: "And for the usual method of teaching the arts, I deem it to be an old error of universities not yet well recovered from the scholastic grossness of barbarous ages, that instead of beginning with arts most easy—and those be such as are most obvious to the sense—they present their young unmatriculated novices at first coming with the most intellective abstractions of logic and metaphysics."[64] David Denby, of course, was no "young unmatriculated [novice]." He writes of his "second coming" to Columbia College as a returning alumnus who had to face Kant during something of a midlife crisis. Sympathy, in this regard, seems due all around the human life cycle!

Among early moderns who reflected upon the instruction of children, Montaigne more notably than Milton endorsed the inducement of pleasure to lead students along the path to virtue, yet Milton's kindred appreciation of motivational psychology warrants full notice.[65] Thus, if the "walls of Jericho" suspended between the beds occupied by Gable and Colbert in Frank Capra's film can effectively signify the problem of skepticism in Cavell's correction of a Kantian perspective on that issue,[66] Milton might readily sanction an appeal to such an alternative means of expression if it helps make a worthy but difficult point.

Further, the foundational presence of two passages from *The Doctrine and Discipline of Divorce* in Cavell's exposition of what he terms, with characteristically suggestive plainness, "the thought of movies"[67] should even interest Miltonists, whose typical concerns include not only works of Miltonic authorship and their sources but also their destinations. The present-day reception of Milton's first tract on divorce demonstrates the continuing vitality of his works as well as the power of his canonical reputation to confer legitimacy upon those bold enough to appropriate his words. Indeed, Cavell's term for his own acquisition of a voice as a philosopher provides an apposite description of this process of appropriation, which he calls "the arrogation of voice" because, among other things, the first of those nouns clearly suggests arrogance as a potential dimension of the action described by the entire phrase.[68]

As a Protestant poet, Milton is comparably alert to his own liability to err in pride—and likewise willing to take that risk. Such alertness is audible, for example, in Milton's characterization of *Paradise Lost* as his "adventur'ous song," since that narrative's most clear-cut adventurer is Satan himself, or in Milton's acknowledgment that his ascent to heavenly themes requires a "bolder wing," since "bold words" are Satan's medium from the outset of the poem. Given these parallels, we can fairly claim that the query Milton addresses to "holy Light," "May I express thee unblam'd?" remains a relevant moral question for Stanley Cavell (*Paradise Lost* 1.13, 3.13, 1.82, and 3.1–3). Even though the possible ruin of sacred truths poses no apparent threat to the secular philosopher, the effort to inherit the authority of such a canonical writer involves kindred hazards of presumption.

Milton first explicitly appears in *Pursuits of Happiness* in the chapter on *The Lady Eve* when Cavell is attempting to account for the absence of children in the genre of remarriage comedy, which this 1941 film directed by Preston Sturges decisively exemplifies. This feature of that genre becomes increasingly important as Cavell pursues his exploration of the counterpart to this kind of movie, which he calls "the melodrama of the unknown woman" and fully discusses in *Contesting Tears*. The inevitable presence of children, however displaced, in such melodramas serves as an index of their dialogic relation to remarriage comedy. But in Cavell's first chapter devoted exclusively to a single comedy of the remarriage kind, he claims that "while marriage may remain the authorization for having children, children are not an authentication of marriage," and then he adds parenthetically: "This is an explicit and fundamental consequence of Milton's great tract on Divorce, a document I take to have intimate implications in the comedy of remarriage, as will emerge."[69]

The emergence of these implications begins to take place shortly thereafter in the chapter already commended for its clarifying remarks about Immanuel Kant via Frank Capra's travelers' tale starring Clark Gable and Claudette Colbert. Cavell quotes at some length from book 1.2 of *The Doctrine and Discipline of Divorce,* where Milton cites Genesis 2:18 about how God's concern for Adam's aloneness occasions the creation of Eve and Milton thence infers "that in God's intention a meet and happy conversation is the chiefest and noblest end of marriage."[70] This Miltonic notion of conversation as the telos of the marital bond becomes clearly an essential constituent of Cavell's subsequent reflections on the films he examines and the human relations they centrally explore. Indeed, once this proof text comes into play, we can note that its idea of marriage as conversation already has appeared prominently in Cavell's title to the book's introduction, "Words for a Conversation," though without mention of the Miltonic inspiration of this term.

It is a sign of the breathtaking sweep of Cavell's generalizations that he draws upon authors and events and their agents in the manner of *grand récit* associated with intellectual history rather than the anecdotes (or *petites histoires*) and "thick descriptions" of recent historical materialism.[71]

For example, in characterizing the overall project that leads to his enlistment of Milton's authority as a spokesperson about marriage, he writes, "It is part of our understanding of our world, and of what constitutes an historical event in this world, that Luther redefined the world in getting married, and Henry VIII—one of the last figures Shakespeare was moved to write about—in getting divorced. It has since then been a more or less open secret in our world that we do not know what legitimizes either divorce or marriage."[72]

Such capacious assertions can have a stunning resonance if we can put our characteristic suspicions on hold long enough to give them a fair hearing. Even in these dread latter days of skeptical postmodernism and the hermeneutics of suspicion, if you are in love with what philosophy is in love with and thus responsive to claims of such breadth, a nearly fitting Miltonic parallel is not far to seek: "Before the Hills appear'd, or Fountain flow'd/Thou with Eternal Wisdom didst converse" (*Paradise Lost* 7.8–9). However, since Urania's conversation with Sophia—*eternal* wisdom, that is—takes place before time has a start, it is certainly an inappropriate analogue for what most often qualifies as scholarly exchange nowadays. We must historicize,[73] if not temporize, our insights and locate them within the course of densely particularized events. The detailed specificity of "thick description" that the prevailing historical materialism increasingly requires can make the brief decade between Luther's marriage and Henry VIII's divorce seem itself an eternity; and Shakespeare, whoever he might be, stands on the horizon of a future we would never reach without the speed of other kinds of thought. Such ecstasies as we may experience in contemplating, say, Milton's poetry or Cary Grant's comic genius we had best keep to ourselves.

However, in time before time as we know it, Urania converses with Sophia, according to Milton's summoning of his muse in book 7; and it is wisdom which Eve comes to see is alone truly fair once she knows Adam, with whom conversing she forgets all time (*Paradise Lost* 4.491 and 639). Such wisdom as the Judeo-Grecian formulation, Sophia, signifies by no means belongs exclusively to Adam any more than Eve holds exclusive title to grace, though a certain kind of grace distinguishes her in her first appearance in the poem (*Paradise Lost* 4.299).[74] The interplay of these sometimes gendered attributes confines to neither sex alone sole claim to their possession. Wisdom, rather, engages in conversation in the beginning and, perhaps, emerges through conversation thereafter—say, in Adam's dialogue with Raphael or when Adam and Eve work their difficult way toward contrition after the "completing of the mortal Sin/Original" (*Paradise Lost* 9.1004–5).

But skepticism shuts down conversation, and the dominant theme of Cavell's philosophizing has been to expose how such abrupt terminations of verbal exchange often represent a flight from our shareable, if not common, humanity, which skepticism refuses even to acknowledge, let alone affirm. Stanley Fish's recent essay, "Why We Can't All Just Get Along,"[75] illustrates how Milton can serve in the role of conversation-stopper by reproducing ancient strategies of skepticism. For example, the effort to track down origins that leads either to infinite regress or simple admission of ignorance served early moderns like Montaigne as occasions for faith in the face of the limits of human understanding.[76] Fish cites two Miltonic versions of ignorance about origins and the divergent conclusions they each entail as an illustration of irreconcilable differences that make conversation nowadays impossible between Christian conservatives and not only government officials but ordinary citizens who play by the current rules of public discourse. A fundamental divergence of first principles derived from such ignorance eliminates all grounds for exchange in each instance; and conversation, in such cases, should logically turn into root and branch extirpation of rival opinions, if not of the rivals themselves, according to one of Fish's more provocative inferences from these observations.[77]

Abdiel challenges Satan's fomenting of rebellion in heaven by asserting the priority of their maker's authority on the very basis that he is their maker.

> Shalt thou give Law to God, shalt thou dispute
> With him the points of liberty, who made
> Thee what thou art, and form'd the Pow'rs of Heav'n
> Such as he pleas'd, and circumsrib'd thir being?
>
> *Paradise Lost* 5.822–24

The rebel responds to this claim by pointed epistemological questions that ask how one can know anything about his own creation, and the inevitable ignorance of origins thus exposed by this interrogation becomes the occasion for Satan's claim of self-creation.

> We know no time when we were not as now;
> Know none before us, self-begot, self-rais'd
> By our own quick'ning power.
>
> *Paradise Lost* 5.859–61

For Fish, the ignorance of origins then becomes the bottom line shared by Adam with the leader of the rebel angels, but from which each derives divergent first principles. In Adam's autobiographical account of coming into being, he likewise acknowledges his ignorance not only of who and where he was but also "from what cause" (*Paradise Lost* 8.270–71). But Adam's questions about his origins yield a fundamentally different answer, not unlike Montaigne's fideism in his "Apology for Raymond Sebond":

> how came I thus, how here?
> Not of myself, by some great maker then
> In goodness and in power preeminent.
>
> *Paradise Lost* 8.277–79

However, Fish then characterizes the choices of both Adam and Satan as epistemologically identical acts of faith that yield irreconcilably different first premises and thus keep their paths of thought inevitably apart. There is no reasoning about these initial choices—however unpersuasive it may seem, for example, that a being with the wherewithal to make himself, such as Satan claims, would promptly forget his inaugural act of self-creation. These acts of faith—whether in God or in materialism, as Fish distinguishes between Adam's choice and Satan's—are what allows thought to get going in the first place; and such fundamental differences make any meaningful conversation thereafter impossible between these two parties or any others whose basic convictions depend upon mutually exclusive first premises such as Christian conservatives and contemporary liberals. Indeed, it is the burden of Fish's argument to demonstrate the fundamental inconsistency of the theses propounded by such Christian thinkers as George Marsden and Stephen Carter, who attempt to find a place for religious values in public dialogue nowadays.

Consent

This breakdown of conversation in the public sphere bears a telling relation to the other passage from *The Doctrine and Discipline of Divorce* that Cavell arrogates to his own purposes in *Pursuits of Happiness* when he is discussing *The Philadelphia Story*.[78] The selection from Milton's tract begins, "He who marries, intends as little to conspire his own ruin as he that swears allegiance"; and it thereafter pursues parallels between civic and marital attachments that serve Cavell in glossing the idea of marriage as "exemplifying or symbolizing . . . society at large," as constituting a relationship of what one (clueless) character in *The Philadelphia Story* calls "national importance"—a phrase Cavell playfully evokes in titling the chapter he devotes to this 1940 comedy directed by George Cukor "The Importance of Importance."[79] This role of marriage in its political dimension is utopian for Cavell inasmuch as such relationships stand for an eventual human community rather than one already attained. Such a utopia can inspire even those whose first principles *are* incommensurable because it can lead them forward, "in the direction of [their] dreams," rather than backward to the reduced circumstances of a relentless epistemology.

Cavell's reflections on Kant—which, as we have seen, could have been an aid for David Denby's ordeal of reading Kant at Columbia—bear crucially upon this utopianism.

> One inflection of the moral law is that its necessity and universality are to be viewed as holding in the "realm of ends," which may be thought of as the perfected human community. This realm is also a world "beyond" the world we inhabit, a noumenal realm, open to reason, standing to reason; but I am not fated to be debarred from it as I am from the realm of things-in-themselves, by my sensuous nature; for the perfected human community *can* be achieved, it may at last be experienced, it is in principle presentable. Yet there is between me and this realm of reason also something that may present itself as a barrier—the fact that I cannot reach this realm *alone.*[80]

But one can enter this utopia in pairs, and in the comedies Cavell explores, the remarried couples represent such an eventual community. They also stand as a rebuke of our present failure to advance any further in the direction of such a possible world.

As Cavell addresses this issue of marriage's both private and public entailments, Milton's concept of marriage as conversation is broadened to include Locke's idea of consent via the Miltonic precedent of an analogy between marriage and a commonwealth. In considering the idea of an original contract as the charter and model of consent, Cavell had earlier, in *The Claim of Reason,* engaged the famous skeptical challenge by David Hume to Locke's claim about the historicity of his idea: "In vain are we asked in what records this charter of our liberties is registered. It was not written on parchment, nor yet on leaves or barks of trees."[81] However, since the drive of Hume's raillery is to establish the authority of the idea of consent on the firmer ground of human equality, Locke's fantastic etiology vanishes under this attack while the concept itself acquires a more secure foothold;[82] and that enables Cavell to address the thornier issue of tacit consent and clear the air of any residual sense of agreements made and obligations assumed without allowance for conscious consideration and express consent. Cavell maintains that Locke's idea of tacit consent only applies to "foreigners (settled or passing through)," whereas "*membership* in the polis requires *express* consent."[83]

Thus, Cavell's intertwining of Miltonic conversation and Lockean consent enables the idea of marriage that he propounds to display unequivocally public and private dimensions. The union of these two terms under the sign of marriage allows Cavell to carry forward the weight and luminosity of basic traditions of thought—their gravity and grace, if you will—into our contemporary discussions of social justice at their liveliest and most consequential. The indestructibility of such Western writers as David Denby ventures to celebrate in his account of temporary withdrawal from his public place in our popular culture of the moment becomes readily manifest in Cavell's agile shifting from high to low and from popular to elite. Rather than retreating from one order of cultural experience to another, Cavell manages to forge links between them or to find such links virtually in place, simply waiting for acknowledgment, if one can see beyond the perspectives professional training routinely disciplines us into. Dissolution may indeed climb from low to high and sink from high to low, as Wordsworth avers in his melancholy sonnet; but such truth as fails not (if there is any) requires a witness who can effectively attest to altered forms in which it subsequently appears, to congruencies between popular and elite cultures, not their mutual exclusivity.

2

ON BLOOM AND CAVELL
ON SHAKESPEARE

*B*oth Harold Bloom and Stanley Cavell are distinguished humanists who have established their considerable reputations in fields
other than Shakespeare studies. Bloom achieved early recognition as a
literary critic and theorist while focusing his attention chiefly upon romantic and modern poetry. Cavell is a philosopher whose thought
mainly develops from reflections upon the ordinary language philosophy
of J. L. Austin and the later writing of Ludwig Wittgenstein, especially
his *Philosophical Investigations*. However, Bloom and Cavell have both
subsequently published significant books on Shakespearean drama. Thus,
Bloom provides a telling comparison in any effort to assess the role of
Shakespeare in Cavell's philosophy and the availability of that philosophy
in Cavell's Shakespeare criticism.

Other shared qualities also link them. Both are Jewish American academics of the same generation who have prospered in Ivy League universities that once excluded Jews from their faculties. Moreover, they have
both hearkened to an American voice in Ralph Waldo Emerson that
decisively influences their approaches to critical interpretation. But
Bloom hears an Emerson significantly different from the sage of Concord
to whom Cavell attends. For example, in Bloom's defense of a beleaguered Western canon, he simply disdains the common charge of elitism.[1] Indeed, he makes precisely that charge against Emerson while, at
the same time, he readily embraces Emerson as a "necessary resource" in
the battle of the books.[2]

Cavell, on the other hand, considers the finest accomplishments of
our popular culture, such as Hollywood movies at their best, to be of
comparable stature with Shakespeare's plays. As he puts it, "[N]othing

else will be poetry for me that cannot compete with the experience of concentration and lift in such words" as these by Irving Berlin:

Heaven, I'm in heaven
And the cares that hung around me through the week
Seem to vanish like a gambler's lucky streak
When we're out together dancing cheek to cheek.[3]

Not only does Cavell's approach to film comedy derive centrally from Northrop Frye's anatomization of that genre in Shakespeare. Cavell also enlists Emerson to fend off the conventional accusation that the movies he first explored in detail as a cinematic genre were merely "fairy tales for the Depression." Cavell cites Emerson on reading in his essay "History" as the best way of initially understanding the lush settings of a thirties film such as *The Awful Truth:* "It is remarkable that involuntarily we always read as superior beings . . . We honor the rich because they have externally the freedom, power, and grace which we feel proper to man, proper to us. So all that is said of the wise man by Stoic or Oriental or modern essayist, describes his unattained but attainable self."[4]

The chapter that follows seeks to elaborate upon these shared aspects of the works and careers of Bloom and Cavell—their Jewish origins and their Emersonian predispositions—as a prelude to comparing their approaches to Shakespeare. Cavell's immigrant experience surfaces explicitly, though briefly, in his reading of the Hollywood melodrama, *Stella Dallas;* and key lines of thought in his study of that film reprise arguments that he made over a quarter of a century earlier in "The Avoidance of Love: A Reading of *King Lear.*" Bloom's *Lear* essay contains a telling fascination with Edmund, a figure who enables Bloom to deploy, in this Shakespearean context, the theory of literary influence that amounts to Bloom's most consequential contribution to literary interpretation in our time.

Immigrant backgrounds also heighten the alertness of Bloom and Cavell to the dialectic of shame and shamelessness in the characters they read and in the personae they themselves project. Both Cavell's marked affinity for Stella Dallas and Bloom's occasional recourse to Groucho Marx bespeak extremes of this dialectic between which these two writers go to and fro. Playing Fiorello in *A Night at the Opera,* Chico puts it this way (with a thick Italian accent): "How we came to America it's a wonderful story, but I'm not going to tell it now." He then proceeds to tell that story, which is, in its way, the story told by that film itself. We can also discern traces of such a tale in the attitudes of both Bloom and Cavell toward Shakespeare and questions of canonicity.

Finally, as writers, both Bloom and Cavell entertain the highest ambitions for their work as artful prose and even poetry. Their frequent fulfillment of such aspirations makes reading them a pleasure more often than we may fairly claim for most other critics. Openness to such pleasure regularly encounters the censure of dogmatic skepticism nowadays. We tend to characterize that phenomenon as "negative critique" or the "hermeneutics of suspicion"; but under whatever rubric it appears, such a perspective tends automatically to recycle cynical routines of unmasking that have grown only too familiar.

Bloom warrants such interrogation more than Cavell, for Bloom's argument-driven prose often strikes the confident tone of convictions, which, though they may be wrong, seem never in doubt. Cavell, however, leads his reader through processes of thought that companionably allow her to witness, not only the sometimes winding paths that can bring our minds to a particular destination, but even some of the remarkable sights we may encounter along the way. Cavell has made a career-long habit of accepting the skeptic's challenge and trying to reconceive, via the idea of acknowledgment, how to respond aptly to this demand for knowledge. As Cavell puts it, "I do not propose the idea of acknowledging as an alternative to knowing but rather as an interpretation of it . . . In an essay on the tragedy of *King Lear* I say, 'For the point of forgoing knowledge is, of course, to know,' as if what stands in the way of further knowledge is knowledge itself; something not unfamiliar in the history of knowledge as expressed in the history of science. Otherwise the concept of acknowledgment would not have its role in the progress of tragedy."[5]

Still, despite Bloom's merely contrarian grousing at too many turns, the experience of such pleasures as *both* of these writers often provide tempts me to violate the current taboo against appreciation in willful homage to literary excellence. Thus, what a young dissenter might once have scathingly termed the excellent foppery of their world now becomes the occasion of an ironically rare, though hardly radical, gesture among academic literati: the praise of literary accomplishment.

Common Backgrounds

Harold Bloom and Stanley Cavell are virtually contemporaries. Only four years separate their dates of birth. This slender margin seems slight indeed, but undoubtedly it entailed specific exactions. For example, in *A Pitch of Philosophy*, when Cavell seeks to explain how, as a failed musician, he became a philosopher, he appeals to the importance of audition in the kind of philosophizing he felt called to practice. In a fine book about Cavell as a philosopher, Timothy Gould prominently registers this dimension of Cavell's work in his title, *Hearing Things: Voice and Method in the Writing of Stanley Cavell*. Likewise, Arnold Davidson aptly dubs Cavell "a diagnostician of the spirit in which things are said."[6] He has a keen ear for tones of voice, something close to perfect critical pitch. Of course, it is the notion of "pitch" upon which Cavell puns in calling his "autobiographical exercises" *A Pitch of Philosophy*. But in linking his life story to his choice of vocation, Cavell's account of an ear injury that resulted from a childhood accident also enables him to make an explanation that Bloom's relative youth spares him from having to make: why he didn't serve in the Second World War.

Both Bloom and Cavell received their professional training during the postwar years of the GI Bill when veterans were the heroes of a generation. As with Gatsby's courting of Daisy, uniformed service opened doors otherwise closed to the rank and file. It also created an atmosphere of respectful seriousness about the study of normative Western culture. But unlike the former Jimmy Gatz, both Bloom and Cavell are also Jews. An elite education thus helped both of them assimilate into the professoriat of Ivy League institutions with a recent history of excluding "their kind."

In *Political Correctness* Stanley Fish recalls looking around the room during an English department meeting at Berkeley in the early sixties and wondering why all the Christian humanists were Jews.[7] He attributes this fact to many immigrants' desire for their children to assimilate, which was readily served, among those who pursued the academic study of literature, by specializing in the English Renaissance. This most mainstream and conventional of literary fields offered fair terms of competition to the grown-up children of newcomers still (though perhaps unconsciously) apprehensive that their cultural differences would adversely single them out and ultimately exclude them from professional opportunities. These potential targets of prejudice and discrimination could gather under the sign of the human and there fairly exercise their rights in pursuing careers.

Paul Alpers, one of Fish's Jewish colleagues among the Christian humanists at Berkeley, makes a comparable point about his Italian American friend Bart Giamatti. The specificity of each group's particular experience—Italian Americans in Giamatti's case, Jewish Americans in Bloom's and Cavell's—warrants full recounting, but this generalization still holds: immigrancy and ethnic difference required adaptation to a normative culture whose dominance a subsequent generation has decisively challenged. And Shakespeare, more than any other writer, exemplifies the cultural hegemony that demanded such accommodation. Moreover, for Alpers, this accommodating quality of Giamatti's scholarship represents a virtue that distinguishes a whole age group. "Now one of the strengths of my generation of Renaissance scholars was our ability to accept the conventions of the works we studied, the 'social agreements they live by,'" Alpers observes; and he continues: "taking literary works on their own terms was enabled by, and at one time entailed, taking our country and our society on their own terms."[8]

More serendipitously, Bloom and Cavell both attended performances of the *Henry IV* plays at the Old Vic in London shortly after the war. "The decisive theatrical experience of my life," Bloom recounts, "came half a century ago, in 1946, when I was sixteen, and watched Ralph Richardson play Falstaff."[9] Richardson was indisposed and did not appear on the day that Cavell and his mother attended part 1 as a matinee and part 2 in the evening. However, Laurence Olivier's performance as Hotspur in the afternoon and Justice Shallow at night made a lasting impression upon the young tourist from California.[10] The impact of Olivier's bravura warrants noting in comparison with the young Bloom's experience of that same production, even though Bloom claims that Olivier "could not divert [him] from the Richardsonian Falstaff."

The Shakespeare criticism of both Bloom and Cavell also emerges in kindred contexts, though, from the perspective of chronology, they seem out of sync. Bloom's Norton lecture on Shakespeare, at Harvard in the fall of 1987, marks the beginning of a series of publications in which the centrality of Shakespeare expands ultimately to book length in *Shakespeare: The Invention of the Human* and competes only with the centrality of Bloom himself in that project. A defiant celebration of an increasingly beleaguered Western canon characterizes Bloom's writings of this period. In 1987 Cavell published *Disowning Knowledge in Six Plays of Shakespeare,* a collection of essays whose earliest work derives from lectures delivered over two decades before in Humanities 5, Ideas of Man and the World in Western Thought, a popular offering in Harvard's Program on General Education. Such a course in many ways exemplifies the humanism frequently targeted by opponents of the canon in recent debate.

In the summer of 1966 Cavell composed the first part of his essay on *King Lear* as lectures for that course. In July of the previous summer, it is important to note, President Johnson initiated a major escalation of U.S. involvement in Vietnam by committing 200,000 more troops to the American effort there. Thus, alarm about that war was greatly intensifying throughout these years, especially on college campuses. During the following summer, 1967, Cavell wrote part 2 of the *Lear* essay, which, he remarks at the time of its republication in 1987, "bears the scars of our period in Vietnam; its strange part 2 is not in control of its asides and orations and love letters of nightmare."

In this context, he then proceeds to acknowledge at greater length his frequent "[concentration] upon the male inflection of the world, Lear's and ours" and the "grating" effect some of its manifestations produce in rereading this early work. "For a political experience to have moved back out from the mind onto the skin and into the senses means that in these twenty years something like a new set of natural reactions has formed, which means a new turn of history."[11]

These events, the Vietnam War and the emergence of feminism—to which one must emphatically add the civil rights movement—constitute what we might fairly label the conditions of possibility that brought into being what Bloom calls the School of Resentment and against which he tirelessly rails in attempting to rescue Shakespeare from diminishment at the hands of such scholars. Moreover, the brands of Shakespeare criticism that Bloom thus deplores convince him that we lost access to *King Lear* during the decades that such approaches as feminism and new historicism prevailed. "There is no *King Lear* in our time," Bloom avers, troping with characteristic aggression upon the title of Maynard Mack's estimable study of that play's performance history.[12]

Many, of course, would vehemently disagree with this claim in many, many ways. As often with Bloom, the problem would arise of where to begin registering such intense and manifold disagreement. *A Thousand Acres,* Jane Smiley's remarkable reprise of Shakespeare's tragedy from Goneril's perspective, seems an apt option, given the accolades that have greeted it. So do Cavell's highly regarded "The Avoidance of Love: A Reading of *King Lear*" and the returns he has subsequently made to this essay's lines of thought, explicitly in his address to the World Congress of the International Shakespeare Association in 1996 and implicitly in his study of *Stella Dallas,* published that same year in *Contesting Tears: The Hollywood Melodrama of the Unknown Woman.*[13]

"Reading well," Bloom tells us, "is one of the great pleasures that solitude can afford you," and reading is how Bloom prefers to take his Shakespeare, most especially *King Lear.*[14] Reading well is such a pleasure,

Bloom continues, "because it is, at least in my experience, the most healing of pleasures. It returns you to otherness, whether in yourself or in friends, or in those who may become friends. Imaginative literature is otherness, and as such alleviates loneliness."[15] This sounds uncannily like Emerson, or at least the Emerson that Cavell has sought to expound and, on occasion, has defended from attacks by, among others, Harold Bloom.[16] Elsewhere Bloom strikes a similar note in thus describing the exchange between reader and text with reference to Falstaff's condemnation by George Bernard Shaw, who, "like all of us, could not confront Shakespeare without a realization antithetical to itself, the recognition of both strangeness and familiarity at once."[17] Such formulations culminate in Bloom's claim that Shakespeare invented us in a grand prolepsis that makes, it would seem, any subsequent contribution from us, at best, merely redundant. Emerson thus expresses virtually the same conviction: "Now, literature, philosophy, and thought are Shakespearized. His mind is the horizon beyond which, at present, we do not see."[18]

"In every work of genius," Emerson famously asserts, "we recognize our own rejected thoughts; they come back to us with a certain alienated majesty."[19] This is the model of reading as provocation to a self-in-the-making that Cavell has persuasively glossed, and it became exemplary of the moral perfectionism that would preoccupy him during the last decade of his teaching at Harvard, 1987–97. The other who becomes the friend is the better or further self drawing us onward in the adventure of becoming who we are next to be. As Thoreau puts it in the "Solitude" chapter of *Walden,* that remarkable book about which Cavell has also written a remarkable book, "With thinking we may be beside ourselves in a sane sense." Thoreau describes the structure of the self as characterized by "a certain doubleness" and seeks to remind us of possibilities of which we tend to lose sight in the reductive everydayness of our roles as neighbors and friends. Thoreau earlier makes a comparable point through some reading he has done in "a Hindoo book." The soul, "from the circumstances in which it has been placed, mistakes its own character, until the truth has been revealed to it by some holy teacher, and then it knows itself to be *Brahme.*"[20]

Just as it is readily open to misappropriation, such care of the self, which is literally "led forth" anew in the process of "education," is an easy target for misguided accusations of narcissism. Moreover, in the recent context of curricular debates, the further charge of elitism promptly followed such accusations, and it was directed both against the sort of courses in which Cavell first presented his reading of *Lear* and against the

Western canon, with Shakespeare at its center, that Bloom undertook to defend in his book of that name, *The Western Canon.*[21] That book, in turn, most directly derives from *Ruin the Sacred Truths,* and both culminate in *Shakespeare: The Invention of the Human.*

Cavell's effort to defend the principle of perfection from charges of elitism figures prominently in *Conditions Handsome and Unhandsome: The Constitution of Emersonian Perfectionism,* where the opening sentence addresses almost precisely this issue by posing the question: "Is Moral Perfectionism inherently elitist?"[22] Although Bloom has condemned the fruits of Emersonian self-reliance in contemporary American society as a religion of selfishness, his repeated attitude to the charge of elitism has been shameless defiance. Thus, Cavell's thoughtful apologia for the Emerson he cherishes strikes a note Bloom never sounds. Yet the pedagogical tone that he takes in *How to Read and Why,* where Bloom intends "no polemics . . . but only to teach reading," allows the Emersonianism he shares with Cavell to become audible, even though Bloom sometimes lapses from steady realization of his aim to avoid polemics.[23] This connection warrants exploring because Cavell, for the specific purpose of teaching, wrests his Emerson from guilt by association with Nietzsche.[24] Moreover, it is Nietzsche whom Bloom regularly invokes, especially in his recurrent attitude of defiance against "resenters" and also in his frequent claim that Shakespeare goes skepticism one better with nihilism.

By uncovering the traces of Emerson in Nietzsche and by clarifying his own affiliation with Nietzsche's American precursor, Cavell lays a more secure claim to the responsiveness in Emersonian thought. He acknowledges what Emerson calls the "unhandsomeness" of our condition, how much exceeds our grasp or slips through our fingers. Indeed Cavell reckons that such an avowal constitutes philosophical progress.[25] Bloom, however, protests too much. His defiance becomes mere routine and thus compromises his receptivity with the shrill tones of the ranter. Self-reliance centrally entails an aversion to cant and conformity, but it acknowledges estrangement through frank avowals of uncanny recognition. It welcomes the stranger home. Bloom too readily converts such strangers into his own familiar, an adversary he summarily overpowers and absorbs; or else he derides and rejects her with equal dispatch.

Emersonian Differences

The roots of Cavell's concern with Emersonian perfectionism run deep into the curricular heartland whence issue recent debates over "great books" and their role in undergraduate education. But when Cavell guardedly offers what could seem a sort of canon of perfectionist works, he specifies texts only after disclaiming anything more than "some imaginary interplay among [them]" and pointedly admitting that he asks "almost nothing of the idea of this interplay."[26] Further, the privileges of membership in Cavell's group of texts are hardly exclusive since it is little more than a list of works cited or mentioned in the pages of his book. Also, as Cavell's work on film amply demonstrates, he is a dedicated exponent of popular culture; indeed, he makes the highest of claims on its behalf and has fought noteworthy battles to make them stick.[27] Thus, in forgoing the defense of an embattled canon, Cavell differs sharply from Bloom, but in their approach to reading they share important similarities that Cavell makes both intelligible and defensible in the face of such political objections against them as Bloom high-handedly attempts to whisk away.

Indeed, one of the texts in Cavell's list poses the very challenge that his opening question about elitism raises. The third of Nietzsche's *Untimely Meditations,* "Schopenhauer as Educator," is cited by John Rawls in *A Theory of Justice* precisely to demonstrate, in the strongest imaginable terms, not merely the inherent elitism of the principle of perfection and its contrariness to the ideal of equal liberty, but also its potential oppressiveness. Rawls claims, in fact, that such an ethical perspective, in elevating the culture of ancient Athens as a prized value, would not merely overlook but even accept slavery as an ultimately unobjectionable social practice in a polity whose high achievements in the arts managed to fulfill primary goals of moral perfectionism.[28]

Though elitism seems a mild charge in such a context, Rawls's citation from Nietzsche's "Schopenhauer as Educator" to exemplify this dimension of moral reasoning especially matters to Cavell because that "untimely meditation" resounds with allusions to Emerson.[29] If the perfectionism in Nietzsche's meditation actually corresponds to Rawls's characterization of the practical injustice of such political principles as he enlists Nietzsche's essay to represent, Cavell realizes that his effort to inherit Emerson by positive acts of affiliation will be tainted.

For instance, one crucial turn in Nietzsche's argument assumes an attitude toward civic virtue that echoes a remark of Emerson's about skepticism as it is embodied in Montaigne. In commending "freedom and again freedom: that wonderful and perilous element in which Greek philosophers were able to grow up," Nietzsche continues thus: "Whoever wants to reproach him [the philosophical genius], as Niebuhr reproached Plato, with being a bad citizen, let him do so and be a good citizen: thus he will be in the right and so will Plato."[30] In his sketch of Montaigne, Emerson expresses comparable sentiments in the following sentences: "The superior mind will find itself equally at odds with the evils of society, and with the projects that are offered to relieve them. The wise skeptic is a bad citizen: no conservative; he sees the selfishness of property, and the drowsiness of institutions. But neither is he fit to work with any democratic party that ever was constituted; for parties wish every one committed, and he penetrates the popular patriotism."[31]

Of course, Nietzsche's Emersonian statement entails numerous complexities. Among other things, despite its tone of utter forthrightness, it offers no clear moral alternative between good and ill; rather, it posits the potential tragedy of a conflict between right and right. *Antigone* is Hegel's famous example of such a moral struggle, as Nietzsche well knew; and the presence of tragic possibilities in the alternatives specified by Nietzsche fully indicates the profound consequences of making a choice at such a juncture. However, the exposition of this particular passage pertains less here than does the audibility of its Emersonian resonances, which are characteristic of other crucial claims of Nietzsche's in his meditation on Schopenhauer.

Nietzsche's transcription of Emersonian sentiments figures significantly in Cavell's recuperation of moral perfectionism because such echoes recur in the passage Rawls singles out as evidence for the shortcomings of that mode of ethical reflection. For Cavell, it is as though Rawls were directly attacking Emerson. In discussing the principle of perfection Rawls focuses upon "the absolute weight that Nietzsche sometimes gives the lives of great men" and the continual effort he occasionally says we must spend "to produce great individuals."[32] The passage that Rawls then adduces as evidence of these proclivities derives from a section in "Schopenhauer as Educator" where Nietzsche again is clearly striking a recognizably Emersonian note. Indeed, Nietzsche's argument at that juncture leads Cavell back to "The American Scholar"; his path is worth following for those with an interest in seeing clearly some nineteenth-century attitudes frequently distorted in current recountings of them.[33]

Comparable parallels between Emerson and Nietzsche emerge if one further explores the immediate context of the passage from Nietzsche that Rawls draws upon. In the first sentence of the paragraph that follows it, Nietzsche observes that "culture is the child of each individual's self-knowledge and dissatisfaction with himself." And he continues, "It is hard to create in anyone this condition of intrepid self-knowledge because it is impossible to teach love; for it is love alone that can bestow on the soul, not only a clear, discriminating and self-contemptuous view of itself, but also the desire to look beyond itself and to seek with all its might for a higher self as yet still concealed from it."[34]

This quest for an unattained self, whose very appearance as an ideal is occasioned by the example of another, constitutes the gist of Emersonian perfectionism.[35] But the opening of "Self-Reliance," which corresponds in telling ways to the above passage from Nietzsche, makes clear that self-alienation causes this ideal's otherness, not its irreducible externality or necessary difference from the self. To repeat Emerson's famous claim with immediately relevant emphasis added: "In every work of genius we recognize *our own* rejected thoughts; they come back to us with a certain alienated majesty."[36] Thus, self-contempt, as Nietzsche describes it, is bestowed upon the self by love in the name of a higher self that we betray by leaving it unrealized; and clear, discriminating self-knowledge enables us to see not merely our shortcomings, but our promise, and to move in its direction. In Emerson's terms, the self that hearkens to the example that attracts its regard transfigures the illustrious model in the process of its realization and becomes just such an example to others—a representative man, in the democratic lingo of Emersonian perfectionism.[37] Both the passive admiration of hero-worship and the fixation of idolatry retard self-transformation and run precisely counter to the procedure Emerson formulates.

Needless to say, this intrapsychic transaction can have a darker side in the punitive stalemate, if not torture, where dreams in which begin responsibilities turn into nightmares of failure. In these grim moods all that seems great and good indicts the self for personally lacking any such qualities; and the overreacher who underachieves suffers torments of his own devising. However, merely psychological description of such a process slights the political convictions embedded in the terms of Emersonian perfectionism and inclines discussion toward the pathology of clinical observation. Even a defender of Emerson's social outlook such as Judith Shklar, in speaking of his democratic "inhibitions," thus obliges herself to reclaim what she intends as tribute from the taint of morbidity her chosen words carry.[38] Cavell, in rebutting Rawls's notion that the principle of perfection is a teleological theory and thus entails political problems of distribution, unequivocally asserts the democratic values at the core of Emersonian perfectionism: "[T]he good of the culture to be found is already universally distributed or else it is nothing—which is to say, it is part of what it is to be a moral person. Emerson calls it genius;

we might call this the capacity for self-criticism, the capacity to conse-crate the attained to the unattained self, on the basis of the axiom that each person is a moral person."[39]

Bloom would not recognize Emerson in so egalitarian a characteriza-tion. Rather, he insists upon Emerson's "spiritual elitism" and epitomizes his outlook as "an elitist vision of the higher individual."[40] However, when Bloom seeks to discredit the pervasive resentment that he attributes to contemporary schools of interpretation, he readily overcomes any dis-comfort occasioned by such qualities as his view of Emerson holds in critical focus. "Group criticism, like group sex, is not a new idea, but seems to revive whenever a sense of resentment dominates the aspiring clerisy. With resentment comes guilt, as though societal oppressions are caused by how we read . . . Emerson, who knew the only literary and critical method was oneself, is again a necessary resource in a time beginning to weary of Gallic scientism in what are still called the Humanities."[41]

King Lear in Their Time

In reading *King Lear*, the play's vastness will reduce any response to par-tiality, and its notorious unbearability is likely to make even the most tough-minded flinch. In the desperate quest for some sign of redemption from the pervasive bleakness of this immense tragedy, one need not recoil as far as Nahum Tate's happy ending in his revised version of the play that was commonly performed on the English stage for over a century and a half, from 1681 to 1839. Even Jane Smiley, however, confirms this common reaction in her grim 1991 novel *A Thousand Acres*. If she has written a *King Lear* for our time, she has accomplished this feat by taking precisely the opposite tack from that of Nahum Tate. Smiley, moreover, has acknowledged her regard for the "ambition to write the saddest novel ever written," a story with "NO REDEMPTION" [*sic*].[42] Yet, in offer-ing us Goneril's version of the Lear plot, she concludes *A Thousand Acres* not only with Ginny's unflinching recognition of her father's utterly benighted and destructive selfishness. She also includes Ginny's acknowl-edgment of the cause of the totally lost generation of her unnecessarily miscarried children. Jess Clark, Smiley's Edmund for our era, has helped her to this understanding of her inability to carry a baby to term; and he has roused her to the anger that accompanies it.

This fugitive from military service during the Vietnam War returns safely home thanks to the Carter amnesty that repatriated those who took flight to avoid the draft and/or active duty. Thus, Jess, in his way, shares the victim's status to which Ginny will finally awaken through recovered memories of her incestuous violation by her father. Indeed, her sympathy for him and her intimacy with him are a prelude to that awakening. Yet Jess himself repeats the sins of her father to the extent such is possible for someone who does not actually stand in that relation to her. He sleeps with Ginny and, then, with her younger sister, Rose (the Regan figure), in the same sequence followed by their father. Thereafter, he abandons them both and thus leaves Ginny to discover his betrayal and Rose's at the same time she recovers the memory of her father's crime against her. Ginny's capacity to see Jess, nonetheless, as a partner in her loss perhaps inadvertently adds a note of grace to the determined bleakness of this novel, whose author aspired to write the saddest story ever told. Thus, we do not have Goneril in the eighties virtually fantasizing marriage with children by Edmund, Shakespeare's coldest villain. If we did, Nahum Tate's happy ending, which includes the marriage of those long-suffering victims of paternal misunderstanding and vindictiveness, Cordelia and Edgar, would here meet its mighty opposite. But we do have a noteworthy nod in that direction, or as Shakespeare puts it: "Yet Edmund was beloved."

"Suffering," however, "is the true mode of action in *King Lear*," as Bloom contends; and such comprehensive pathos tests the limits of any reader's capacity for honest engagement with representations of human agony.[43] Partiality, on the other hand, is a quality that an Emersonian reader would happily accept. As Cavell has demonstrated, the resistance to inclination entailed in the Kantian morality of duty involves a flight from subjectivity that Emerson's transcendental philosophy does not embrace.[44] Asserting the interest, if not necessarily the absolute validity, of a given reader's response amounts to a kindred endorsement of the inevitable limits of human perspective. Thus, if we examine the responses to *Lear* by Harold Bloom and Stanley Cavell, we may be forgiven the partiality that derives from a certain selectiveness without which we could not efficiently make such comparisons. Moreover, the partiality of their particular readings constitutes the true subject of such an approach; it is what the comparisons seek to illuminate.

For Bloom, the "play's central consciousness perforce is Edgar's . . . [because] Lear's lack of self-knowledge, blended with his awesome authority, makes him unknowable to us."[45] However, Bloom resists any diminishment of Lear's stature, for "to lose Lear's greatness is to abandon a part of our own capacity for significant emotion."[46] Moreover, for

Bloom, Lear shares a deep affinity with Bloom's virtual alter ego among Shakespearean characters, Falstaff. Lear and Falstaff together constitute "Shakespeare's two supreme visions of advanced old age."[47] Bloom's Falstaff is "the Socrates of Eastcheap," and Bloom always seems ready to play this role himself, like the stand-in for Ralph Richardson on the day Cavell missed his chance to share Bloom's transforming experience of Richardson's performance of Falstaff. The "Socrates of Eastcheap" affirms his endless youth. By this positive gesture, Falstaff transcends denying the antiquity that Lear laments.[48]

Still, Bloom locates Edgar at the center of the play's self-understanding, and he is particularly impressed by Shakespeare's arbitrary violation of the historical line of succession to settle upon this obscure figure whose only claim to fame is an odd one. He rid the land of wolves. Once death has taken its high toll of nearly all the play's main characters, such a task seems representative of all that's left to do in England. Revival of the monarchy could only occur virtually *ex nihilo;* meanwhile, there's some cleaning up to do.

Though Bloom assigns Edgar such a significant position in his response to the play, his fascination with Edmund far exceeds his interest in the legitimate brother. Edmund "out-Iagos Iago," to whom Bloom has dedicated an entire volume in the Chelsea House series he edits called "Major Literary Characters." It is almost as though tradition has failed Bloom in the disproportionate attention it has lavished upon the inferior villain. Tellingly, Edmund also provides occasions for Bloom to introduce a biographical variation on his agonistic theory of authorship. He proposes that Edmund's charismatic nihilism derives from Shakespeare's basing his character upon Christopher Marlowe, whose death in 1593 deprived Shakespeare of his worthiest living rival and whose work provoked Shakespeare's emulation for years thereafter. As "a pagan atheist and libertine naturalist," Edmund plays "the roles that Marlowe's life exemplified for his contemporaries."[49]

Moreover, Edmund provides Bloom with an occasion to exemplify once again his argument that Shakespeare excels all others in the representation of character or, as his book's subtitle puts it, the invention of the human. By the process that Bloom characterizes as self-overhearing, Edmund begins to undergo a change otherwise unprecedented in his life's span when he observes, in his dying breath, "Yet Edmund was beloved." This change promptly leads Edmund to a sudden resolution to do some good "despite [his] own nature" (5.3.238, 243). To appreciate the Emersonianism in Bloom's formulation, we may simply ask: what self could Edmund be overhearing at this moment but his better or further self, to which he has been overdeterminedly deaf heretofore? He returns too late to its "alienated majesty." Cavell makes a comparable claim about Edmund when, in "The Avoidance of Love," he observes that "evil is not wrong when it thinks of itself as good, for at those times it recaptures a craving for goodness, an experience of innocence which the world rejects."[50]

Cavell's *Lear* essay focuses upon shame as the pervasive motive that drives the action of this tragedy. In the first scene Lear dodges the making of an honest avowal of his own need for love by staging a public ceremony. Even his talk of "[crawling] toward death" and his anticipation of Cordelia's "kind nursery" sound like involuntary revelations of infantile sentiments rather than frank confessions of need. Lear seeks to exact lavish tribute from his daughters while denying the inevitability of his dependence upon them. Likewise Gloucester can only brazen out his initial acknowledgment of paternity in Edmund's case. He hedges its expression with ribald jokes whose bluff appeal for Kent's connivance might promptly embarrass a less stoical interlocutor. Shortly thereafter, the easy arousal of his suspicions of Edgar reveals Gloucester's insecurity even about the bond whose legitimacy might have spared him such anxiety. Any exposure of contingency seems to threaten such figures with inadmissible evidence of their human vulnerability. Thus, they must hide or deny or otherwise seek cover from revelations of their neediness.

Cavell is also exceptionally critical of Edgar's delay in identifying himself to his father Gloucester. In his autobiographical writing Cavell has located his alertness to this sentiment in the context of his own relationship with his father.[51] Moreover, as we have seen, Cavell has linked his own, vocationally decisive, affiliation with J. L. Austin—Cavell's philosophical father, if you will—to his immigrant father's lack of any "language ordinary or natural to him," a limitation that could easily cause considerable social anxiety, though the elder Cavell regularly overcame this shortcoming with adeptness in storytelling.[52] Indeed, Cavell interestingly describes what Bloom would call a primal scene of instruction when Austin curtly censured him for taking too casually the philosophical problem of universals: "I felt an utter, quite impersonal, shame," Cavell notes, "shame, and a kind of terror, as if before the sacred task of philosophy, for having been faithless to its calling."[53]

"Impersonal" seems a curious word to describe someone in the throes of so intense a moment. Perhaps it is merely a post-factum fantasy of detachment that represses the very pain that makes such an experience memorable, though self-deception of this kind is hard to imagine in a mind so aware of itself as Cavell's. Perhaps it records a crucial occasion in the apprenticeship of a *professional* philosopher who has, nonetheless, pointedly challenged the validity of philosophy's professionalization.[54] Moreover, Cavell has been taken to task for "disingenuously" identifying himself as an "amateur" in both Shakespeare and film studies, two chief areas outside philosophy where he has made sustained forays into criticism.[55] I cannot explain with certainty Cavell's choice of the word "impersonal" to describe the shame he experienced in Austin's censure, but it warrants notice in the context of the exception he has taken to those who characterize the manner of his writing as "personal." Furthermore, Cavell notes this "misguided description" in relation to Rael Myerowitz's comparisons of Cavell's references to his Jewish background with those of other Jewish American academics such as Harold Bloom.[56]

At the risk of such a mistaken personalization of Cavell's writing on *Lear,* I want to note the overdetermining presence of shame in "The Avoidance of Love" as a source of that essay's abiding power. Shame, and the avoidance of eyes that shame enforces, becomes for Cavell the explanatory key for opening the mysteries of motivation that drive the action in *King Lear* from its outset. As Cavell forcibly posits this thesis, he drives home the urgency of his claim by accosting the reader with an intimate imperative: "Think of being ashamed of one's origins, one's accent, one's ignorance, one's skin, one's clothes, one's legs or teeth."[57] Moreover, in establishing the grounds for his argument about the motivational force of shame, Cavell echoes Burckhardt's famous assertion that, during the Renaissance in Italy, "man became a spiritual *individual, and* recognized himself as such."[58] "With the discovery of the individual," Cavell opines, "whether in Paradise or in the Renaissance, there is the simultaneous discovery of the isolation of the individual."[59] However, a less immediately apparent allusion here leads one not to Burckhardt but to his young colleague in Basel, Friedrich Nietzsche, whose genealogy of tragedy repeatedly emphasizes the Apollonian *principium individuationis* that constitutes the Sophoclean agons of such characters as Oedipus and Antigone. According to Nietzsche, tragic experience, in the Attic tradition, entails painful separation into discrete selfhood, and Greek tragedy reenacts the ordeal of that traumatic process.

Cavell, however, remains eloquently agnostic on Burckhardt's historical claim. His unwillingness to take a definite stand on this question of timing enables him to escape the trap of positivism in investigating subjectivity. Moreover, it allows him to evoke dimensions of human inwardness that elude exact temporal charting or precise association with some grand progenitor. At this juncture he thus forbears from commitment to a position analogous to Bloom's attribution of the invention of the human to Shakespeare.[60] Rather, he strikes an Emersonian note in tandem with the echo of Nietzsche, both of which reinforce the claim he is making about tragedy: that such suffering provides a kind of knowledge; undergoing a loss, not *grasping* something, thus becomes a condition for philosophical progress. In "Experience," Emerson puts it this way: "It is very unhappy, but too late to be helped, the discovery we have made, that we exist. That discovery is called the Fall of Man. Ever afterwards we suspect our own instruments."[61]

Stella Dallas **and** A Thousand Acres

This idea recurs under the Nietzschean rubric of "the pain of individuation" in Cavell's discussion of *Stella Dallas*, where he offers an ensemble of influences and analogues—not only from Emerson and Nietzsche, but also Descartes, Thoreau, and Ibsen—that converge to support his concluding assertions about Stella's actions in that melodrama.[62] This film tells the story of a mill-hand's daughter who aspires to become part of the glamorous world she sees at the movies. Stella marries "above her class," and when her marriage fails, her daughter, Laurel, is torn between the parents' different worlds. Stella ultimately lets Laurel go live with her father and his new wife. Cavell rejects the standard reading of this film as a tear-jerker about noble self-sacrifice and social exclusion. Stella lets Laurel go for reasons quite different from any spell that upper-class glamour once cast upon the vulnerable heart of a restless working-class girl.

Cavell's essay on *Stella Dallas* summons memories at two important moments that impart a sense of his deeply personal involvement with the argument he advances. The first comes early and is hard to miss:

> When my mother asked for an opinion from my father and me about a new garment or ornament she had on, a characteristic form she gave her question was, "Too Stella Dallas?" The most frequent scene of the question was our getting ready to leave our apartment for the Friday night movies, by far the most important, and reliable, source of common pleasure for the three of us. I knew even then, so I seem always to have remembered it, that my mother's reference to Stella Dallas was not to a figure from whom she was entirely disassociating herself. Her question was concerned to ward off a certain obviousness of display, not to deny the demand to be noticed.[63]

The prominent placement of such a recollection in an essay entitled "Stella's Taste" suggests an intimate concern with questions of value that do not legitimately warrant ethical or political monitoring at the level of public policy. Rather, they fall into the class of what early modern Protestants called "things indifferent," where personal preference should exercise authority and rights of association should be entirely voluntary. But matters of taste have a way of acquiring consequences beyond the sphere of personal discretion. They readily become instruments of shame, humiliation, and exclusion. The key issue in Cavell's reading of *Stella Dallas* centers upon who wields these instruments. Can Stella *not* know what she is doing? At crucial points in the plot, does she not exercise conscious control over how she looks and decisively calculate the impact her appearance is making? Does she not clearly express her *distaste* for a social world she once aspired to join, which thus becomes, for Stella, a world well lost despite the inevitable pain of separation?

Cavell emphasizes Stella's willful management of her appearance in opposition to views that stress both her lack of control in this regard and her ultimate victimization as an outsider unable to cross rigid boundaries of social class.[64] Thus, Cavell disputes the view that Stella gives up her daughter Laurel in a gesture of noble self-sacrifice so she can gain membership in a world to which Stella aspires but cannot enter. Retrospectively, in the introduction to *Contesting Tears,* Cavell goes so far as to characterize his reading of this film as an effort "to demonstrate the *overturn* of the received archetypal story of self-sacrifice, to reveal it instead in the Stanwyck *Stella Dallas* as a story—or as the cover for a story—of self-liberation and self-empowering."[65] These rival responses to questions raised by this melodrama's poignant finale create an inviting occasion for moral reflection. However, the personal depth of Cavell's engagement of these issues in reading this film again warrants particular attention, especially because he does not so prominently highlight his stake in this later turn of his argument. When Cavell invokes "the issue of immigrancy" in America, where "the demand for conformity becomes withering, both absolute and obscure," he adds, in a terse aside, "I speak from experience."[66]

Stella's decision to let Laurel go into a social world where Stella's taste and manner mark her as an outsider corresponds to a pattern of assimilation familiar to many immigrant families in America. In Cavell's career, this pattern is reflected more clearly in his relations with his father than in those with his mother. As Cavell has remarked,

I was prepared for ordinary language philosophy and Austin's way of doing it by my father's dilemma. My father reached the point of my birth with no language "ordinary" or "natural" to him. His Polish and Russian were gone, his Hebrew was childish, his Yiddish frozen, and his English broken to begin with. Yet, like Austin, he had a knack for telling stories that hit home, that went right to the quick of some moral or philosophical issue. My father's struggle to be at home with his life here could set my teeth on edge. He worked in a pawnshop, and I sometimes worked there too. So I know it was an honest business, and an honorable one, too. He showed painstaking consideration for the hardships that brought people there. He had nothing to be ashamed of. I could have told him that.[67]

In *The Present Age* Kierkegaard compellingly satirizes modern knowingness as it appears in the diminishment of relations between fathers and sons into merely clinical observation. The lukewarm evasions of such detachment regularly tempt our intellectual nature to settle upon what passes for knowledge or the attitudes of mind associated with such a relation to others. We withhold acknowledgment as though we knew in advance how things stand, though such prudent forbearance mostly spares us the pain of an honest reckoning with our own needs and limitations in our relations with others. Cavell, who published an essay on Kierkegaard in his first book, *Must We Mean What We Say?* (1969), also includes him in a list of those he calls nineteenth-century philosophers of identity—Emerson, Thoreau, and Nietzsche are the others—in the account of the adolescent crisis that leads into his memory of a decisive confrontation with his father, a turning point after which they began to forgive each other.[68] This passage from *The Present Age* well describes the sort of detached knowingness that a crucial moment of candor allowed Cavell and his father to get well beyond.

A father no longer curses his son in anger, using all his parental authority, nor does a son defy his father, a conflict which might end in the inwardness of forgiveness; on the contrary, their relationship is irreproachable, for it is in the process of ceasing to exist, since they are no longer related to one another within the relationship; in fact it has become a problem in which two partners observe each other as in a game, instead of having any relation to each other, and they note down each other's remarks instead of showing a firm devotion.[69]

For Cavell, as with Kierkegaard, such calculation and reserve represent a profound moral failure. From this perspective, the severity with which Cavell judges Edgar's delay in revealing himself to his father Gloucester acquires greater intelligibility. Indeed, so far as Cavell's severity exceeds our measured sense of rightness in that case, it bespeaks his view of the consequentiality of such a failure. Moreover, it signals the sensibility that he subsequently manifests in his responsiveness to the plight of Stella Dallas and in his descriptions of his biological and professional fathers—the former's struggles with shame and Austin's awakening of shame in Cavell.

Ironically, it is over just such an issue that Jane Smiley allows Ginny, the narrator in *A Thousand Acres,* to announce what you might call Smiley's intention to write a novel. In reprising the *Lear* plot, when Smiley stages her version of the division of the kingdom, she lets her narrator's musings patently interrupt the action as it is unfolding. She deliberately slows down the on-going action for the sort of meditative interlude that a play by Shakespeare would use a soliloquy to represent. But a novel can deploy such a pause for reflection without endangering the progress of the plot so emphatically. In fact, Smiley has acknowledged that it is this freedom with point of view that attracts her to the novel as a literary form and that initially attracted her to the "novelization" of this particular Shakespearean tragedy.[70]

Thus, between Caroline/Cordelia's initial demurral over her father's offer and Larry/Lear's prompt exclusion of his youngest daughter from inheriting a third of the family farm, Smiley inserts a page and a half of Ginny's ruminations about her views of her father. They sound uncannily like an effort to gain the sort of detachment that Kierkegaard condemns in *The Present Age.* " 'Perhaps there is a distance that is the optimum distance for seeing one's father,' Ginny opines. 'Well, that is a distance I never found.' "[71] Of course, Kierkegaard is commenting upon relations between fathers and sons, not those between fathers and daughters. Still, what Bloom calls the patriarchal sublime could not survive Ginny's quest for perspective. What Cavell dares to condemn in Edgar would also resist censure in her case. Indeed, it would be scandalous to pass such a judgment against Ginny, and besides, who would want to do so? Starting, as it does, from the premise of father-daughter incest, Smiley's *Lear* for our time completely disarms such criticism, once one accepts that central premise.

Shame, Shamelessness, and the Uses of Shakespeare

Among the foremost qualities that distinguish Bloom's Shakespeare criticism and his overall project of reclaiming the Western canon, shamelessness seems a strong contender for first place. His wholehearted embrace of Falstaff is symptomatic but hardly unique. Bloom rides roughshod over fields of knowledge where angels might fear to tread. His troping upon justly famous commonplaces of contemporary criticism amounts to contrarian trumping of whatever rival opinions might initially seem obstacles in his way. Thus, they can become opportunities for striking turns of phrase as Bloom advances his own claims.[72] When Falstaff playfully taunts Hal for a casual allusion to scripture, the phrase he uses, "damnable iteration," offers an apt analogue to Bloom's practice. It is not an exact parallel to that ruin of the sacred truths that Marvell feared Milton might cause and that Bloom invokes to epitomize the relations he explores between poetry and belief in major works of the Western canon. Rather, it smacks of a flirtation with scandal whose consequences needn't prove too costly in the end. It attracts a desired attention and thus satisfies a need to be noticed that regularly goes unfulfilled among academic critics.

In *The Book of J* Bloom makes a brash gesture at claiming the mantle of Shakespeare from, if not God, at least the messenger of His (to many) holy word—in this case the court historian of King David in 2 Samuel, to whom source critics attribute the authorship of the private history of Israel's first king. "Since David is as complex and dialectical a consciousness as Hamlet," Bloom writes, "describing his personality is a Shakespearean task."[73] Then, with no more pause than a period, Bloom begins his description of David. When Bloom's brazen performance in this book elicits the truly apposite criticism that he "lacked the audacity to go all the way and identify J as Bathsheba the queen mother," he announces himself "happy to adopt the suggestion belatedly" and thereafter uses the two designations interchangeably.[74] Elsewhere, when Bloom recommends that Marlowe's Barabas should be played by Groucho Marx—"the sublime Groucho," as Bloom dubs him—we are again witnessing his deployment of one of the resources upon which he routinely draws to confront audaciously the narrowing of human possibilities.[75]

But, of course, in this case he is boldly facing down basic evidence of the legacy of European anti-Semitism. Groucho Marx, it seems, should play Harold Bloom playing Falstaff in his assault upon the School of Resentment.

Cavell has thoughtfully explored the foundational presence of immigrant experience in the comedies of the Marx Brothers.[76] Moreover, he is acutely aware of the proximity between the ridiculous and the sublime, and he has acknowledged his apparent courting of "outrageousness" in using film comedy to gloss the ideas of such thinkers as Immanuel Kant and Ludwig Wittgenstein.[77] His study of opera and the ineffable subjectivity voiced by divas overlaps tellingly with his work on Hollywood melodrama and Shakespeare. He aptly invokes Groucho in "the sublime Marx brothers' *A Night at the Opera*" to illustrate the easy passability of whatever may seem definitely to mark a boundary between the ridiculous and the sublime. In Cavell this passage itself moves from Debussy to the Marx brothers via late Shakespeare—in particular, the finales of *The Winter's Tale* and *Antony and Cleopatra* in which, respectively, Hermione's statue comes to life and Cleopatra readies herself to join her Antony beyond the grave.[78]

Like Bloom, Cavell also entertains explicit ambitions of the highest sort for his writing as writing, as we have seen. In enumerating features that distinguish the literature of moral perfectionism Cavell notes that such "philosophical writing, say the field of prose, enters into competition with the field of poetry, not—though it feels otherwise—to banish all poetry from the just city but to claim for itself the privilege of the work poetry does in making things happen to the soul, so far as that work has its rights."[79]

Cavell's literary ambitions, at their height, are fully shared by Bloom, whose use of prose poetry at decisive turns in his critical works declares an intimacy between criticism and poetry that makes the two indistinguishable except via such an obvious formal sign as versification.[80] However, it is when Bloom's agonistic theory of authorship overtakes his representation of the process of reading that he most strikingly differs from Cavell. Bloom's persistent effort to advance this cherished thesis leads him to allow argument to drive his prose too exclusively. His extreme emphasis upon conflict and willful misreading occludes the responsiveness that interpretation at least initially requires.

Perhaps the ridiculous and the sublime, and even shame and shamelessness, are discernible only by canons of taste that political interpretation must forego in its quest for an egalitarian culture. Animated by righteous indignation, not by resentment, it must tirelessly unmask aesthetic discriminations whose true foundations are supposedly race, class, and gender. When Bloom identifies "the patriarchal sublimity" of *King Lear* as the feature he wishes to foreground, perhaps he is indulging merely in an exercise in nostalgia rather than a bold reversal of pernicious trends. His penchant for superlatives, not only in degree but in kind, leads him to celebrate sublimity rather than to decry patriarchy. If Jane Smiley's *A Thousand Acres* has become *King Lear* in our time, Cavell's reading of *Stella Dallas* has at least given him a way to sustain his end of the conversation with the next generation in its preoccupation with gender issues. Meanwhile, Bloom has drifted into monologue, overhearing only his old self and deaf to the next self, the onwardness of the self, as Emerson puts it.

In his pedagogical mood, Bloom invokes Emerson's claim in "The American Scholar" that the best books "impress us with the conviction that one nature wrote and the same reads." Despite the struggles for mastery of strength against strength that Bloom employs to characterize the memorable writing of strong poets, there subsists even in that contest a prior experience of reading founded upon impressionability. "If *King Lear* is fully to find you," Bloom continues, "then weigh and consider the nature it shares with you; its closeness to your self . . . Be open to a full reading of *King Lear,* and you will understand the origins of what you judge to be patriarchy."[81] The question whether Bloom's call to openness will led to the promised end that he specifies warrants asking; and the fullness of any reading will inevitably betray some partiality, however minutely accountable to the text under review such a reading may aim to be. But the chance that some change will take place in a self that freshly overhears itself in the lines of *King Lear* seems a safe bet. Even Edmund could testify to that.

3

FROM SKEPTICISM TO PERFECTIONISM

When a thought of Plato becomes a thought to me, . . . time is no more.[1]

In this chapter I describe the reception of Renaissance skepticism by the contemporary philosopher Stanley Cavell. I begin by characterizing that mode of Renaissance thought and proceed to show the ways in which Cavell has made use of Montaigne and Descartes in responding to Shakespearean tragedy. The influence of Emerson upon Cavell helps to explain his evolving manner of linking skepticism and tragedy and his response to these phenomena in Shakespeare and philosophy. Like Montaigne, Emerson wrote an essay on "Experience," but for the American philosopher, that essay marks an irrevocable encounter with skepticism and a realization of our vulnerability to its devastating incursions into our everyday lives. By remaining open to what the Frenchman ultimately shrugs off, Emerson not only demonstrates a capacity for tragic understanding that Montaigne fails to realize, he also becomes an exemplar of the perfectionism that Cavell comes to embrace.

Since Cavell's skepticism emphasizes the problem of other minds rather than doubts about the external world, it inspires the response of perfectionism. This mode of thought depends upon the other as a provocation to self-transformation whether that other appears in the form of a friend or a text or as some other stimulus to fresh transformation and change. This dynamic potential in texts recalls Renaissance modes of writing, in which the practice of imitation involves both literary models and models of conduct, a practice in which aesthetics and ethics overlap and permeate one another. The second part of this chapter begins by describing a key moment in the Renaissance reception of Plato—

Cardinal Bembo's discourse on love in Book Four of *Il libro del cortegiano*—which derives from the tradition of thought that Cavell pointedly uses to illustrate fundamental features of perfectionism. This doctrine of love can serve as a guide to the Neoplatonic philosophy of love that permeates the lyric tradition of Elizabethan poetry. Exemplary lyrics of this kind are then reanimated by perfectionist readings and imitations by such contemporary poets as Anthony Hecht and Philip Larkin in poems that demonstrate the power of such idealism despite our current wariness in precisely this regard. The second part of this chapter also seeks to illustrate this kind of perfectionist reading by exploring in some detail the relationship between Larkin's "Sad Steps" and the sonnet from Sir Philip Sidney's *Astrophil and Stella* that it explicitly evokes, "With how sad steps, O moon, thou climb'st the sky."

Stanley Cavell's Renaissance Skepticism

Renaissance skepticism chiefly warrants that name inasmuch as it depends upon the rediscovery and circulation of Sextus Empiricus's *Outlines of Pyrrhonism,* and we can witness the impact of that text upon a key example of this mode of Renaissance thought in Michel de Montaigne's "An Apology for Raymond Sebond." In that essay Montaigne strives to distinguish between dogmatic skepticism, which he particularly associates with Cicero's *Academica,* and the more mitigated variety, which he associates with Pyrrhonism. The Renaissance takes its name from the revival of classical culture that such developments exemplify, and the revival of ancient skepticism in particular follows a trajectory in which such key figures as Montaigne and Descartes represent alternative modes of doubt. Montaigne balks at the absolutism of radical doubt because he senses the paradoxical claim to knowledge that it implicitly registers. Knowing that everything is subject to doubt means one knows something. Descartes, on the other hand, embraces that absolutism. He pushes complete doubt as far as it can go, until he is stopped by his own line of reasoning and forced to acknowledge his inability to doubt his own existence as a doubter. In the Second Meditation, that leads him to admit the undeniability of his own existence.

Stanley Cavell's Renaissance skepticism emerges most notably in his readings of Shakespeare's plays, and in his essay on *Othello,* he brackets his reflections on that play with considerations, initially, of Descartes and, ultimately, of Montaigne. Indeed, you might say that the later skeptic provides the epistemology of Cavell's interpretation of this tragedy and the earlier skeptic provides its tropology or moral interpretation. More-over, the appearance of these philosophers in chronologically reverse order complements another wrinkle in time that distinguishes Cavell's overall argument about Shakespearean tragedy. Cavell claims that this dramatic genre, in Shakespeare's hands, anticipates the absolute nature of Cartesian skepticism. The so-called hyperbolic doubt of such an uncom-promising thinker is figured in the irreversible course of Othello's quest for an unattainable certainty about Desdemona and in his inability to settle for anything less than the achievement of this impossible goal. In her recent book, *Satisfying Skepticism,* Ellen Spolsky takes explicit issue with precisely this feature of Cavell's Shakespeare criticism, its alignment of tragedy and Cartesian skepticism. She observes that, "during the early modern period (as always), there were choices between interpretations of doubt. It was, as I claim, the literary genre of tragedy, not the structure of skepticism, that produced the impression of its inevitability."[2]

Actually, this topic of the skeptic's choice figures importantly in Ca-vell's subsequent discussion of *The Winter's Tale,* and it strikes me as implicit in Cavell's turn toward moral reflection via Montaigne in dis-cussing *Othello.* Thus, I am not sure that there is a difference of opinion here but, rather, a misunderstanding. Somehow, a well-meaning Pyrrho-nist intervention in Othello's sudden ordeal seems an untenable proposi-tion. It sounds as though recommending that the unhinged commander simply calm down and learn to live with uncertainty (because, after all, you never really can be too sure about anything, even uncertainty) would actually put a stop to his rash and murderous course of action. Perhaps it should, and perhaps Othello has chosen not to heed any such sound advice; but this sort of hypothesis captures nothing of the tragic emotion communicated by Othello's agon nor any of the fellow-feeling it can awaken in a responsive audience. The loss of such emotions, and the sense of inevitability that goes along with them, would amount to the loss of a dimension of human experience that tragedy helps us access and understand. Moreover, as Cavell's writing demonstrates, this drastic or hyperbolic quality corresponds to the temptations and threats of skepti-cism in many of its manifestations.

Tragedy and Cartesian skepticism map onto one another in Cavell's thought because they both force issues to extremes. However, the Carte-sian solution to the challenge of radical doubt depends on a demonstra-tion of God's existence, beginning in the Third Meditation and relying on the so-called ontological argument in the Fifth. Such lines of skeptical thought only exacerbate Othello's dilemma because they entail a misrecognition of the human beloved as the divine and a consequent misplacement of Desdemona onto the altar of divinity, where she cannot but fail to meet the expectations put upon her. Once Descartes is convinced of his own existence, he turns to God to assure himself that he is not alone in the universe. Othello turns to Desdemona for such assurance, and he confuses her with God in the process. The Christian theology of incarnation, which collapses the distinction between human and divine, facilitates such a fateful error; but Othello's denial of Desdemona's human nature derives from a prior avoidance of his own, a refusal to see himself as a dependent and needy creature. The high-minded self-image that Othello entertains (and powerfully articulates) makes him vulnerable to revelations of his sexual nature, which is unbearably reflected in the passion that he himself arouses in Desdemona. This horror of the human that Othello thus manifests elicits Cavell's appeal to Montaigne, whose embrace of his own finitude exemplifies the acceptance of human shortcomings that Othello so violently shuns.

The Montaigne whom Cavell thus enlists to exemplify the instruction that he receives from this Shakespearean tragedy amounts to the three essays explicitly named and briefly engaged in the final pages of "Othello and the Stake of the Other." These are "Of Some Verses of Virgil," "Of the Power of the Imagination," and "Of Experience"; and Cavell illustrates the apposite moral philosophy that Montaigne might enable us to bring to bear upon the tragic loading of Othello's bed by citing an exemplary sentence about the human condition from the first of these essays: "What a monstrous animal to be a horror to himself, to be burdened by his pleasures, to regard himself as a misfortune!"[3]

Notably, Cavell does not rest content with the authority he has conferred upon Montaigne as a moral philosopher by thus summoning his critical observations about our chronic discomfort with the conditions of human life. Rather, he asks this question: "Is Montaigne's attitude fully earned, itself without a tint of the wish for exemption from the human?" He then proceeds to find in Shakespeare's tragedy a "possible rebuke to Montaigne for refusing a further nook of honesty," a rebuke of the sort that you might say he also finds in Descartes and elsewhere in Shakespeare, both of whom press skepticism to a further limit than Montaigne allows it to go. Moreover, this wish for exemption from the human generally characterizes Cavell's understanding of skepticism, and he subsequently finds a version of it in *Coriolanus* that prompts yet another reference to Montaigne, this time to "Of the Cannibals." Coriolanus's unfitness for civil conversation reveals an attitude toward language that views speech as a kind of cannibalism. Coriolanus either aggressively employs an uncivil tongue or, rather than engage in such verbal exchange, he may see "his salvation in silence." However, as Cavell observes, "Silence is *not* the absence of language; there is no such absence for human beings; in this respect, there is no world elsewhere."[4]

These references to four of the *Essays* amount to the sum of explicit mentions of Montaigne in Cavell's writing on Shakespeare, and I am unaware of others elsewhere in Cavell's works except for a pair of allusions to "To Philosophize Is to Learn How to Die."[5] Thus, Cavell's Renaissance skepticism is a decidedly minor topic unless we entertain other senses of this phrase. For example, Cavell's vocation as a philosopher begins in response to the challenge of skepticism, and he has steadily engaged that issue as it emerges in reflections upon ordinary language as a rebuke to metaphysics and the spells it sometimes casts upon thought. Austin and Wittgenstein inspire this mode of thought in Cavell, which ultimately leads him to the happy recognition of their affinity with American Transcendentalism. For Cavell, the preoccupation with the near, the common, and the low, in Emerson and Thoreau, sounds a note entirely consonant with major concerns of ordinary language philosophy and the everydayness it seeks to cultivate, explore, and recover. Of course, both of these New Englanders represent a literary development in the nineteenth century that F. O. Matthiessen famously dubbed an "American Renaissance," but that mere coincidence of terms hardly matters compared to the spiritual kinship as readers and writers that links Montaigne and Emerson and, through Emerson, Montaigne and Cavell.

Emerson; or, the Skeptic—and the Perfectionist

Emerson, of course, selected Montaigne as one of his half dozen "representative men" in his book of that title, and "Montaigne; or, the Skeptic" appears as the central chapter in that book, which he published in 1850. Indeed, some critics have found an Emersonian self-portrait in his sketch of the French essayist, and Emerson himself says that upon first reading Montaigne's *Essays,* he felt as if he himself had written them, as if, we might add (paraphrasing Emerson) he were encountering his own "rejected thoughts" in the work of another "with an alienated majesty," as he describes that experience in "Self-Reliance."[6] Like Montaigne, Emerson also wrote an essay, "Experience," whose title and whose skeptical reflections bear a notable resemblance to Montaigne's "Of Experience," and Cavell has dedicated a lengthy essay to what he calls "Finding as Founding: Taking Steps in Emerson's 'Experience,'" though the Renaissance text whose presence Cavell specifically overhears in Emerson's essay is *The Winter's Tale*.

Cavell's reading of Emerson has led him increasingly to affiliate his own way of philosophizing with a mode of thought that he calls perfectionism. The dialectical affinity between perfectionism and skepticism primarily depends on the role of the other in both of these modes of thought as Cavell represents them. The skepticism that defies a settled solution pertains to the existence of other minds. The transformation of the self that perfectionism invites depends upon the magnetic draw of another (via a text or a conversation or numerous other conceivable means). This other awakens us to our further self and encourages our progress in becoming what we are, as Nietzsche transcribes Emerson's description of our unattained but attainable self.

Because Cavell tends to associate his practice of philosophy not with a set of problems but with a set of texts, he stresses the activity of interpretation, or the reading of texts, as a way of doing philosophy.[7] This devotion to texts as a point of departure for philosophical writing contains within it a powerful idea of "renaissance," or rebirth, that the prevalent historicism in Renaissance studies has tended to discredit or overlook. While the New Historicism is commonly viewed as a response to New Criticism, its customary rejection of literary formalism in favor of more politically attuned accounts of the texts it surveys has inclined it to subordinate, not only the formal qualities of these writings, but also their formative power in the present moment. Stephen Greenblatt expresses the purpose of literary history as an effort to awaken the dead,[8] whereas you could say that Cavell's perfectionism seeks to awaken the living. However, as David Sedley points out, Greenblatt's method of interpretation often entails a dynamic oscillation between skepticism and wonder. This perceptive appreciation of how Greenblatt's thinking frequently works by a movement between alternative modes of response offers a fair account of the engaging energy in much of his prose. The responsiveness thus described displays a clear affinity to the ambitions of Cavell's perfectionist criticism, though Greenblatt's professed fascination with the dead de-emphasizes the immediacy and verve that his writing often communicates and the compelling interest that it can provoke.[9]

Cavell speaks of the kind of philosophical writing he does as competing with poetry in its aspiration to "[make] things happen to the soul."[10] Moreover, he cites Emerson's claim about literary experience in which historical differences become temporarily irrelevant: "[w]hen a thought of Plato becomes a thought to me,—when a truth that fired the soul of Pindar fires mine, time is no more." Such a claim is not idle romanticism because it does not seek to transcend history. Rather, it seeks to find ways to begin history anew, ways in which we can become part of time's story as it proceeds. As Emerson's great inheritor, Friedrich Nietzsche, would argue, "when the past speaks it always speaks as an oracle: only if you are an architect of the future and know the present will you understand it."[11]

In "Of Experience," when we hear Montaigne lament the inadequacies of law and medicine, he stresses their failure to perform the jobs they are supposedly intended for and their inability to measure up to the experience of life upon which Montaigne would rather found his convictions. By this stage in the composition of the *Essays,* Montaigne has passed beyond his intensely skeptical phase, and the pervasive epistemological concerns of "An Apology for Raymond Sebond" have given way to a more robust confidence in the evidence of his own lived experience as a guide in life. Systematic efforts to codify knowledge for the adjudication of human conflicts or the diagnosis and treatment of physical illness routinely miss the mark and betray, not only the limitations of human intelligence, but the prideful denial of such shortcomings and the presumption that results from failure to acknowledge them. Montaigne would rather live by the lights of his own experience than rely upon the professional authority of such demonstrably fallible experts. Yet Montaigne also admits that emotion is a significant part of his experience, and he acknowledges the vagaries of feeling that condition human understanding. Even though his honesty on this score may be a prelude both to fideism in religion and conventionality in social life, his willingness to accept the pervasive reality of such influences distinguishes his representation of subjectivity from the clarity and distinctness of ideas that Descartes insists upon in overcoming his skepticism.[12] Both Montaigne and Descartes find answers to skepticism, but Montaigne's includes a much more capacious embrace of the self's experience. If Descartes's *cogito* subjectivizes knowledge, you might say that Montaigne's essaying of the self subjectivizes ignorance; but he claims, in the process, a subjectivity far more inclusive of recognizable human experience, of what it feels like to be a person.

In "Montaigne; or, the Skeptic," Emerson observes: "There is a power in moods, each setting at nought all but its own tissue of facts and beliefs. There is the power of complexions, obviously modifying the dispositions and sentiments. The beliefs and unbeliefs appear to be structural; and as soon as each man attains the poise and vivacity which allow the whole machinery to play, he will not need extreme examples, but will rapidly alternate all opinions in his own life. Our life is March weather, savage and serene in one hour."[13]

Montaigne's willingness to inhabit and articulate, not only the lucid moments of his experience, but also the vagaries, serves as a precedent for Emerson. Cavell aptly calls the subject of Emerson's essay, "Experience," "the epistemology, or say the logic, of moods," and he specifies "the moral of that essay as contained in its late prayerful remark, 'But far be it from me the despair which prejudges the law by a paltry empiricism.' That is, what is wrong with empiricism is not its reliance on experience but its paltry idea of experience."[14] Of course, Montaigne is emphatic not only about his feelings but also about the physical conditions of his life and especially his own body's aches and pains upon which he elaborates at great length in his essay "Of Experience," among other places. As Cavell has explained, Emerson's "Experience" also relies upon a palpable fantasy of embodiment. Despite lamenting his painful inability to get his grief over his son Waldo's death any nearer, Emerson demonstrably incorporates the anguish of his loss into his own bodily feelings and virtually becomes pregnant with his pain before he can achieve any release from it. This moving act of visceral imagination hardly seems a mere illusion of male parthenogenesis in which Emerson's creative act of writing this essay usurps the woman's part in giving birth to his child. Indeed, one feels that, if Emerson got his grief any nearer, he would die in the process.

We can recall that, in his essay on *Othello,* Cavell ultimately chastens Montaigne with the question whether he is not turning away from "a further nook of honesty" about the human condition. Ironically, "the exemption from the human" that Montaigne may be seeking is precisely an exemption from the absolute nature of Cartesian doubt—a vertigo of uncertainty that Othello's ordeal dramatizes with the full terror and pity that tragic action can arouse. Thus, Descartes's *Meditations* reopen the challenges of dogmatic skepticism that Montaigne's Pyrrhonism had supposedly laid to rest, and Shakespeare's dramatic art anticipates that event. Similarly, for Montaigne, who visited Torquato Tasso during his six-year confinement in Ferrara, the Italian poet's misfortune represents primarily an example of the folly of overconfidence in human reason (which is especially frail in it finest manifestations) and the catastrophe that such an excess of intellectual pride can entail.[15] For Emerson, whose understanding of Tasso derives from Goethe's play about him, Tasso stands for "true tragedy" of a distinctly Hegelian kind, a conflict between rights that occasions "genuine grief . . . a grief we all feel, a knot we cannot untie."[16]

But, for Cavell, despite his attraction to a performative interpretation of the *cogito,* Descartes's rationalism itself mainly offers just a logical proof in response to the terrifying challenge of absolute doubt, whereas a life—one's own life, mine or yours—needs to be claimed by more than reason alone. Though Montaigne's more capacious articulation of his lived experience offers a more robust voicing of the terms upon which one might enter such a claim, his response to dogmatic skepticism still exemplifies a doomed approach to the obstacles presented by the human capacity for doubt. For Cavell, skepticism, finally, is not to be refuted but to be lived, and it is Emerson who follows such a course and thus can exemplify a viable response to this chronic threat and temptation of the human predicament.

Clearly, Emerson inspires Cavell's turn toward perfectionism and his consolidation of his identity as a philosopher of that kind. Moreover, since Emerson finds in Montaigne, as a representative man, an instance of the skeptic, he also finds in him an adequacy as an exemplar that Montaigne succinctly dismissed with this famous dictum: "Every example is lame."[17] Thus, both tragedy (which Cavell consistently reads in Shakespeare as one variation or another of the skeptical crisis)[18] and the overcoming of skepticism via the responsiveness of perfectionist reading receive significant expression in the works of Emerson, whom Cavell seeks to adopt as the founding father of American philosophy and a neglected, if not willfully repressed, precursor of his own manner of writing and thinking.

In *Nature,* Cavell claims, Emerson has not yet found his philosophical voice. Rather, that early essay serves as a contrast to subsequent ones, like "Self-Reliance" and "Experience," for "in *Nature* Emerson is taking the issue of skepticism as solvable or controllable whereas thereafter he takes its unsolvability to the heart of his thinking."[19] However, the skepticism that we must live, because of its unsolvability, is not primarily that which pertains to the external world. Metaphysics can raise questions about the reality of objects that we perceive, but we seem to be able adequately to manage our life among them by simply ignoring such questions, should they ever arise in the first place. However, what we have to go on with other people is, ultimately, the evidence of our own experience in all of its rough mixture of clarity and ambiguity. We reach others via self-knowledge, which we often acquire, modify, abandon, etc., in the process of making the effort to know and understand them.

This is the grounds of knowledge, such as it may be, that Montaigne insists upon in "Of Experience": "Then whatever may be the fruit we can reap from experience, what we derive from foreign examples will hardly be much use for our education, if we make such little profit from the experience we have of ourselves, which is more familiar to us, and certainly sufficient to inform us of what we need."[20] Even a paltry empiricism, Montaigne here claims, begins at home.

Whether we like that or not, this constitutive feature of our knowledge of others makes it a moral science, so perhaps it is unsurprising to hear Emerson acknowledge in his essay on Montaigne that: "The final solution in which skepticism is lost, is in the moral sentiment, which never forfeits its supremacy. All moods may be safely tried, and their weight allowed to all objections. The moral sentiment as easily outweighs them all, as any one. This is the drop which balances the sea."[21] Notably, however, in "Self-Reliance," when he decries the condition of his contemporaries who have lost this necessary basis for moral action, Emerson slyly alludes to Descartes, as though what Emerson calls the diseases of thought were founded, not only upon a dependence on the thought of others, but upon that of the wrong thinker as well: "Man is timid and apologetic; he is no longer upright; he dares not say 'I think,' 'I am,' but quotes some saint or sage."[22] Montaigne may exert the stronger appeal, but the Cartesian shaking of the foundations requires notice. Moreover, that shaking ultimately elicits a countermove fully congruent with David Sedley's articulation of a dialectic between skepticism and sublimity. Once Emerson has decried the shame bespoken by our conformity, he echoes Jesus on the lilies of the field and commends the roses under his window. They "make no reference to former roses or to better ones; they are for what they are; they exist with God today. There is no time to them. There is simply the rose; it is perfect in every moment of its existence."[23]

Inasmuch as Emerson's citation merely echoes Descartes's *cogito,* it reflects the timidity it decries, the unthinking automatism of what Emerson ironically calls "the *virtue* most in request . . . conformity" (emphasis added). However, at this turn in his essay, he defines the virtue he celebrates by contraries: "Self-reliance is its [conformity's] aversion." The irony in thus strategically quoting Descartes, and the tone in which readers can hear these words said, enable the writer to inhabit them, rather than merely to mouth them as though he were simply impersonating the discoverer of this truth. So far as Emerson realizes one of the lessons that we have seen Cavell draw from *Coriolanus*—that there is no world outside of language, and "in this sense there is no world elsewhere"—he fully appreciates that it is not mere repetition that leaves words open to the emptiness of vacuous misappropriation. Emerson writes of the conformists' embarrassing inanity, "Their every truth is not quite true. Their two is not the real two, their four not the real four; so that every word they say chagrins us and we know not where to set them right."[24] However, he does not mean that two plus two no longer makes four, or that such persons mistakenly think that it makes three or five. Rather, he means that they stand in a false relation to whatever truths they may enunciate. Words recur, or we would not have a usable language; and the validity of certain claims makes them worth repeating. However, the spirit in which we repeat their formulation makes all the difference, and we can only know this from the inside and, as Cavell puts it, acknowledge it in others from the outside. Such an idea would be preposterous to Descartes, whose attachment to mathematical certainty not only reflects his early training and intellectual activity, it also signifies the sort of knowledge he mainly values once the problem of the self's existence has been decisively resolved.

In the Second Meditation, Descartes flirts with something very much like the problem of other minds: "when looking from a window and saying I see men who pass in the street," he hypothesizes, "I really do not see them, but infer that what I see is men. . . . And yet what do I see from the window but hats and coats which may cover automatic machines?"[25] But this is a momentary impulse to which Descartes will not return when he wonders, in the Third Meditation, whether he is alone in the universe. Rather, he turns to God for an answer to that question. Once grounded in the indubitable conviction of his own existence, the Cartesian subject turns toward God and the clear and distinct ideas of which He provides assurance. A sharp division between subject and object prevails thereafter, and interest in the external world of things rather than persons comes to predominate once the subject has overcome its initial ordeal of self-doubt. Descartes turns toward other concerns and abandons the considerations of self-study that continually engage Montaigne and enable him to speculate with empathy and due caution about others as well. But if we come to a secure knowledge of our own existence through such an internal reckoning, we are left with knowledge of the mind as the only sure evidence of the existence of another.[26] That knowledge, however, is irretrievably blocked to us unless we are willing to forgo an appetite for certainty and, like Montaigne, we can come to know the shadowier and less distinct parts of ourselves. They can provide us with a meeting place upon which we can encounter others and begin to essay our self-knowledge as clues to understanding others.

Perfection's Heirs

Amid a circle of distinguished courtiers, Cardinal Bembo famously expounded a doctrine of love that went the rounds of numerous other courtly circles throughout Europe during the sixteenth century. Central to that doctrine is Bembo's claim that God is like a circle, whose circumference is beauty and whose center is goodness.[27] We have all been there, to that city of words called the ducal palace in Urbino that Castiglione founded in *Il libro del cortegiano* or to other such literary utopias designed for our moral benefit. Indeed, the phrase "city of words" provides perhaps the best self-characterization, as a work of literature, of the earlier volume from which I have borrowed that phrase, Plato's *Republic;* it also serves Cavell as his title for his own collection of "pedagogical letters on a register of the moral life," as he describes his lectures on moral perfectionism. In *The Republic* Socrates explains how the wise man will enter politics "at least in his own kind of city," a phrase promptly revised to specify such a place as "the city we were founding and described, our city of words," which Socrates further calls "a model laid up in heaven, for him who wishes to look upon, and as he looks, set up the government of his soul."[28]

Plato and Bembo both take us on spiritual journeys upward, yet their English inheritors, Sidney and Shakespeare, were as likely to reverse directions and descend. The momentum in their sonnets, though hardly just one-way, often tends emphatically downward, toward the world and the flesh, or makes decisive turns in that direction after periods of ascent. Indeed, like the widespread availability of Platonic texts, after concerted efforts to recover them in fifteenth-century Italy and especially in Florence at Ficino's academy, the very earthwardness of such journeys epitomizes a key element of the humanistic culture in which they participate. The human being in the world, not God in His heaven, increasingly becomes the focus of the *studia humanitatis* that seek to replace the *studia divinitatis* of the medieval university. But it is the kinetic sense of being on the move that links the perfectionism of the Neoplatonic elements in Sidney and Shakespeare with viable manifestations of such philosophizing both in classical antiquity and also nowadays.

Stanley Cavell has recently defended the principle of perfection against charges of elitism from no less an authority than John Rawls in his magisterial treatise *A Theory of Justice*.[29] In the process Cavell has not only fulfilled his discernible ambition and reclaimed the perfectionist mode of reflection as a worthy option for present-day democratic thinking, he has also provided potentially more refreshing perspectives from which to view past lyrics than dominant approaches in early modern studies now tend to offer. Whereas Stephen Greenblatt speaks of the literary historian's task as conjuring the dead,[30] a perfectionist, by contrast, might claim for such texts the capacity to revive readers who have, sadly enough, come to inhabit the dead zone of impercipience and unresponsiveness to signs even of their own vitality.

"In every work of genius," Emerson observes, "we recognize our own rejected thoughts: they come back to us with a certain alienated majesty."[31] When contemporary critics hear the word "genius" in this assertion, they are likely to lament what John Rawls deems the perfectionist's tendency both to give "absolute weight" to "the lives of great men" and to urge that humanity "continually strive to produce great individuals."[32] Rather, as Cavell remarks about Emerson, "For him, genius is, as it is with Plato, something each person has, not something certain people are. Emerson's remark about genius is a kind of definition of the term: If you find the return of your thoughts to be caused by a work in this way, then you are apt, and in a sense justified, to attribute this return to the genius of the work."[33]

This way of reading past texts, of course, stands at odds with current methods that emphasize difference rather than identity and that rely upon models of history—whether synchronic or diachronic[34]—that facilitate such an emphasis. Identity and the attention to shared features, on the other hand, can enable apposite entertainment of ideas of cycles, as in what Erik Erikson calls the human life cycle with its various stages along a trajectory that allows for recycling or what Erikson calls "epigenesis."[35] Just as romantic poets or, for that matter, the first psychoanalyst discovered that childhood is not merely a stage along life's way but a dimension of the self, likewise characteristically youthful or adult sentiments and behaviors are not exclusively confined to a particular developmental moment in the Eriksonian scheme of things.

Of course, such a model dangerously flirts with "essentialist humanism," the prime anathema of our prevalent mode of historical interpretation, which seems bent upon translating even the most secular epiphany into a misrecognition. While this habit of critique helpfully eliminates bogus notions of continuity from our sense of the past, it also stifles the breath of inspiration that readers and writers have customarily imbibed from past texts of recognized merit—classics, if you will. Moreover, it may be worth venturing to diagnose the spirit in which such charges are often pressed. In studying the reception of a work of literature our own receptiveness may be exposed to a revealing test. Cavell's crucial distinction between knowledge and acknowledgment would help in this effort.[36] On one hand, we may recognize our sharable, if not common, humanity only by daring to acknowledge it and then being willing to modify such convictions in the event of misrecognition. On the other, we allegedly may "know" essentialist humanism when we see it simply by a hyperbolic sense of human "otherness" or historical "anachronism" that preemptively denies the possibility of any common ground by its fixation upon differences. Such a dogmatic insistence upon difference precludes identification before it even has a chance to begin.

The African-American writer Ralph Waldo Ellison acknowledged that he bore from the outset "a heavy moniker" for "such a small brown nubbin of a boy"; but, when he recollected his boyhood days in Oklahoma City, he tried to show the worlds of promise and possibility to which he and the friends of his youth readily aspired. In formulating their high hopes they even dared to imagine themselves as "Renaissance men."[37] Poets of our era similarly have striven to inherit, on their own terms, sonnets by Sidney and Shakespeare; and the success of their efforts belies easy claims of the exclusive otherness such works supposedly represent. Anthony Hecht, in "A Birthday Poem," written for his second wife, Helen, summons a couplet from Shakespeare's Sonnet 53. The query of its opening lines, as Hecht puts it, "[echoes] down the ages in [his] head": "What is your substance, whereof are you made,/That millions of strange shadows on you tend?" The terms "substance" and "shadows" strike a Neoplatonic note, part of whose resonance Hecht further employs in the title of the volume in which this poem first appeared, *Millions of Strange Shadows*.[38]

But elsewhere in this collection, Hecht registers, with special vividness, his preoccupation with another Shakespeare sonnet, sonnet 151 ("Love is too young to know what conscience is"). In "Going the Rounds: A Sort of Love Poem," Hecht invokes Shakespeare as "our arch-scholiast of the spirit's agon." This lyric then painfully exposes the aptness of Tudor moralism to the speaker's disappointment in love, despite the condescension with which he initially brings such views to bear. The "rounds" mentioned in the poem's title bespeak, among other things, the kind of literary circle that harks back to the medieval pattern of *de casibus* tragedy and its concern with the instability of human affairs.

"What goes up must come down" is the cliché Hecht effectively employs to express "the ultimate, sick/Joke of Fortuna," whose mutability ironically is later exemplified by the pompous speaker's own jilting. The ribaldry of Sonnet 151 offers another parallel round of prideful ascent and downfall in its racy play upon the cycle of male sexual arousal and detumescence. The speaker in Hecht's poem deifies love in these provocative terms, which are utterly reminiscent of the system of sexual puns upon which Shakespeare founds Sonnet 151: "That goddess is remorseless, watching us rise / In all our ignorant nerve, / And when we have reached the top, putting us wise."

Sidney and Larkin: A Perfectionist Reading

The ribaldry of such learned allusions perhaps seems merely titillating, if not effete, and thus betokens potential pitfalls of the very elitism from which Cavell seeks to exonerate the principle of perfection. More thorough consideration of Hecht's poem and the collection in which it appears could easily free both from such charges, but that effort would lead me from my current purpose of demonstrating the present vitality in past texts, their capacity to awaken the living. The uses Hecht makes of Shakespeare's sonnets bear a kinship to Philip Larkin's allusive arrogation of Sir Philip Sidney's thirty-first sonnet in *Astrophil and Stella* ("With how sad steps, O moon, thou climb'st the skies"),[39] which better demonstrates the sort of dynamic exchange a perfectionist response can produce.

The brief citation in the title of Larkin's lyric, "Sad Steps," like the meditative moon-gazing described therein, indicates the poet's willful affiliation of his poem with Sidney's thirty-first sonnet. Larkin's opening line, however, promptly reveals the abrasive attitude with which he means to engage whatever romantic pathos the Sidney connection may suggest: "Groping back to bed after a piss."[40] Larkin thus begins his poem with confrontational vulgarity, made especially prominent here by his choice of a rhyming word and its final position in this first line. He then proceeds to a crescendo of contempt in the sarcastic exclamations addressed to the moon midway through the fourth tercet: "Lozenge of love! Medallion of art!" This scornful mockery virtually reverses the traditional placement of the pious devotee who ascends above the sublunar flux to attain the perspective of *contemptus mundi*. Indeed, Larkin, or the speaker of these lines, indulges temporarily in a kind of *contemptus caeli*, like one of those atheists whom George Orwell aptly describes as not so much disbelieving in God as having a personal grudge against Him.

This first movement of Larkin's lyric runs, as follows, from blunt realism to anti-romantic derision:

> Groping back to bed after a piss
> I part thick curtains, and am startled by
> The rapid clouds, the moon's cleanliness.
>
> Four o'clock: wedge-shadowed gardens lie
> Under a cavernous, a wind-picked sky.
> There's something laughable about this,
>
> The way the moon dashes through clouds that blow
> Loosely as cannon-smoke to stand apart
> (Stone-coloured light sharpening the roofs below)
>
> High and preposterous and separate—
> Lozenge of love! Medallion of art![41]

Whereas Sidney's sonnet dramatizes a playful interrogation of the moon, Larkin's upward glance occasions his drift into sharp derision before he recoils in a desolating recognition of the sort Eliot enunciates in "East Coker" without Larkin's immediate sense of personal identification: "O dark dark dark. They all go into the dark,/The vacant interstellar spaces, the vacant into the vacant[.]"[42] In contrast, when Astrophil conditionally establishes his "fellowship" with the moon, Sidney is ironically toying with what Ruskin condemns nearly three centuries later as the pathetic fallacy. Upon this shaky premise Astrophil presumes to question the moon as a fellow sufferer of painful disappointment in love, an interrogation made all the more paradoxical because of the moon's traditional location "above the varying shore of the world" on the cosmic border, the first heavenly circle, where constancy begins.[43] There, in Renaissance cosmology, "constant love" should be virtually a structural principle.

However, Astrophil's sympathetic ascent to the circle of the moon yields a rich harvest of surprisingly mundane rhetorical questions that dramatizes Stella's hardness of heart with such ingratiating restraint as often distinguishes Astrophil's tone from the angry frustration of earlier English Petrarchism like that of Sir Thomas Wyatt. This upward journey also resembles more explicitly Neoplatonic pilgrimages in *Astrophil and Stella* which sometimes end, however, in abrupt reversals—suddenly aborted missions of the would-be spiritual traveler. Sonnet 5 ("It is most

98

true, that eyes are formed to serve"), for example, and Sonnet 72 ("Desire, though thou my old companion art") wittily reveal the earth-
boundedness of the aspiring lover when their concluding lines bring
Astrophil down with a gentle jolt. Likewise, Sonnet 71 ("Who will in
fairest book of nature know") stages an orthodox journey toward transcendence whose high hopes at the poem's close founder surprisingly—if
one has not yet grown accustomed to this Sidneyan routine. While
David Kalstone elaborates upon this sonnet as "a rare example of what
appears to be a direct response to a poem by Petrarch," he also notes that
both the Italian model and its English imitation are each a "characteristic
achievement."[44] Indeed, Sidney's Neoplatonic perfectionism becomes
explicit in this poem's lovely phrase "perfection's heirs," which itself
might yield the Italianate pun *l'aura di Laura*. That pun can help us to
characterize these sonnets as airs about an ideal woman that are continually complicated by the carnal realities of the desire her beauty arouses.
Such complications account for the repeated reversals of the high-
minded ambitions that routinely set Astrophil on Neoplatonic quests that
seem predestined to fail.

In *The Defence of Poesy* Sidney's reformed Christianity and its emphatic
sense of human fallibility supply him with the means to understand the
inevitable failure of such missions. There Sidney celebrates poetry as the
highest form of learning, whose "final end is to lead and draw us to as
high a perfection as our degenerate souls, made worse by their clayey
lodgings, can be made capable of."[45] The redundancy in the phrase "final
end," which is more blatantly driven home only two paragraphs later in
the phrase "ending end," baldly declares the teleological structure of
Sidney's perfectionism. Astrophil's continual inability successfully to
cross the dividing line between the visible and the intelligible, between
beauty and virtue, reveals the subversive power of a rival telos. Stella's
beauty resists translation into abstract terms and thus regularly disables
Astrophil's high-mindedness, despite the best of intentions.

Although he recognizes in Plato an important precursor, the perfectionism that Cavell espouses finds its fullest expression in the onwardness
of the Emersonian self. Though taking steps and finding a way, moved by
the attraction of its "unattained but attainable self,"[46] its final destination
remains willfully vague. The Emersonian self lacks the clearly teleological
structure of Sidney's Neoplatonism, which, ironically, mirrors the same
formal structure that leads John Rawls to reject "the principle of perfection" as "a teleological theory" and to strike, via Nietzsche, at Emerson's
supposed fixation upon "the lives of great men" and the "[production]

of great individuals."[47] But unlike the Neoplatonist, the onward momentum of the Emersonian self is not directed upward. The Emersonian scholar discovers "materials strewn along the ground"; he "[embraces] the common" and "[sits] at the feet of the familiar, the low."[48]

In this regard he may be the heir of such imperfections as Elizabethan sonneteers like Sidney and Shakespeare often expose when the exactions of Neoplatonic idealism bring them down to the acknowledgment of failure or even to defiance. Unmeetable demands can occasion productive reckonings and the redirection of desire within the realm of human possibility. "My mistress' eyes are nothing like the sun," Sonnet 130 notoriously proclaims.[49] It then proceeds to blazon forth a catalogue of happily unrealized ideals and welcome shortcomings. Such praise and celebration are wrested from standards too high and too narrow to measure fairly the realities of actual attachment. Rather, anti-idealism can expose the perverse strictures of such unrealistic expectations.

Though less blatant than Sonnet 130, the antiplatonism of Sonnet 98 ("From you I have been absent in the spring") effects a descent through the very circles that the aspiring soul is meant to mount en route to an ecstatic union with the Summum Bonum. Bembo's guidance in *Il libro del cortegiano* provides an exact map of this poem's itinerary, if you just follow it backwards. We begin on high with the apotheosis of "proud pied April, dressed in all his trim," and "heavy Saturn," ironically kicking up his heels in spontaneous, irresistible merriment at the season's freshness. Then, we savor the collective loveliness of birds and blossoms— what Wallace Stevens calls all sorts of notes, all sorts of flowers[50]—before turning to particulars like "the lily's white" and, unforgettably, "the deep vermillion of the rose." Platonic ascent is meant to go in the other direction, heavenward; but, instead, we finally fix upon the absent beloved, of whom all the previously mentioned items are "but figures of delight/ Drawn after you, you pattern of all those." These lovely items, from heaven to earth, are all "shadow[s]" of the beloved. Of course, as Astrophil well knows, it is supposed to be the other way around; but then, it hardly ever works like that for him either. Stella is meant to be a particular realization of a universal ideal whose perfection, as it turns out (for Astrophil), she actually embodies and thus becomes a model for others.

If we return to Philip Larkin and the moon, we can perhaps achieve a perspective upon his lyric and its relation to Sidney's sonnet that is less "deconstructive and diachronic" than that David Cowart proposes in analyzing what he calls the "literary symbiosis" between these two poems.[51] Cowart's notion of "symbiosis" and of the subsequent lyric's "reconfiguration" of elements drawn from the Elizabethan sonnet already strikes a more constructive note that a less "intertextual" approach than his might also apply to the experience represented in Larkin's lyric as well. We left Larkin's speaker deriding a kind of sentimental "lunacy," if you will, while directing these taunts at the moon and, implicitly, at sappy romantics spellbound by the sight of it: "Lozenge of love! Medallion of art!" But this sarcastic ejaculation suddenly changes course:

> O wolves of memory! Immensements! No,

> One shivers slightly, looking up there.
> The hardness and the brightness and the plain
> Far-reaching singleness of that wide stare

> Is a reminder of the strength and pain
> Of being young; that it can't come again,
> But is for others undiminished somewhere.[52]

The sarcasm's change of course is occasioned by a chilling sense of the moon's remoteness and isolation, expressed both in the exclamation, "Immensements!" and in the descriptive phrase "far-reaching singleness." From this perspective any illusion of "fellowship" with the moon is untenable. What Sidney's mild irony makes perceptible Larkin dramatizes by bringing derision up short, far short, as an alternative means to self-indulgent romanticism for crossing an unbridgeable gap. Such illusions as Astrophil entertains upon the dubious basis of whatever "judgment" can be claimed for "long-with-love-acquainted eyes" (precisely none, I would suggest) are only undone by Sidney obliquely, whereas they are starkly exposed by the fierceness and sudden recoil of Larkin's speaker.

Yet the violence of the outburst in Larkin's lyric also records a kind of traumatic breakthrough, a crisis of recognition that yields a different disposition toward the young, who, it now becomes clear, were the initial object of contempt. Desolation settles upon the speaker who has so bitterly burlesqued romantic moon-gazing, but the "wolves of memory" hunt him down and bestow "a reminder of the strength and pain / Of being young." It is also a reminder of the present "otherness" of that stage of life and its lostness to the speaker: "it can't come again." The occasional recycling of characteristic qualities that distinguish stages in the human life cycle, what Erikson calls "epigenesis," is plainly no option here. But the speaker's tone of contempt has vanished; and, to effect that change, memory has briefly conferred upon him a sort of fellowship with those he once scorned, a receptiveness to their difference from him now. Acknowledgment of loss replaces derision of youthful romanticism. Daylight will surely come after this night's unexpected musings, but its modest work of mourning may not promise morning, as Thoreau's punning celebration of such a spiritual passage might move some to sing. It is just a small victory over cynicism—but a victory nonetheless.

Sidney, however, conceives of poetry as an instrument of moral education unequaled among learned pursuits. It can decisively affect not only our hearts and minds but our conduct as well. In *The Defence* Sidney shows no restraint in the superlatives he summons in his climactic assertion of poetry's preeminence in the humanities: "[V]irtue is the most excellent resting place for all worldly learning to make his end of, so poetry, being the most familiar to teach it, and the most princely to move toward it, in the most excellent work is the most excellent workman."[53] But to imagine that a poem can occasion even the slightest change of heart, one must affirm the truth of sentiments only personal experience can ultimately prove—and only to one's fallible self. As we have noted before, even a paltry empiricism begins at home. Moreover, there seems no end to the suspicions anybody (oneself not least) can raise to counter such a claim: Are you sure about that? How do you *really* know? I wonder . . . So begins what Cavell aptly calls the skeptic's "recital," occasioned by what philosophers traditionally term the problem of other minds.[54] Of course, we cannot know another's inner experience with absolute precision. We can only acknowledge it, and in doing so, we run the inevitable risk of getting it wrong.

As though anticipating such potentially unsettling doubts, Sidney both opens and closes *The Defence* with studied nonchalance. He initially describes himself as "having slipped into the title of a poet," his "unelected vocation"; and he ultimately disparages "the triflingness" of *The Defence* and commiserates with "all that have had the evil luck to read this inkwasting toy."[55] Similarly, in *Astrophil and Stella* Sidney eloquently exploits poetic traditions via disclaimer, a gesture that frequently constitutes the most fertile paradox of his lyric art. In sonnet after sonnet Astrophil denounces the confections of "dainty wits," the grandiose speeches of "[s]ome lovers," and the motives of those who "search in every purling spring/Which from the ribs of old Parnassus flows." He directly asserts his own freedom from such literary affectation: "I never drank at Aganippe well."[56] This ploy, of course, enables Sidney handsomely to parade his elaborate cultivation of poetic resources.

Thus, he can ostentatiously inherit from Ovid and Petrarch and many another noteworthy precursor while seeming to scorn self-conscious displays of artistry and learning. The plainspoken forthrightness with which Astrophil voices feelings contrary to those of such canonical models gives his subsequent claims the ring of truth. Moreover, sonneteering itself is an activity that raises suspicions of affectation. When it figures in a game proposed by one of the company at the ducal palace in Urbino, Unico Aretino, it promptly occasions such doubts.[57] In a group where *sprezzatura* will become a guiding principle, so demanding a form requires an unseemly show of effort. Sonneteering entails violation of the maxim which governs the conduct of the perfect courtier, as this group conceives of this ideal figure: *ars est celare artem.*[58]

In the first part of "Going the Rounds," Anthony Hecht follows Sidney's procedure as he views, with considerable jaundice, circumstances that apparently correspond to the conventional wisdom and "moral pearls" he sardonically summons to master them. Compared with Larkin's stark idiom, Hecht's manner occasionally sounds like otiose name-dropping, until he shifts into the second part of his poem. There, it first turns out that the joke is on him; and, by the end, he can voice an earnest avowal of devotion, once manifold irony has cleared a place for the expression of such sentiments.

If we were talking merely about the efficacy of a shift in stylistic registers, say from the erudite to the demotic, the moment might invite discussion of Wordsworth's imitation of the thirty-first sonnet in *Astrophil and Stella,* which opens by repeating the first two lines of Sidney's sonnet ("With how sad steps, O moon, thou climb'st the skies;/How silently, and with how wan a face").[59] The project announced in the preface to *Lyrical Ballads,* with its emphasis on the "language really used by men," indicates Wordsworth's affinity, at least, for the sort of tone, if not diction, that Sidney often employs in tension with conspicuous allusions to Ovid, Petrarch, and other such estimable precursors. But Wordsworth's sonnet, despite the link in literary history that it supplies between Sidney and Larkin, is eminently forgettable and leaves no discernible trace upon "Sad Steps," except perhaps the inadvertent echo of an echo. "Wordsworth's sonnet is the product of its age," Cowart writes, "a standard Romantic celebration of nature."[60] Indeed, Larkin's speaker initially reacts against the automatism of such a response and exhibits, in the process, the equally mechanical reflexes of a grumpy old man. Fortunately, he later manages to "part thick[er] curtains" than those that concealed the night sky. Thus, he catches a cautionary glimpse of himself, a self who, if not a stranger, was certainly estranged from the person who thus achieves a further self by following the lead of this surprising recognition.

The poem thus renders a perfectionist moment in which the self undergoes a transformation and *becomes* what it is by recovering what it has previously rejected. This perfectionist mode of thought runs through the poems we have discussed and links philosophers as apparently remote from one another as Plato and Cavell. At one daring turn in his essay on *Macbeth,* Cavell finds himself wanting to say something about his guiding principles as a critical thinker. High aspiration leads him abruptly to Plato: "The great responsibility of philosophy is responsiveness—to be awake after all the others have fallen asleep."[61] This image of the philosopher's wakefulness amid sleepers evokes the figure of Socrates at the end of the *Symposium.* It expresses Cavell's wish to follow out an interpretive intuition and the line of thought entailed therein; it is the maxim for that pursuit.

In Castiglione's reprise of that Platonic moment, the company at the ducal palace in Urbino realizes that Bembo's discourse has induced ecstasy: they have completely lost track of time. To paraphrase my epigraph from Emerson's "History," when a thought of Plato becomes a thought to them, time is no more. Once the group begins to entertain suggestions for tomorrow's topic of discussion, they learn that it is already tomorrow. When one of them looks out the window after Bembo's climactic paean to love, Venus alone, the morning star, hovers on the horizon as a final sign of the rapture they have all shared.[62]

The differences between these courtiers' blissing out in high Renaissance Urbino and Philip Larkin's undergoing a momentary change of heart in Hull after the last world war threaten easily to multiply out of control. The dyspeptic mood of the English welfare state seems remote indeed from nostalgic yearnings at signorial courts in Italy after the French invasion of 1494 had revealed their utter vulnerability. And which, if any, of these representations of radically diverse occasions would tellingly connect with the experience of either "a small brown nubbin of a boy" in Oklahoma City early in this century or the African-American laureate he would become decades later? It is impossible decisively to say. Such texts exist merely as cities of words, or even more modest settlements, that we may feel moved to try inhabiting. They are models "laid up in heaven, for him who wishes to look upon, and as he looks, set up the government of his soul."[63] We can claim with confidence that our participation in the politics of these cities has only utopian consequences—no more, no less.

4

FROM CYPRUS
TO RUSHMORE

*I*n Stanley Cavell's writings on film there are two major arguments about early modern developments that also recur influentially in his writings on Shakespeare. Most prominently, there is Cavell's claim that Shakespearean tragedy anticipates Cartesian skepticism. Shakespeare dramatizes the withdrawal of the world made manifest in our uncertainties about external reality, and he extends that skepticism in dramatizing doubts about other minds, which disappoint the human desire for secure and unassailable conviction about them.[1] Additionally, there is the claim that marriage, in the early sixteenth century, lost all public foundations of credible legitimacy, whether they were based in church or state. Once Henry VIII got divorced and Martin Luther got married, the institution of marriage never recovered its generally uncontested stability during previous epochs.[2] These arguments come together decisively for Cavell during the time he composed the fourth and final section of *The Claim of Reason,* which concludes with his celebrated essay on *Othello.* As Jay Cantor noted long ago, this essay bears a deep connection to the work on Hollywood movies that Cavell was advancing during the same period when he was bringing his philosophical magnum opus belatedly to a conclusion.[3]

Thus, if we examine Cavell's film and Shakespeare criticism from this period together, rather than parceling it out into discrete phenomena such as conventional disciplinary procedures would encourage, if not demand, we can detect a cluster of recurrent concerns. They pervade this work and show how Cavell's philosophy becomes available through his criticism in both these areas. Such issues emerge as relations between popular and elite culture, the genres of film and Shakespearean drama (especially if they bear upon marriage and skepticism), the provocation of Emerson as a founder of American thought and a forerunner of ordinary language philosophy; and further questions emerge about receptivity and responsiveness, about a fit audience both for Cavell's kind of writing and for the kinds of work to which it responds.

Othello and *The Philadelphia Story*

Cavell's essay on *The Philadelphia Story* frequently appeals to Shakespeare. It makes both central and incidental points in terms of plays as various as *A Midsummer Night's Dream, King Lear, The Tempest, Othello,* and *The Winter's Tale.* For example, mention of *The Winter's Tale,* which typifies the structure of remarriage basic to the film genre Cavell is exploring, leads to a reference to "its companion piece," *Othello.* This reference, in turn, leads to the observation that the "three males of *The Philadelphia Story* may be construed as dividing up Othello's qualities."[4] The Shakespearean terms of this last comment seem rather arbitrary, arriving not exactly from nowhere but from a surprising point of departure. Inasmuch as *Othello* has played no previous part in the discussion under way, what is it doing here?

An obvious answer involves Shakespeare's widespread canonicity and his works' consequent availability for illustrative purposes. This function of Shakespeare can help satisfy the need for a common culture as a basis of intelligent exchange about matters of human consequence typically addressed by philosophers and other literati. The familiarity of classic Hollywood comedies made Cavell believe them potentially another such source of shared experience to tap for public conversation of an engagingly serious sort. This conjunction of the popular and the canonical affords Cavell the best of both worlds: the immediate vitality of familiar and beloved movies, and the pervasive authority of Shakespeare's high status in the literary canon. Movies enliven discussions upon which Shakespeare confers seriousness.

Northrop Frye's approach to Shakespeare underwrites Cavell's anatomization of film genres in his books on Hollywood movies, and he is quite explicit about this debt from the very beginning of *Pursuits of Happiness.* Frye's influence is especially evident in Cavell's employment of the idea of the green world, that place of perspective at which unhappy couples must arrive to re-imagine their relations completely enough to get back together. Comedies of remarriage frequently call this place Connecticut, but it is ultimately a place in the heart where getting together again becomes possible. However, Frye's approach pervades Cavell's film criticism more broadly. Because it entails the identification of structures and types and themes at a high level of generality, it allows Cavell to move with apparent ease between diverse works whose exact relations sometimes defy more precise specification.

What Cavell calls the logic of the genre of remarriage allows him to construe this kind of work as an open system of variously recurring elements or features. He is less interested in codifying these elements than in exploring the arguments they give rise to, once their recurrence is noted.[5] Once Cavell observes that he has previously interpreted *Othello* "as, so to speak, a failed comedy of remarriage," he has created a tenable opportunity for further comparisons with other such works. The kinship of genre invites or, at least, sanctions further detection of family resemblances between a comedy of remarriage, such as *The Philadelphia Story,* and *Othello*. For example, what are their male figures like? Do they share any revealing qualities? Some such unexpressed line of inquiry yields the further observation that the "three males of *The Philadelphia Story* may be construed as dividing up Othello's qualities."

A more profound connection between Cavell's essays on these two works emerges in their discussion of virginity. In his essay on *Othello* Cavell introduces this theme quite dramatically: "We know—do we not?—that Desdemona has lost her virginity, the protection of Diana, by the time she appears to us. And surely Othello knows this!" Here the interrogative mood promptly unsettles any complacency in "our" claim to such knowledge, and then an exclamation anxiously seeks to reestablish that claim on a more certain footing. Cavell thus evokes the high stakes that ride on the question he glancingly broaches before citing Northrop Frye's *The Secular Scripture* to gloss the matter more fully: "Deep within the stock convention of virgin-baiting is a vision of human integrity imprisoned in a world it is in but not of, often forced by weakness into all kinds of ruses and stratagems, yet always managing to avoid the one fate which really is worse than death, the annihilation of one's identity."[6]

This issue pertains directly to *The Philadelphia Story,* whose "success" as a comedy of remarriage contrasts with the failure of *Othello* in this regard. That Cavell was thinking about these works in tandem becomes evident not merely through the excursus on how the three males in the movie divide up Othello's qualities. By 1979, when *The Claim of Reason* was published, Cavell was also teaching these works together in his large undergraduate course in Harvard's Program on General Education.[7] This course, in which the first part of Cavell's essay on *King Lear* initially emerged as lectures during 1966 and 1967, had undergone notable revisions that included the substitution of *Othello* and *The Winter's Tale* for *King Lear,* as well as the addition of Descartes's *Meditations on First Philosophy,* Freud's *Three Essays on Sexuality,* and *The Philadelphia Story,* among other changes and adjustments in the syllabus. Thus, Cavell's writing again reveals a fundamental connection to his teaching of undergraduates, whose assigned readings make decisive appearances in the essays here under review.

In the foreword to his first book, *Must We Mean What We Say?,* Cavell raised the question of "an audience for philosophy," and he concluded that volume with his essay on *King Lear.* Similarly, *The Claim of Reason* concludes with an essay on *Othello,* the Shakespearean tragedy that Cavell had begun teaching in Humanities 5, Ideas of Man and the World in Western Thought in 1977, two years before he published that book of philosophy. The presence of bright undergraduates, whose specifically professional training was not immediately a concern in this sort of course, should not be underestimated as an aid to Cavell in imagining what he called "an audience for philosophy." Just as the appeal of both Shakespeare's widespread canonicity and the popularity of Hollywood movies served him to make his philosophy more available to the uninitiated, the lecture hall helped to give life to the conversational feeling of direct address so prevalent in his mature thought. The embodied presence of others moves thought, almost irresistibly, toward more open dialogue. That those others are not in attendance as avowed aspirants to some specific career goal helps assure that the terms of such exchanges will remain general, except when they are employed to explore details of works that those present are expected to have studied as assigned reading.[8]

As Shakespeare's most domestic of tragedies, *Othello* offers an apposite context in which to explore the mysteries of marriage. During the time Cavell was thinking through the central issues of that play, he was also fastening upon Milton's definition of marriage as a central idea of his study of the Hollywood comedy of remarriage. Milton characterizes marriage as "a meet and happy conversation," and this description should naturally appeal to a philosopher with a deep interest in film comedy of the thirties and forties. Not only does the tradition of Western philosophy derive centrally from the dialogue form represented most illustriously in the writings of Plato. The advent of sound also inspired screenwriters, during the thirties and forties, to make lovers especially talkative; and the

dialogue in the movies that Cavell so carefully reads often takes philosophical turns.

In *The Philadelphia Story* Cavell notes that Dexter Haven (Cary Grant)
not only evaluates the conversation of Tracy Lord (Katharine Hepburn)
with pointed criticism, he also performs a part that Cavell repeatedly
construes as that of a philosopher. Tracy's inaptitude for conversation or,
if you will, marriage, betrays the "spiritual virginity" to which she has
cleaved in becoming a "married maiden" as Dexter's first wife. Dexter's
part in the exchanges on screen sometimes reveals what Cavell elsewhere
calls "the philosophical power of passiveness."[9] At one turn he calls this
"Dexter's mysterious power to control events," though he subsequently
backs away from that reading as a poor or prejudicial interpretation while
he continues his quest for Dexter's "authoritativeness, or charisma." In
this context Cavell's attribution of Othello's "capacity of authority" to
Dexter makes sense; but Othello's lack of patience, his inability to suffer
passion consciously rather than yield prematurely to its violent dictates,
runs precisely counter to Dexter's ability to let things happen without
untimely intervention.

Cavell applies to Dexter such terms as "true therapist," "magus," and
"sage" before he makes the most forthright of his assertions in this regard:
"Dexter's demand to determine for himself what is truly important and
what is not is a claim to the status of a philosopher."[10] Appearing as it
does in an essay entitled "The Importance of Importance," this assertion
has a particular resonance. That title itself echoes the self-importance of
Tracy's fiancé, George Kittredge (John Howard), in his wishful interest
in any publicity their marriage might receive in *Spy* magazine. When he
notices a copy of *Spy,* whose editor hopes what he dubs "The Philadelphia Story" will be its "most sensational achievement," George asks
Tracy, "Is there anything in there about the wedding?" Then he sheep-
ishly explains to her why he anticipates such attention. "Well, I thought,
yours being one of the oldest families in Philadelphia and my getting to
be fairly important . . . It's luck, of course. I just thought . . ."

Later, under a barrage of criticism from Dexter, Tracy reveals her own
inclination to adopt George's viewpoint. By evading what Dexter calls
"terribly important" self-knowledge, she accepts the unexamined life
and the external indicators of value upon which it must depend. She
defends her fiancé from Dexter's disparaging characterization by claiming, "Already he's of national importance." But, shortly thereafter, when
George declares to Tracy, "We're going to represent something," she
palpably recoils from the pedestal upon which he figuratively seeks to

install her. It is precisely George's unconscious acquiescence to what others deem important that distinguishes his view of the world and way of inhabiting it from Dexter's achievement of a philosophical perspective that allows him to decide independently about questions of value. As Cavell puts it, "George lives his life outside in, so he is never free from the idea that something external to his life can give it importance."[11] Gradually, this understanding of George is beginning to dawn on Tracy.

The emphasis that Cavell places upon the identification of Dexter as a philosopher invites speculation about just what kind of a philosopher, in Cavell's eyes, Cary Grant is here portraying. I stress the subjectivity involved in thus construing this actor in this role because Cavell places a similar stress upon this dimension of film criticism. Cavell had earlier insisted that movies, in contrast to plays, explore mere types, rather than characters. Indeed, he had invoked Othello and Desdemona to exemplify characters, as distinct from types. For Cavell, these Shakespearean figures illustrate this striking divergence between the two media, but then he goes on to concede that, "[o]f course there is a sense of character explored [in film]. It is our own."[12]

Emerson and Receptivity

Cavell makes the analogous assertion that estimable texts read us as much as we read them when he discusses the American transcendentalists, Emerson and Thoreau, with whose philosophizing he feels a direct connection.[13] Such texts can thereby expose our numbed sensibilities. The writer on trial, if you will, is not the author of the literary *objet d'art* under review. It is the reviewer himself. Since Cavell also uses the terms "texts" and "readings" to characterize his film criticism, these terms are virtually interchangeable with their counterparts in his literary criticism. This ethical principle of criticism, that texts read us as much as we read them, applies in both contexts, the interpretation of film and that of literature. At one point in his essay, "The Thought of Movies," Cavell formulates this principle with the claim that the practice of criticism tests the critic's character more than it tests his intellect.[14]

Cavell's formulation at this turn alludes unmistakably to Emerson's famous assertion in "The American Scholar" that character "is higher than intellect."[15] Though Cavell does not explicitly mark this reference, it is hard to miss once one has become aware of the pervasiveness of Emersonian thought and phrasing in Cavell's work as early as the mid-seventies. Moreover, the very title of the essay in which he advances this

Emersonian claim, "The Thought of Movies," provocatively refuses to split the difference between character and intellect or subject and object. The essay itself addresses the problem of detecting allusions, in particular those to Shakespeare, a habit of mind for which Cavell has been censured. But the equivocal genitive of its title confronts the problem of "the source or possession of philosophy" that Cavell first broached in the foreword to *Must We Mean What We Say?* when he glossed Hamlet's manic lines to Horatio and cordially welcomed their strange but suggestive ambiguity.[16]

> There are more things in heaven and earth, Horatio,
> Than are dreamt of in your philosophy.[17]

This vulnerability to texts can produce problematic moments. Cavell's Emersonian argument is a response to a serious charge leveled by an otherwise favorable reviewer of *Pursuits of Happiness*. In his chapter on *The Philadelphia Story,* Cavell hears Tracy Lord's celebratory outburst, "I think men are wonderful!" as an allusion to Miranda's exclamation in *The Tempest,* "How beauteous mankind is!" The reviewer deems this bit of imaginative audition an instance of "hysterical impropriety," and Cavell seeks to exonerate himself from this charge by a variety of arguments.[18] These include the seemingly incidental observation that both sentences contain the same number of syllables, a similarity of sound that could indicate a conscious echo whereby a memorable line receives approximate reformulation. But the important argument interprets Tracy's breakthrough here as the same as Miranda's. It is an acknowledgment of her dawning awareness—and the wonder of it—that there are two distinct or separate sexes.

Cavell's persistence in calling this moment in *The Philadelphia Story* an allusion to *The Tempest* unflinchingly makes an extremely strong claim. Using another term, say, analogue, would allow Cavell to moderate this claim without losing much of the commentary he wishes to make. This alternative term would keep in play the congruencies between Tracy's exclamation and that of Miranda, the spontaneity and candor of recognition that both express; but perhaps it would not satisfy what Cavell calls, in "The Thought of Movies," his "need for Shakespeare." This need arises from Cavell's conviction that evaluative distinctions between popular and elite or low and high culture simply do not apply to works of such reputedly different orders as Shakespearean drama and the Hollywood movies that he admires. Art and entertainment or, if you will, instruction and pleasure are indistinguishable in memorable works whose impact goes deep even though perhaps not for long. Both the evanescence and profundity of such experiences take our measure revealingly. In this case at least, Cavell is committed to correcting the undervaluation of the popular rather than overvaluation of the elite.

This ambition further reveals Cavell's Emersonian affinities. On the one hand Emerson spoke of nothing less than a "revolution . . . to be wrought by the gradual domestication of the idea of Culture," and he announced in this regard his inclination to "embrace the common" and to "explore and sit at the feet of the familiar, the low." The studious attention that Cavell has lavished on mainstream Hollywood movies of the first decades of the sound era constitutes his dedication to the Emersonian project voiced in such lines. On the other hand, the innumerable Shakespearean contexts, allusions, and analogues that Cavell brings to bear, discovers, or invents bespeak his acceptance of Emerson's strongest assertion about the bard. "Now, literature, philosophy, and thought are Shakespearized. His mind is the horizon beyond which, at present, we do not see."[19]

In Cavell's essay on *The Philadelphia Story,* "The Importance of Importance," these uses of Shakespeare are all in evidence. Cavell sifts through a variety of telling options, such as *Othello* and *The Winter's Tale,* before he emphatically situates the movie under scrutiny in especially strong relation to *A Midsummer Night's Dream.* In his discursive anatomization of the film genre he identifies as the Hollywood comedy of remarriage, the central premises that Shakespeare affords Cavell include the transformation of the woman (such as Hermione in *The Winter's Tale*) and what Northrop Frye calls the green world (such as the wood around Athens in *A Midsummer Night's Dream* or the pastures of Bohemia in *The Winter's Tale*). But what Emerson calls the Shakespearization of literature, philosophy, and thought becomes more apparent in moments that might tempt Cavell's critics to level such a charge as "hysterical impropriety." By seeing Shakespeare nearly everywhere, Cavell courts the outrageousness he has previously acknowledged risking in the process of bringing together the high and the low, the popular and the elite orders of culture.[20]

In his essay on *The Philadelphia Story,* another inviting occasion for leveling this charge occurs in Cavell's remarkable discussion of this film's final moments. This concluding sequence represents the camerawork of Sidney Kidd (Henry Daniell), the editor and publisher of *Spy* magazine, capturing, if you will, the movie's three stars in a still photograph. This picture then becomes a page of (perhaps) *Spy* or even the wedding album, which is then turned to another such page, as the film emphatically declares the end of its story and begins to offer the closing credits. To describe these frozen images of Tracy Lord and her two most eligible suitors, Cavell has recourse to Shakespeare and asks, "[I]s there not some lingering suspicion that the picture of the trio was already a kind of wedding photo?—that somehow, as Edmund madly says in the final moments of *King Lear,* "I was contracted to them both./Now all three marry in an instant."[21]

The arguable "madness" of Edmund's assertion and Cavell's plainly equivocal diction—"some," "kind of," "somehow"—are surely meant to take the critical pressure off such a citation by openly indicating its tentativeness as just a passing thought, uncanny enough in its fit to warrant mention. The Shakespearean resonance, however, significantly upgrades this evanescent moment of Cavell's generally stylish prose, which easily shifts registers from informality to statelier measures, as the quotation from *King Lear* reveals in its context. But if one follows this line of thought where it leads, one arrives at a place in *King Lear* unlikely to remind anyone of the conclusion of *The Philadelphia Story.* Making the link on the grounds of anything besides the sonorous authority of an echo from Shakespeare seems untenable; hence, it would amount to "hysterical impropriety" to insist upon it for other reasons.

Thus, Cavell seems to be simply drawing upon the cultural capital of the swan of Avon himself, the most bankable of bards. Shakespeare's words can be used to impart unjustifiably high value to humdrum occasions otherwise deemed unworthy of eloquence. But such an argument can be turned upside down. The very occasions that we consider routine and prosaic may hide in plain sight nothing less than the significance of our lives. Cavell characterizes the adventure that his philosophy undertakes as a quest whose object is the ordinary, the everyday, whose capacity to disappoint us remains withering. The best of those films too easily dismissed as merely formulaic products of the Hollywood studio system require such eloquence if we are to resist our inclination to take them for granted. Willful indecorum may be precisely the tactic necessary to overcome an habitual devaluation of excellence that we refuse to acknowledge.

This claim puts into practice not only Emerson's homage to the familiar, at whose feet he chooses to sit. It also implements his assertion that character is higher than intellect by taking the risk of giving offense. The critics who consider Cavell's approach to classic Hollywood movies pretentious and over-intellectual are making the same kind of distinction.

Their chosen terms indicate defects of character more than intellectual shortcomings. Cavell strikes such critics as a name-dropper seeking to show off his familiarity with the canonical in-crowd while engaging in discussion of the culture of the masses. Concerns with who's in and who's out inevitably entail value-laden discriminations that the quest for a democratic culture must aim to adjudicate fairly. Cavell describes his ambition in terms that emphasize inclusion without abandoning the effort to celebrate excellence.

The typecasting of Cary Grant in *The Philadelphia Story* as a philosopher, therefore, makes Cavell's own sense of what he calls the philosopher in American life relevant to his assessment of Grant's performance of his role in this film. Cavell is exploring, or revealing, a dimension of his own character in thus construing Grant's Dexter Haven in such terms. Cavell had previously glossed Grant's opening pose in *Bringing up Baby* as "a special discovery of Howard Hawks's about Grant's filmic presence, his photogenesis, what it is the camera makes of him."[22] The pose Grant assumed there was that of Rodin's statue, *The Thinker*. The banality of this posture's fame leaves it as routinely open to parody as Hamlet's world-historical attitude of contemplation when he fixes his gaze upon the skull of Yorick; and it is for purposes of parody that Hawks appropriates Rodin in this film at this moment. Yet this parody builds upon Grant's discernible capacity for thoughtfulness that can be, and was (elsewhere), inflected otherwise and employed to project what comes across convincingly as philosophical seriousness. Hawks's discovery about Grant is his ability to project what it is that thinkers—like Cavell, for example—do.

Cavell delivered a lecture entitled "The Philosopher in American Life" not too long after the publication of *The Claim of Reason*. It has been called (somewhat hastily, to my way of thinking) a sort of summary of that exhaustive study.[23] In the intervening years, however, Cavell had also published *Pursuits of Happiness,* which thus indicates other concerns that had continued to hold his attention and strike him as sufficiently philosophical to warrant sustained reflection. In "The Philosopher in American Life," Cavell elaborates upon his discovery of ordinary language philosophy in writers whom he deems the founders (or finders) of American thought, Emerson and Thoreau. He thus announces a sort of homecoming for the kind of philosophy he had practiced for several decades under the inspiration of different precursors, specifically J. L. Austin and Ludwig Wittgenstein.[24]

Moreover, Cavell detects in Thoreau's *Walden* a disposition strikingly akin to what he discerns in Cary Grant's portrayal of Dexter Haven. In this text, where "the sentence is everything," Cavell focuses upon a single such period in whose "few drops," as he puts it, "[a]ll of *Walden* is condensed." In that sentence Thoreau writes, "You only need sit still long enough in some attractive spot in the woods that all its inhabitants may exhibit themselves to you by turns." Cavell glosses this pregnant assertion in various revealing ways, especially when he discerns in the phrase "by turns" the meaning "by conversions" as one of the options; but he generalizes the capacity of this sentence to epitomize *Walden* in the claim that this book "has a power of stillness, say silence, that is sufficiently attractive to be looked to as redemptive."[25] In *The Philadelphia Story* the patience Dexter shows in letting events take their course initially leads Cavell to speak of his "control" over them. His subsequent revision of that term to stress Dexter's "power not to interfere in them" corresponds to what he terms the "power of stillness" in Thoreau and, in a later essay, "the philosophical power of passivity" in Emerson.[26]

The turn or conversion that we witness in *The Philadelphia Story* is that of Tracy Lord, who undergoes, before our eyes, a metamorphosis from goddess to human being. Tracy herself announces this change in her final conversation with her father, just before she remarries Dexter; and the passionate rhetoric of Mike Connor (James Stewart), in his declarations of love to Tracy during the night before the wedding, have mightily assisted this transformation and our awareness of the process. But another such change, whose momentousness well warrants the term conversion, has taken place *before* all the events that we witness on screen in the main body of the movie (i.e., with the exception of the brief opening routine that comically portrays the separation of Dexter and Tracy as a married couple).

Dexter is a recovered alcoholic. His drinking was the pathological manifestation of the "gorgeous thirst" he still claims as his own in his sober state during the main events of the movie. He attributes his recovery from active alcoholism, which is the change he's been through, to books. Mike, who is a fiction writer financially constrained into tabloid journalism, notices his own volume of stories among the books on Dexter's shelf on that fateful night before the wedding. This discovery leads the inebriated Mike to attribute "unsuspected depths" to Dexter, the very sort of inwardness that Tracy had become willing to assign to Mike after reading parts of his book at the library. Indeed, she had fixed upon a favorite story, whose title, Mike informs her, derives from a Spanish peasants' proverb: "With the rich and mighty always a little patience." Dexter, however, disclaims any specific memory of Mike's book, which he encountered while substituting one addiction for another, reading for drinking. Nonetheless, Dexter embodies the virtue of patience commended by the proverb.

Dexter, of course, is no peasant; and what suits him, as opposed to Mike, for Tracy's hand in (re)marriage is a question inevitably raised by this film. It pointedly concerns Cavell both at the beginning of his essay and at its conclusion. When I taught this film at Ruhr University, I was informed by one of my students that the German title for *The Philadelphia Story* is *The Night before the Wedding;* and, more recently, while teaching it in Lisbon, I learned that the Portuguese call it *Scandalous Marriage*. In the light of this information, it amused me to imagine, as I watched the opening credits roll over a ghostly replica of Independence Hall, that perhaps European audiences come to think that *that*'s where Americans get married or, at least, we get married in places like that. In a sense we do, given the constitutional separation of church and state and our inheritance of the protestant demotion of marriage from the status of a sacrament to that of a civil ceremony.

Tellingly, Cavell's thought in this regard depends initially upon Martin Luther's argument to precisely this latter effect in "The Pagan Servitude of the Church," but it gains particular support from John Milton's first pamphlet petitioning the English Parliament to relax the legal constraints upon divorce, *The Doctrine and Discipline of Divorce*. In the preface to this tract, from which Cavell appositely cites in his essay on *The Philadelphia Story*, Milton prominently makes an analogy between the misery of citizens under a tyrannical government and the "household unhappiness" of a bad marriage. For parties to either arrangement—or, in a bad marriage, for husbands, at least—Milton goes on to assert the legitimacy of attempting to shed the bonds of their oppressive condition.

This analogy between political and domestic arrangements is crucial for Cavell in interpreting the Hollywood genres that he anatomizes and reads in both of his books about them. Marriage can indeed stand for something of national importance, if only as a utopian ideal that we employ both as a rebuke of things as they are in our present political arrangements and as a sign of an eventual human community we may aspire to create. Cavell makes this explicit in what he identifies as his most blatant transgression of the mutual frontier between film and philosophy when he employs Kant and Wittgenstein to explore the concepts of human finitude and the limits of knowledge in his essay on *It Happened One Night*. Cavell there suggests that, in such couples as actors portray in remarriage comedies, we can discern "'the realm of ends,' which may be thought of as the perfected human community."[27]

But in *The Philadelphia Story* we witness a lack of inclusiveness that entails not only the banishment of George Kittredge, "man of the people," as Mike ironically dubs him in voicing a suspicion that will ultimately prove true. George's ambition to climb the social ladder is clearly uninformed by any sense of values worth promoting, and tones of envy and resentment have become expressly audible in his clumsy efforts to make himself clear. But we also hear Tracy make distinctions of personal worth in terms that explicitly assert the limits of class differences in deciding such matters when, for example, she remarks that "Mack the night watchman is a prince among men. Uncle Willy is . . . a pincher." Finally, the most capacious and potent formulation of this sort comes from Mike as he summarizes for Tracy the lesson he has learned on the night before the wedding and lifts the clouds of class suspicion with which his persistent skepticism has previously shadowed Dexter: "Well, you see, I've made a funny discovery: that in spite of the fact that someone's up from the bottom, he may be quite a heel. And that even though someone else is born to the purple, he still may be quite a guy."

Still, Mike is also unacceptable to Tracy as a husband. She greets his proposal with a moving acknowledgment of gratitude for his gallantry in which Katharine Hepburn plumbs a depth of feeling indicative of the high degree of emotional resonance achieved in this film's closing sequence. But Tracy rejects that proposal and leaves us with the challenge of explaining Mike's ultimate unsuitability as a candidate for her hand. Cavell appeals at this juncture to the laws of genre and notes that the film informs us—first ironically in Dexter's words, but then seriously from Tracy's mother—of a fact that we cannot doubt. Tracy and Dexter grew up together and thus share the capacity to create a childhood past that enables them to enjoy a mutual playfulness such as we witness in other couples in remarriage comedy, like Grant and Hepburn in *Bringing up Baby* and Grant and Irene Dunne in *The Awful Truth*.[28]

The logic or grammar of this film genre involves such requirements in the forms of life that it imagines, and the extent to which such patterns are natural or "merely" conventional is a measure of the depths they sound in exploring the human heart. Cavell does not work out in any detail the ways in which ideas and expressions from Wittgenstein, such as "grammar," "family resemblances," and "forms of life," overlap or coincide with his thinking about genre. However, the deep connection that he discerns between the conventional and the natural in Wittgenstein's later philosophy supports his inclination to perceive broader human truths in the fundamental structures of the film genres he examines. Cavell cites this apposite thought from Pascal's *Pensées* to underwrite such claims: "Custom is our nature."[29]

Other instances of this genre include couples for whom differences of class constitute no insuperable obstacle to remarriage, as both *It Happened One Night* and *The Lady Eve* readily illustrate. Thus, the claim that Dexter and Tracy remarry simply on the basis of class membership that ultimately excludes other rivals not only overlooks prominent elements of the film script that specifically address such issues. It also fails to see that Cavell's argument for why this pair remarries employs terms that allow comparable couples within the genre he is exploring to overcome class barriers. The childhood such pairs must share is not a stage along life's way, and it is not a passage through a particular kind of childhood available only to the wealthy established few. It is a dimension of the self, a capacity for play that lives on in adults of all ages who have not lost permanent touch with this aspect of their humanity.

We witness this quality in *It Happened One Night* when Ellie and Peter (Claudette Colbert and Clark Gable) pretend to be married and become quite merry together in their enjoyment of pretending to be miserable. The detectives searching for Ellie read this misery as evidence that they *are* a married couple, in the legal or literal sense of the term. Thus, they think they know she's *not* the young woman they're seeking. We can read this moment allegorically, as another sort of sign—one with a spiritual sense that informs us, retrospectively, that they were married just then in the fun of their charade. Thus, when they have gotten back together and return to another motor court, where they will knock down the walls of Jericho, we can fairly interpret this occasion as a remarriage. We can further note that the proprietors of that establishment are mystified by their behavior on that occasion. About this couple in the front office, we can have no doubt that they are a legally married couple. Ellie has recently made what we may aptly term a "hair-breadth's scape i' th' imminent deadly breach" from precisely this condition, if we wish to indulge in resonant citations from Shakespeare. Thus, the film shows us scenes from a marriage in both public and private senses of that term. As viewers, we occupy a position where both of these senses can become visible, whatever we may choose to make of them.

North by Northwest and *Hamlet*

Cavell broaches this issue of the relationship between the public and the private at the conclusion of his essay on Alfred Hitchcock's *North by*

Northwest: the successful pursuit of happiness in marriage amounts to a "state secret" in America. Toward the end of this romantic thriller, when the pre-Columbian figure of a Tarascan warrior shatters on a ledge of Mount Rushmore, Cavell notes, in an apposite turn of phrase, it "produce[s] some film." This sight of some film on screen awakens our awareness (if it has slumbered) that we have been watching a film; and it thus invites us to reflect upon what we have been watching. Just moments earlier, for example, Roger Thornhill (Cary Grant) was trying to rescue Eve Kendall (Eva Marie Saint) from Phillip Vandamm (James Mason), the foreign agent who had purchased this figure at an auction in Chicago. The camera shows Thornhill climbing up a diagonal beam supporting Vandamm's cantilevered house atop Mount Rushmore, and it reveals a ladder-like form that looks like empty frames of film running alongside the cantilever. When Thornhill turns to look over his shoulder, we see six darkened window frames, which constitute even more clearly another ladder-like form that looks like empty frames of film running up the side of Vandamm's house. Three of these windows light up when Eve enters her upstairs room to which Thornhill must mount to save his beloved and those very secrets of state that turn out to be kept on film. In a sense he is trying to enter the film or, rather like us, come into possession of its secrets.

Just before Thornhill completes his climb up to Eve's room, he witnesses a dramatic encounter on the floor below between Vandamm and his main accomplice, Leonard (Martin Landau). It includes this exchange about Eve, with pointed reference to the pre-Columbian figure:

L. You must have had *some* doubts about her yourself, and *still do.*
V. Rubbish.
L. Why else would you have decided not to tell her that our little treasure here has a bellyful of microfilm?
V. *You* seem to be trying to fill *mine* with rotten apples.
L. Sometimes the truth does taste like a mouthful of worms, sir.
V. What truth? I've heard nothing but innuendoes.

In this dialogue, the manifold complexities of this scene include a succinct evocation of what Christian doctrine calls the Fall of Man. Leonard, who will immediately hereafter speak of his "woman's intuition," plays the biblical role of Eve and offers Vandamm the fruit of the tree of knowledge to discredit Eve Kendall's fidelity. Vandamm will soon slug Leonard in response to this humiliating revelation of knowledge he now cannot disown; but, when Vandamm winces over the resulting pain in his hand, this previously unflappable embodiment of *sang froid* reveals the intimate anguish of the betrayal just disclosed, not merely the ache of a sore hand.

In an equally, if not even more, indirect or restrained allusion to that mythical event in the beginning of human experience, Cavell posits a connection between ordinary language philosophers and American transcendentalists. He claims that the "ordinariness" upon which both sorts of thinkers train their attention "speaks of an intimacy with existence and of an intimacy lost, that matches skepticism's despair of the world."[30] In "Experience" Emerson's way of describing our lost intimacy with the world explicitly asserts its relation to the Genesis story, and this description becomes increasingly pertinent to Cavell as he proceeds with his writing about Hollywood movies. "It is very unhappy," Emerson observes, "but too late to be helped, the discovery we have made, that we exist. That discovery is called the Fall of Man. Ever afterwards, we suspect our instruments. We have learned that we do not see directly, but mediately, and that we have no means of correcting these colored and distorting lenses which we are, or of computing the amount of their errors. Perhaps these subject lenses have a creative power; perhaps there are no objects."[31]

When Cavell turns to such melodramas as *Stella Dallas,* he makes this Emersonian connection especially clear in its centrality to his thinking about the achievement of human selfhood.[32] But this line of thought also has roots in Cavell's earliest writing about Shakespeare. In his reading of *King Lear,* "The Avoidance of Love," Cavell echoes Jacob Burckhardt's famous assertion that, during the Renaissance in Italy, "man became a spiritual *individual,* and recognized himself as such," and he compounds this reference with an allusion to the Fall of Man as Emerson psychologizes this mythical event in "Experience."[33] "With the discovery of the individual," Cavell opines, "whether in Paradise or in the Renaissance, there is the simultaneous discovery of the isolation of the individual."[34]

This medley of associations could be expanded. For example, a less immediately apparent allusion here, in Cavell's reading of *King Lear,* leads one not to Burckhardt but to his young colleague in Basel, Friedrich Nietzsche, whose genealogy of tragedy repeatedly emphasizes the Apollonian *principium individuationis* that constitutes the Sophoclean agons of such characters as Oedipus and Antigone. According to Nietzsche, tragic experience, in the Attic tradition, entails painful separation into discrete selfhood, and Greek tragedy reenacts the ordeal of that traumatic process. Tracy Lord's epiphany about men in *The Philadelphia Story* serves as an occasion for Cavell to apply this line of thought in a comic setting by emphasizing Tracy's "admiration at the sheer fact of their separateness, wonder as it were that there should be two sexes, and that the opposite one is *as such* admirable."[35] Cavell's sense of selfhood's coming into being through acceptance of separateness (and acknowledgement of otherness) thus constitutes the bedrock of individual identity as he conceives of its dawning in our minds. "Becoming the one you are"—another phrase Cavell borrows from Nietzsche to describe the process Tracy undergoes in *The Philadelphia Story*—requires both this awareness of difference and distinctness, and its acknowledgment.[36]

This medley of associations can give us an idea of what selfhood means to Cavell, and we can supplement it with an apposite addition that reveals the constructive relations between art and selfhood that Cavell insists upon when he addresses the question of the value of art. In the following passage from *The World Viewed,* he begins by recapping an historical argument most readily identified with Burckhardt, but Cavell promptly shifts it in the psychological direction of Nietzsche's favorite philosopher, Emerson. Once Cavell has taken that turn, he openly declares his sense of the only intelligible claim of value to be made on behalf of art: "At some point the unhinging of our consciousness from the world interposed our subjectivity between us and our presentness to the world. Then our subjectivity became what is present to us, individuality became isolation. The route to conviction in reality was through the acknowledgment of that endless presence of self. . . . Apart from the wish for selfhood (hence the simultaneous granting of otherness as well), I do not understand the value of art."[37]

The study of such films as *The Philadelphia Story* and *North by Northwest* attracts Cavell because they perform this function. He communicates his sense of their value in part by reading them in tandem with Shakespeare, but they themselves occasionally invite this approach by allusions to the plays. *North by Northwest,* for example, signals this connection in its title, which sounds almost exactly like a phrase from *Hamlet.* Numerous other aspects of this movie also link it by analogy with Shakespeare's tragedy. For example, Thornhill is abducted by two men, Licht and Valerian, "mere errand boys," as the latter remarks, "carrying concealed weapons." Like Rosencrantz and Guildenstern, they take their fellow passenger on an unsuccessful journey meant to put an end to his life. At the auction in Chicago, Thornhill, like Hamlet, puts on an antic disposition and feigns a sort of madness as a method of eluding dangerous foes. At the direction of the Professor (Leo G. Carroll), Thornhill and Eve Kendall stage a play-within-the-play (or movie) in the cafeteria at Mount

Rushmore to deceive Vandamm and dampen his suspicions, just as Hamlet arranges such a production to "catch the conscience of the king." Thornhill's mother (Jesse Royce Landis), like Gertrude, is essentially unavailable to assist her son in the nightmare of mortal danger that has descended upon him. She habitually expresses debilitating doubts about him, and in her mockery of both his accusations and fears of his enemies, she seems virtually in league with them. Eve Kendall, the agent under cover in Vandamm's circle, is caught, like Ophelia, in a tangle of circumstance that compromises her relations with Thornhill and mortally threatens her own well-being.

But a pervasive preoccupation with acting constitutes an especially deep kinship between these two works as meditations upon the nature of human identity. *North by Northwest,* on its most obvious level, is a story about mistaken identity that arbitrarily casts Roger Thornhill in a role he cannot shed. His repeated protestations about this mistake only earn him ironic praise for his "performance," a compliment he returns to his tormentors when they impersonate friends. The misidentification of Thornhill as George Kaplan involves an irony about human selfhood that raises fundamental questions about naming and being. As one of the agents around the conference table at the United States Intelligence Agency puts it: "How could he be mistaken for George Kaplan when George Kaplan doesn't even exist?"

An exchange between Thornhill and Eve registers this theme in terms powerfully suggestive of *Hamlet.* It occurs in the dining car of the Twentieth Century Limited when they first meet. Eve has noticed the initials that appear on the matchbook Thornhill produces to light her cigarette.

T. My trademark—rot.
E. Roger O. Thornhill. What does the O. stand for?
T. Nothing.

Perhaps, for the average moviegoer (whoever that might be nowadays), this erotically charged meeting of glamorous strangers on a train seems merely another Hollywood scene of seduction and hardly brings *Hamlet* to mind. It certainly is that, and Hitchcock knowingly lets it unfold in the recognizable manner and mood of such proceedings. But the monumental familiarity of such a line from *Hamlet* as Marcellus's "Something is rotten in the state of Denmark" seems an undeniable echo in this exchange, once one has begun to take the demonstrable connection between *North by Northwest* and the Elizabethan tragedy seriously.

Indeed, precisely how to take that connection is a question of character in the old-fashioned sense—Victorian let's call it. But the exchange itself and the issues it brings into focus might be labeled postmodern, or even posthuman. The self is a cipher constituted temporarily by the circumstances that inform it, and it will change or, perhaps, vanish when conditions change. (Or, as the bad guys put it—and we've learned how to take instruction from them—Roger Thornhill *is* George Kaplan.) The erotic intensity of this moment and its sequel, however cool the irony with which they are portrayed, also signals the self's dissolution at the onslaught of drives beyond its conscious control or the self's vulnerability to refashioning under the irresistible pressure of irrational forces. At the Prairie Stop on Highway 41, where Eve subsequently sends him, Thornhill will survive the crop duster's assault; but he will emerge from that encounter like a new man with a fresh claim upon her that imparts unexpected value to the attraction between them. During the auction in Chicago, after Thornhill's own "hair-breadth's 'scape," he confronts her and Vandamm. Vandamm is bidding on the pre-Columbian figure of the Tarasacan warrior and continues to do so, but Thornhill looks down at Eve.

T. I bet you paid plenty for this little piece of—sculpture—
V. Seventeen fifty.
T. She's worth every dollar, take it from me. She really puts her heart into her work. In fact her whole body.

Eve's tears well up during this exchange. Though Thornhill takes no evident note of her anguish, this statue begins to cry, and soon this angry rational man will begin to act crazy.

Of course, Thornhill is improvising under the urgent inspiration of a death threat; and, like Hamlet, he strategically feigns madness. But how a critic elaborates upon such a likeness raises those other questions of character that Cavell's film criticism has elicited. Michael Wood, for example, broaches them under the rubric of "failures of tact," which he deems "so large as to make one wonder whether they can be failures of another kind."[38] For Wood, such transgressions exceed the bounds of decorum to such an extent that he wonders if they are not symptomatic of a defect of character. Thus, we arrive at a moralized version of critical decorum, which certainly gestures in the direction of Cavell's own conviction that texts (and films) worthy of our critical attention read us as much as we read them. In another context, however, Cavell makes this more relevant observation about tact as it evolves into a moral issue:

"Our (moralized) idea of tact tends toward the idea of not mentioning something, not touching on it; not toward an idea of touching it pertinently, fittingly, painfully if necessary."[39]

In his essay on *North by Northwest,* Cavell ostensibly seeks to demonstrate that film's relationship to *Hamlet* while exploring the affinity between the genres of the romantic thriller and remarriage comedy. From certain perspectives, the popularity of Hitchcock's blockbuster, like that of *The Philadelphia Story,* and the high cultural status of Shakespeare's premier tragedy make the probing of their relationship a test of the critic's character. If doing so at all strikes some as merely tactless, Cavell is willing to court such outrageousness because the payoff is considerable. Not only does he wish to acknowledge and claim the full range of his experience of art. He also wishes to tap into both the dignity of a classic text and the vitality of a popular movie. Reading works of these potentially incompatible kinds together can impart an exciting combination of seriousness and energy to writing that can both rise and descend to such a challenge. There is power at the crossing of these apparently rival alternatives, and Hitchcock's film itself exemplifies this potent mixture. Cavell aspires to a prose that can serve as a vehicle for this risky challenge. If his writing fails, it will warrant the charge of pretentiousness, and Cavell's critics will rightly strive to let the air out of his overblown ambition.

Cavell's arguments about *Hamlet* and Hitchcock's movie, though hardly negligible, seem less important than his performance of certain passages from them as related texts. Their relationship provides Cavell with an occasion for some remarkable writing. Simply to call that relationship Cavell's McGuffin subordinates those arguments too glibly; but the idea of interpretation as performance, a notion Cavell himself elaborates in the introduction to *Pursuits of Happiness,* applies tellingly to this essay's best features.[40] Giovanna Borradori once asked Cavell whether he considered himself "more a writer than a philosopher," and he acknowledged that the road that led him to philosophy was an attempt to find a way to write that he could believe in.[41] He has also affiliated himself with philosophical writing, like Thoreau's, in which "argument" has no part. Rather, Cavell conscientiously redefines the role of argumentation as "accepting full responsibility for one's own discourse," and he seeks to find for himself another philosophical way of accepting that responsibility.[42] If the wish for selfhood constitutes the only intelligible value of art for Cavell, it also amounts to a clear and central value of his philosophical writing. Cavell's writing amounts to both a manifestation of his own selfhood as a writer, coming into being as his prose unfolds, and a provocation to selfhood for his readers as the experience of that prose strikes home in them.

It should go without saying that the monumentality of *Hamlet* readily dwarfs anyone who would venture directly to emulate Shakespeare's achievement. Crawling around on the face of Mount Rushmore, like the man-moth in Elizabeth Bishop's poem of that title, amounts to a fairly good image of how that particular tragedy would take the measure of such grand aspirations. Adding a pair of homicidal villains in hot pursuit of those insect-like humans helps us to know what it would feel like seriously to undertake such a daunting challenge. That Cavell initially writes about *Hamlet* from such an oblique angle as Hitchcock's *North by Northwest* reveals his awareness that the critical tradition also crowds the approaches to this play in such a way as nearly to block direct access. When Cavell later comes to write an essay explicitly about *Hamlet,* it is the shortest of the seven essays he has written about individual plays. It thus reveals a kindred reticence about sustained interpretation of this play. Its opening paragraph even features Cavell's self-description of his "forays into Shakespeare" as "amateur."[43] Richard Halpern calls Cavell's disclaimers of this sort "disingenuous," but how does he *know* that?[44] Cavell's first two essays on Shakespeare come at the end of lengthy volumes of mainly philosophical writing. Cavell did not make these "forays into Shakespeare" without carefully establishing his intellectual credentials beforehand, and they are quite different from those of the "professional" Shakespearean.

Notably, Cavell's two essays about *Hamlet* have ideas about selfhood in common, and they share a preoccupation with Freud. In the later essay, Cavell makes this second connection especially clear by his uncustomary employment of explicitly psychoanalytical terms and concepts. The technical concepts of the "primal scene" and "primal fantasies" sponsor Cavell's quest into the problem of origins and what he deems Hamlet's traumatic misappropriation of the ghost's message. However, Cavell stresses Hamlet's melancholy and stalled process of mourning, which is contrary to the drift of Freud's own considerations of *Hamlet.* Freud's discussions of *Hamlet* begin with an emphasis upon mourning and melancholy, but he then shifts to a dominant concern with Oedipal guilt and rivalry.[45] Cavell views the ghost's description of the older Hamlet's murder as young Hamlet's fantasy of how that crime was committed. That misconstruction of the actual murder displaces a primal fantasy of witnessing parental intercourse, a scene which, of course, could as well be a scene of conception. Thus, separation from the mother and what Cavell calls "the acceptance of birth" become central challenges that stymie Hamlet.

Cavell makes an observation that links his discussion of *North by Northwest* with this way of thinking about *Hamlet* in a series of answers to the question why Eve Kendall is Roger Thornhill's to rescue: "in addition to incorporating at least two of the women [the bad and the good] from *The Thirty-Nine Steps* she also incorporates the mother, perhaps the mother he never had, protecting him from the police by hiding him in a bellying container that shows she holds the key to his berth."[46] Cavell's pun here nicely conveys his meaning and raises the matter of origins that he claims Hamlet displaced in his primal fantasy. About Hamlet Cavell further argues that he experiences Gertrude's sexual power and the independence of her desire in this fantasy as annihilating of his own power. Stalled in his capacity to mourn, he regresses to the earlier trauma of separation from the mother and flounders anew in the unresolved struggle to make the break into a life he can own, to claim his existence. In a later essay, Cavell summarily revisits this issue in *Hamlet* and provides it with a happier or, at least, less morbid ending, which the striking difference in Hamlet's state of mind in the last act makes credible. He focuses upon the moment when Hamlet overcomes his skepticism, like Descartes, by announcing his existence, "This is I/Hamlet the Dane." "This announcement," Cavell argues, "is undertaken by Hamlet as some preparation, or explanation, for his leap into Ophelia's grave, as if facing the death of love is the condition of announcing one's separate existence."[47]

In romantic thrillers like *North by Northwest,* happy endings are expectable outcomes, though achieving that goal can entail many dangerous turns and suspenseful delays. Thornhill is exposed to annihilating forces and faces death at several turns, one of which Eve gives him directions to reach. At the Prairie Stop on Highway 41, as we have seen, his survival of the crop duster's assault gives him a claim upon Eve. Roughly made, that claim brings tears to her eyes at the Chicago auction while Vandamm continues bidding on the pre-Columbian figure with the bellyful of microfilm. When Thornhill and Eve face death together on the heights of Mount Rushmore, Cavell finds the occasion to invoke lines from Hamlet's mad ranting at Ophelia in the sequel to his third soliloquy, "To be or not to be." A discernible relation between his reading of the movie and his subsequent interpretation of the play thus comes into focus. Such connections make the broader lines of Cavell's thought more apparent. In the essay on *Hamlet,* for example, Cavell makes a revealing pun on the title, "Hamlet's Burden of Proof," in the opening paragraph, where he refers to "the burden of [his] story" or its "refrain." The pun helps Cavell clarify a recurrent argument that connects many of his writings, and it is about the achievement of selfhood by overcoming skepticism. But, he insists, it is no substitute for the texts that he reads or, I would hasten to add, for those that he writes:

> In turning to the surprising place of skepticism in Hamlet's burden, it is important for me to repeat: the burden of my story in spinning the interplay of philosophy with literature is not of applying philosophy to literature, where so-called literary works become kinds of illustrations of matters already independently known. It would better express my refrain to say that I take the works I am drawn to read out in public (beginning with those I have listed of Shakespeare) as studies of matters your philosophy has (has unassessably, left to itself) intellectualized as skepticism, whether in Descartes's or Hume's or Kant's pictures of that inescapably, essentially, human possibility.[48]

In the finale of his interpretation of Hitchcock's film, Cavell's performance—this *is* the right word for such writing—achieves a breathtaking eloquence. Earlier Cavell has spoken directly in the voice of Alfred Hitchcock, a gesture indicative of the liberties his writing takes. He inquires into the nature of a source and, speaking for Hitchcock, he offers a swelling sequence of answers that ends with suspension points, indicating that he could go on and on, if he wished. But, he abruptly concludes, "You see my point." The question of sources, like the problem of origins, can overwhelm you with an infinite regress, the skeptic's signature argument. In Cavell's finale about *North by Northwest,* however, *Hamlet,* a key one of those sources, becomes almost an unmarked part of the text. In describing Thornhill and Eve creeping along the face of Mount Rushmore, Cavell turns the mood of the Shakespearean play inside out, to suit the movie at hand, as we have already seen him doing with Edmund's near-final lines in describing the end of *The Philadelphia Story.* In evoking the next-to-last scene in *North by Northwest,* Cavell assimilates the pathology of Hamlet's regression to the lively openness to childhood, which he calls a way of having a shared past such as films in the genre of remarriage comedy, like *The Philadelphia Story,* require of their central couples: "These tiny creatures are crawling between heaven and earth, a metaphysical accomplishment, as if becoming children again. Hamlet, feeling like a child, claims this accomplishment for himself as he declares there shall be no more marriages."[49] Hamlet, however, is not merely tapping into a capacity for play developed in an earlier stage of life. The morbidity of regression possesses him, and he must emerge from its spell, accepting his birth or stepping from a grave, announcing his existence and taking it upon himself. Of course, Hamlet's anguish bespeaks more than just *psycho*pathology when he queries, "What should such fellows as I do crawling between earth and heaven?" and subsequently declares, "I say we shall have no more marriage." There is something rotten in the state of Denmark, not just in Hamlet's state of mind.

On Mount Rushmore Roger O. Thornhill rescues Eve Kendall from the ledge of the cliff where she dangles with no secure footing. He lifts her (magically, cornily, like in the movies!) into an upper berth on the Twentieth Century Limited in *North by Northwest*'s clever sentimental ending. As Cavell notes, this gesture repeats Grant's hand-in-hand hoisting of Katharine Hepburn onto a scaffold in *Bringing up Baby*. In that remarriage comedy the couple's capacity for play is fully in evidence, though it may only be suggested in other such films, like *The Philadelphia Story,* where the couple "grew up together" and thus share a childhood past. The backdrop of Independence Hall, over which the opening credits roll in *The Philadelphia Story,* signals the "national importance" that the pursuit of happiness in marriage can entail, as does the setting of Mount Rushmore in *North by Northwest*. Tracy Lord must awaken from death to be fit for remarriage, as she announces, in a paraphrase of Browning, by describing herself as "Not wounded, sire, but dead."[50] Thornhill returns from the dead or, at least, a near fatal assault, to make a claim upon Eve Kendall, who dispatched him to the encounter with the crop duster. The monumentality of Mount Rushmore is a way for Hitchcock to emulate the monumentality of *Hamlet,* as is the face of Cary Grant, which dissolves into those on Mount Rushmore in the montage of the presidential faces over Grant's face on the runway in Chicago before his departure for Rapid City, South Dakota, on Northwest Airlines. This is the face of the same actor who, in *The Philadelphia Story,* mugged for the photographer from *Spy* magazine by miming a scene from Appomattox. "Grant and Lee," Dexter Haven declares when he shakes George Kittredge's hand after Tracy introduces them to the press as Damon and Pythias. This same face appears lathered in the mirror of the restroom where Thornhill shaves with a tiny travel razor. "Big face," he remarks to a curious bystander. "Small razor."

He really does look presidential, but whose is this face in the camera? Who is Cary Grant? According to Cary Grant, he is somebody who everybody wants to become, including himself.[51] According to Cavell, he is a person in whom the camera can discover a "true therapist," "magus," and "sage"—a claim to the title of philosopher. Perhaps these observations only reveal that Cavell is like everybody else, Archie Leach included, even though *he* did become Cary Grant. Cavell also wants to become Cary Grant and probably, like Coleridge, Cavell also believes he has a smack of Hamlet himself. Is this a bad thing? When faced with the charge of pretension for the connections he makes between film and philosophy, Cavell admits that, "as is typical of a certain kind of American, I find what I do to be pertinent to any and all of my fellow citizens, and I secretly believe that if they saw it as I do, they would all immediately devote themselves to doing it too."[52] That secret is now out, but in trying to make the philosophy he does available through Shakespeare and Hollywood movies Cavell risks the charge of impertinence. In writing about *The Philadelphia Story* and *North by Northwest* as texts that rival Shakespeare and sound depths more profound than what Hamlet calls "your philosophy," Cavell recounts his own American dream. But who is to say he is not simply dreaming?

An Epistemology of Moods

Cavell characterizes Emerson as an epistemologist of moods, and he serves as a model for Cavell's refusal to split the difference between subject and object. In a kindred characterization of Cavell, Arnold Davidson calls him a "diagnostician of the spirit in which things are said" and thereby stresses the connection between speakers and their speech just as Cavell stresses the weddedness of observers to the observations they make, the objects they claim to see.[53] "The secret of the illusoriness [of life]," Emerson avers in "Experience," "is in the necessity of a succession of moods or objects. Gladly we would anchor, but the anchorage is quicksand. This onward trick of nature is too strong for us. *Pero si muove.*"[54] Cavell glosses these sentiments in the following manner:

> The succession of moods is not tractable by the distinction between subjectivity and objectivity Kant proposes for experience. *This* onward trick of nature is too much for us; the given bases of the self are quicksand. The fact that we are taken over by this succession, this onwardness, means that you can think of it as at once a succession of moods (inner matters) and a succession of objects (outer matters). This very evanescence of the world proves its existence

129

to me; it is what vanishes from me. I guess this is not realism exactly; but it is not solipsism either.[55]

Such "proofs" of the world's existence do not require argument in the conventional sense. Moreover, they could as well be demonstrations of one's own existence, inhabiting, as we do, those border towns where subject and object meet and melt into one another. By accepting full responsibility for our own discourse, we claim our existence. When Hamlet declares that he has "that within which passes show," he mystifies what he has not yet begun to claim as his own; but then, the play is only just beginning. Like the "O" in Roger O. Thornhill, these melancholy words could stand for nothing; we'll have to wait and see. Claudius gives Hamlet an argument in return:

> But to persever
> In obstinate condolement is a course
> Of impious stubbornness, 'tis unmanly grief,
> It shows a will most incorrect to heaven,
> A heart unfortified, a mind impatient,
> An understanding simple and unschool'd.[56]

Claudius aggressively wields the moral psychology of Christian examination of conscience. He pronounces a verdict that is judgmental in the extreme, but it coincides in good part with the analysis of Hamlet's inner state as an impasse in the process of grieving. Hamlet has yet to complete the work of mourning, but we will witness his efforts to advance *and* to avoid such labors, especially on that boundary between the world (ours and his) and the self (ours and his) occupied by the soliloquy in Elizabethan dramaturgy. As Cavell observes, Hamlet reaches a point where he can, and does, announce his existence, an inner state that can turn its face outward. Hamlet calls it "readiness" and "perfect conscience" soon after he makes that announcement.

Giving word to the world as it vanishes in a succession of moods and objects does not exactly suggest the Shakespearean soliloquy, which tries to come to a temporary halt in the midst of such onward proceedings, to call time out for reflection. Rather, it more precisely suggests stream-of-consciousness, with its ability to render inner and outer matters at once, a way of writing that gives a new lease on life to realism in narrative.[57] Among innumerable options, it can be a tale told by an idiot, such as Benjy in *The Sound and the Fury,* or the passionate affirmation of a modern-day Penelope, such as Molly Bloom in *Ulysses.* In Saul Bellow's *Herzog,* the epistolary mania of Moses Herzog sounds a bit like what Cavell calls his "love letters of nightmare" to his fellow Americans in describing some of the unruly passages in "The Avoidance of Love: A Reading of *King Lear*" some two decades after its composition.

> *Dear General Eisenhower. In private life perhaps you have the leisure and inclination to reflect on matters for which, as chief executive, you obviously had no time. The pressure of the Cold War . . . The old proposition of Pascal (1623–1662) that man is a reed, but a thinking reed, might be taken with a different emphasis by the modern citizen of a democracy. He thinks, but he feels like a reed bending before centrally generated winds.* Ike would certainly pay no attention to this. Herzog tried another approach. *Tolstoi (1828–1910) said . . . On the other hand GWF Hegel (1770–1831) understood . . .* But that's all wrong! thought Herzog, not without humor in his despair. I'm bugging all these people—Nehru, Churchill, and now Ike, whom I apparently want to give a Great Books course. Nevertheless, there was much earnest feeling in this, too.[58]

Much "earnest feeling" and energy of a more wholesome sort animate Cavell's best writing. In an expository form of stream-of-consciousness, they sometimes give it the power more realistically to render processes of thought and association than arguments and evidence alone can manage. Cavell's essay on *North by Northwest* partakes of such writing's inwardness while fully accepting responsibility for its own discourse. That discourse is founded upon responsiveness to the texts under review and their capacity both to read their reader and expose shortcomings in his response and to inspire insights and understanding that can only be conveyed in a less restrained, more expressive prose than academic convention usually allows. At the very outset, Cavell acknowledges the weakness of his position. Driven as he is by a desire to respond philosophically to film, to respond to the philosophy in film, he simply gets lost. This condition seems more threatening than a limitation because of the boundlessness in which it sets Cavell adrift. However, after an open avowal of this lostness, he begins to find words and move ahead. Cavell thus discovers what elsewhere he describes as the philosophical power of a weak position, which inspires in turn compelling literary expression.[59]

Roger O. Thornhill, whose middle initial stands for nothing, becomes, like other roles for such a star as Cary Grant, a mere cipher whose identity Grant absorbs. It's a nice face, a big face, as Eve and Thornhill, respectively, put it. On screen it can even be bigger than those of the presidents on Mount Rushmore, but it can also become ours when we become possessed of the thought of this movie. It can stand for something, and Cavell makes a special effort to disclose this representative power in his reading of this film's final moments. In doing so, he not only incorporates lines from *Hamlet,* as I have indicated; he also silently invokes Matthew Arnold's "Dover Beach":

> Thornhill proposes marriage as he and the woman hang from a precipice; a gallant concept, as if marriage were a presence of mind, requiring no assurance of a future. Close-ups of the pair on the surface of the monument faces show them as if on an alien planet. There is no longer nature on the earth; earth is no longer an artifact by analogy, intimating God; it is literally and totally artifact, petrified under the hands of mankind. To place your film in competition with such an achievement is to place it in competition with film's own peculiar power of preserving the world by petrifying it, or anyway fixing it in celluloid. The couple in remarriage comedies are isolated at the end, expected to legitimize marriage without the world, which has no help for pain. The surface of Hitchcock's Mount Rushmore strikes me as a place of absolute spiritual isolation, civilization engulfing even empty space . . . To fall from Mount Rushmore, as I am imagining it, would be to fall off the earth, down the vast edges drear of the world.[60]

The unmarked presence of Arnold's poem here in two phrases, "no help for pain" and "the vast edges drear of the world," indicates the seriousness of both Cavell's sentiments and his ambitions for his prose. Perhaps this tone of seriousness is no longer audible or even supportable, given the spirit of our times. If we remember too readily Anthony Hecht's satirical appropriation of Arnold in "The Dover Bitch: A Criticism of Life," for example, or President Lyndon Johnson's selective misappropriation of some lines from Arnold's last stanza, which he attributed to Robert Lowell in a clumsy effort to claim the high ground in a public controversy during the Vietnam War, we may simply have become too hardened in our cynicism to be reached by such writing as Cavell's. Echoing Arnold on such an occasion—or taking instruction and delight in recognizing the reference to his poem—may merely seem snobbery of "the worst kind," as Tracy Lord puts it, intellectual snobbery. Cavell threads his prose about Hollywood movies like a sampler with what Arnold notoriously labeled "the best that is known and thought in the world." While Cavell would include those films under that rubric, to some he seems to reveal in his manner of writing the sort of elitism that opening the canon to include works of popular culture often aims to eliminate. But I certainly don't hear this prose that way, and I am unpersuaded by those who readily do, especially if they simply leave their reaction at that. Perhaps we have simply forgotten that we have a culture worthy of our highest aspirations and requiring our liveliest performances if we wish to inherit it. What could have caused such "forgetfulness"? That is a hard question in need of a probing response, but an atmosphere of censorious moralism in the guise of egalitarian openness has too often hobbled ambitions that arise from such convictions about the cultural legacy we may wish to make our own.

Presence of mind and petrifications of art are deeper mysteries than such dogmatic skepticism can fathom, however familiar and understandable this sort of attitude has become. The tears of Eve Kendall at the auction in Chicago betoken an anguish neither Vandamm nor Thornhill notices, and they also escape what Leonard calls his woman's intuition, which Vandamm recognizes as jealousy. The statue cries, but we must "awake our faith," as Paulina exhorts the onlookers at Hermione's statue in *The Winter's Tale,* to believe in those tears, which we too might otherwise not even notice. They will elude us, as will the feelings that they evince, and we will remain metaphysically asleep to this compelling evocation of human subjectivity.

In its blatant dramatization of the transition from presence of mind to the petrifications of art, the end of *The Philadelphia Story* flaunts its apprehension of this challenge posed by film art and flies in the face of our apprehensiveness about it. We witness the makeshift remarriage of Dexter and Tracy as a motion picture of people who move about and are then suddenly frozen in a still photograph. Except for the closing credits, the film is over after that still turns into a page that turns to another still, as in a wedding album or studio production book. This final gesture from movement to frozen stillness reminds us with a jolt that we have "only" been watching a movie.

About this moment, as we have seen, Cavell asks, "[I]s there not some lingering suspicion that the picture of the trio was already a kind of wedding photo?—that somehow, as Edmund madly says in the final moments of *King Lear,* "I was contracted to them both./Now all three marry in an instant."[61] In response, we might plainly ask, "Isn't this citation of Shakespeare in this context quite off the wall, out of the blue, merely gratuitous?" Edmund is dying amid the carnage his treachery has greatly helped to cause. The Philadelphians are scrambling happily to accommodate eleventh-hour changes on a festive occasion whose sacramental status is questionable not only because of Luther, Henry VIII, and all that, but also because the officiant, old Parson Parsons, like "most of the others" in attendance, couldn't recognize the supposed groom anyway. What happens in *Lear* is death-ridden. "Yet Edmund was beloved," and he makes a vain last-minute effort to do some good before he dies. What happens in *The Philadelphia Story* is a return to life after Tracy has announced about herself in the wee hours of the night before the wedding, "Not wounded, sire—but dead."

In the passage where he compares Desdemona and Othello to movie roles to distinguish between characters and types, Cavell celebrates the film under discussion, Vigo's *L'Atalante,* as "the best film ever made about the idea of marriage." He then proceeds to claim that, from the resonance of Vigo's camera, "we learn more than we knew of wedding processions, how they can feel like funeral processions, presumably because they can communicate the dying of the bride to her past." Also, you will recall, this passage concludes with a reformulation of film's capacity to explore human character. Despite its preoccupation with types, "there is a sense of character explored. It is our own."[62]

Recalling this passage from "More of the World Viewed," written only a few years before he composed his essay on *The Philadelphia Story,* "The Importance of Importance," can help us recover the kind of thinking that sometimes informs Cavell's use of Shakespeare in his essays on film. It differs significantly from the method of Shakespeare criticism then emerging and so prevalent in the decades thereafter. Rather than thick description of a particular event, it senses the kinship of analogy on the mythic grounds of basic human experiences such as life, death, and rebirth in the present instance, solemnized by ceremonies such as weddings and funerals. Stephen Greenblatt, who characterized the new approach to Shakespeare study as New Historicism and has proven its foremost practitioner, describes the literary historian's task as conjuring the dead.[63] He offers that description in addressing the question, "What is the history of literature?" His emphasis falls on the pastness of the past and the challenges of recovering it in all its strangeness and difference from the present. The scholar Greenblatt aptly singles out at this turn in his reflections is Horatio, whom his companions thus identify when they urge him to apply his expertise in accosting the ghost of Hamlet's father on the battlements of Elsinore: "Thou art a scholar, speak to it, Horatio."

Long ago Cavell glossed, and indeed welcomed, the ambiguity some have detected in this scholar's alleged possession of philosophy as it is expressed by Hamlet's declaration, "There are more things in heaven and earth, Horatio,/Than are dreamt of in your philosophy."[64] In doing so he perhaps revealed a proclivity for "amateur forays," not only into Shakespeare, but into philosophy as well. The ordinariness of ordinary language philosophy amounts to a stand against the spellbinding arcana that the professional, the esoteric, and the merely private sometimes claim on their own behalf. As Cavell has continued to cultivate his affinity for Emerson's philosophy, his declared ambition has been to awaken the living, not to conjure the dead, and to pursue lines of thought and topics of reflection theoretically open to all and likely to occur to many when the mood is upon them. Presence of mind such as Cavell brings to bear upon the texts and movies he reads involves a different sense of the past from that which Greenblatt articulates. Cavell invokes this sentence from Emerson's "History" to help define it: "When a thought of Plato becomes a thought to me, . . . time is no more."[65] His attraction to the principle of perfection has required him to defend it against charges of elitism, but his willingness to go against the current has enabled him to offer welcome alternatives to intellectual fashions of the moment.[66] He has followed out lines of thought long evident in his work but regularly available for surprising renewals during a period occasionally infatuated with supposedly revolutionary ideas that quickly become stale commonplaces.

5

READING CAVELL READING
THE WINTER'S TALE

*I*n an especially telling way, Stanley Cavell's essay on *The Winter's Tale* demonstrates the unusual power and influence of his work in Shakespeare studies. Despite its virtual lack of explicit reference to current or even traditional writings on this particular play, Cavell's essay has received serious consideration among consequential recent interpreters of *The Winter's Tale*. Stephen Orgel's introduction to the Oxford edition of this play indicates the unique magnetism of Cavell's thought. In this setting, where a review of the play's reception history is very much the order of the day, Cavell's comments about Mamillius's death seem to have basically opened up, or established, a new avenue of inquiry. Orgel quotes Cavell at length and in a kind of splendid isolation during a focused consideration of this topic.[1]

The pathos of this loss derives mainly from its ultimately forgotten impact, as though Mamillius's death were finally negligible, if not irrelevant, to the larger ambitions of restoration and continuity that are fulfilled by the play's apparently happy ending. But this neglect of Mamillius's fate also concerns other key themes of the play and of Cavell's reading of Shakespeare which only compound its importance. Idolatry, for example, and its equally extreme counterpart, iconoclasm, become expressions of dogmatic skepticism and the destructive force it releases in its flight from uncertainty. When, in an effort to satisfy his doubts about his son's paternity, Leontes claims that Mamillius's nose is "a copy out of [his]," this phrase suggests a nexus of interests that links questions of skepticism with ideas of imitation as well as idolatry and its violent alternative, iconoclasm.

Besides Cavell, no other contemporary interpreter of the play inspires such attention from Stephen Orgel, its most thorough and well-informed modern editor; and others follow his lead. David Lee Miller features Cavell's arguments prominently in his chapter on *Hamlet* and *The Winter's Tale,* "Witnessing as Theater in Shakespeare," in *Dreams of the Burning Child: Sacrificial Sons and the Father's Witness.* Though Miller's provocative book ranges widely, he is primarily a Renaissance scholar, and the Shakespeare chapter thus bespeaks his professional expertise most revealingly. It is fully informed by a knowledge of current readings of the play by such scholars as Stephen Orgel, Janet Adelman, and Valerie Traub; but its point of departure among readings of *The Winter's Tale* clearly derives from Cavell's essay on that play and, specifically, from its dismay with the apparent negligibility of Mamillius's death.[2]

We can see similar indications of Cavell's influence in other important writings on *The Winter's Tale* during the last decade. In Maurice Hunt's ample account of "The Critical Legacy" in *The Winter's Tale: Critical Essays,* Cavell's essay is given a full-page summary that installs it securely among memorable recent interventions.[3] Ironically, in Hunt's introductory essay, Cavell's work receives as much attention as that of Northrop Frye, whose work on comedy and romance profoundly influenced a generation of Shakespeareans and inspired Cavell himself so decisively that he was aptly enlisted to write a foreword to the 1995 reissue of Frye's *A Natural Perspective: The Development of Shakespearean Comedy and Romance.*[4] Likewise, in T. G. Bishop's long chapter on *The Winter's Tale* in *Shakespeare and the Theatre of Wonder,* which seeks "to put together the two approaches to the play that seem to [him] to have generated the most powerful insights," Cavell is the prime representative of "that [approach] which investigates the operation of networks of knowledge and sexual fantasy, for which the central figure is Leontes."[5] Within these networks questions of idolatry and imitation, skepticism and iconoclasm acquire compelling force via Cavell's manner of raising them and making their insistent pressure keenly felt.

It is especially noteworthy that "Recounting Gains, Showing Losses: Reading *The Winter's Tale*" has been so influential upon professional practitioners of Shakespeare criticism because, uniquely among Cavell's essays on Shakespeare, it makes virtually no mention of any such critics. The only (and remotely) possible exception to this claim is an essay by George Santayana, "The Absence of Religion in Shakespeare," to which Cavell briefly alludes by recapping its main argument in half a sentence.[6] But actually this reference better reveals the general humanistic contexts to which Cavell appeals in situating his reflections on Shakespeare's romance; and the other writers whom he invokes with varying degrees of specificity—Freud, Wordsworth, Wittgenstein, Nietzsche, Empson, Austin, Hume, Descartes, Thoreau, and Emerson—further this impression. Moreover, this list of writers also suggests the original context in which Cavell's essay appeared because it mixes thinkers and writers especially associated with skepticism or romanticism or both. Cavell's reading of *The Winter's Tale* was originally presented as the fourth and final Beckman lecture; and, in 1988, the year after *Disowning Knowledge in Six Plays of Shakespeare* appeared, Cavell published these lectures in his book *In Quest of the Ordinary: Lines of Skepticism and Romanticism*. The subtitle precisely indicates Cavell's conscious attention to lines of thought that began irresistibly to emerge in the fourth section of *The Claim of Reason,* which Cavell had brought to a conclusion with the essay that later appeared in *Disowning Knowledge* as "Othello and the Stake of the Other." If we think of the four Beckman lectures as a sort of book-within-a-book, we can see a very clear pattern in the way Cavell appeals to Shakespeare to bring his more sustained exercises in philosophical and literary reflection to a satisfactory conclusion. *Must We Mean What We Say?* concludes with Cavell's famous essay, "The Avoidance of Love: A Reading of *King Lear*," just as *The Claim of Reason* concludes with Cavell's reading of *Othello*.[7]

If Cavell has failed to attend carefully to recent work on *The Winter's Tale,* Shakespeareans have repaid this neglect by ignoring his work on film. Since his writings on the Hollywood comedy of remarriage derive major premises and points of comparison from Shakespearean drama and its critics (especially Northrop Frye), such oversight warrants correction. More importantly, however, the current boom in studies of Shakespeare and film, though it has generally focused upon issues relating to adaptation, has frequently produced work whose methods could find a precedent in Cavell's writing. Recently, for example, *Shakespeare Quarterly* has published two essays on *Hamlet* whose thematic approaches and whose concern with matters of popular culture, if they are anticipated by any previous work of this kind, can certainly find a precursor in Cavell's 1981 essay on *North by Northwest*.[8] Cavell's recent lecture, "Two Tales of Winter: Shakespeare and Rohmer," continues this mode of criticism by examining the Shakespearean romance that served as a primary basis for Cavell's anatomization of the Hollywood genre of remarriage comedy, *The Winter's Tale,* in tandem with Eric Rohmer's *Conte d'hiver*.[9]

This chapter aims to read Cavell's readings of Shakespeare, especially of *The Winter's Tale* and of such other relevant works as Preston Sturges's

The Lady Eve and Eric Rohmer's *Conte d'hiver*. As an exercise in reading readings, this chapter is, at least, doubly transitive. First, it seeks to illuminate pertinent thoughts of Stanley Cavell, one of America's foremost philosophers and the only such thinker who has dedicated sustained attention to Shakespeare, both in their relation to Shakespeare's plays and in their own right as they bear upon those plays. Second, it also seeks to illuminate the objects of his attention, especially when they are Shakespeare's plays and films that bear upon Shakespeare and Cavell's thinking about Shakespeare's works.

Shakespeare, Sturges, and Rohmer

"Recounting Gains, Showing Losses" appears as the final essay in the first edition of *Disowning Knowledge* (1987), but the introduction to that collection better serves to demonstrate the degree to which romanticism and skepticism had combined to influence Cavell's thinking about Shakespeare by the late eighties. At the end of the third Beckman lecture, Cavell's reading of Wordsworth's "Ode: Intimations of Immortality" clearly occasions the compelling thoughts about Mamillius that so impressed Orgel and D. L. Miller at the opening of the fourth of those lectures.[10] These are thoughts about the death of a youth and about the death of youth and about the possibility of adult recovery after such losses. After Cavell hauntingly notes that, at the end of *The Winter's Tale,* a dead seven-year-old boy "remains unaccounted for," such thoughts give rise to the painfully importunate inquisition that Cavell unleashes in his essay's second paragraph.

> Or is this prejudicial? Shall we say that the absent boy is meant to cast the shadow of finitude or doubt over the general air of reunion at the end of the play, to emblematize that no human reconciliation is uncompromised, not even one constructible by the powers of Shakespeare? Or shall we say that in acquiring a son-in-law the loss of the son is made up for? Would that be Hermione's—the son's mother's—view of the matter? Or shall we take the boy's death more simply symbolically, as standing for the inevitable loss of childhood? Then does Perdita's being found mean that there is a way that childhood *can,* after all, be recovered? But the sixteen years that Perdita was, as it were, lost are not recovered. Time may present itself as a good-humored old man, but what he speaks about in his appearance as Chorus in this play is his lapse, his being spent,

as if behind our backs. Then is the moral that we all require forgiveness and that forgiveness is always a miracle, taking time but beyond time? Any of these things can be said, but how can we establish or deliver the weight or gravity of any such answer?[11]

But in the introduction to *Disowning Knowledge,* Cavell stands back to assess his Shakespeare writings more generally and to describe his critical practice. That description reveals the inspiration of Emerson and Wittgenstein in much of Cavell's thinking: "My aim in reading," Cavell declares, "is to follow out in each case the complete tuition for a given intuition (tuition comes to an end somewhere)."[12] To formulate a sort of maxim for his Shakespeare criticism, Cavell here transcribes Emerson's endorsement of intuition in "Self-Reliance," to which he appends a version of Wittgenstein's assertion, in *Philosophical Investigations,* about the terminability of explanations. Emerson writes, "We denote this primary wisdom as Intuition, whilst all later teachings are tuitions," and Wittgenstein writes, "Explanations come to an end somewhere."[13]

Cavell merges these two claims in his statement of critical purpose, absorbing the very words of his estimable precursors into his self-characterization as a reader of Shakespeare. In the process of this appropriation of others' words and ideas, Cavell forces upon us a question central both to Shakespeare's play and to Cavell's manner of thought and writing. It is the question of idolatry. Shakespeare's play raises it with regard to the lawfulness of Giulio Romano's art and Paulina's "business" with it. Similarly, Cavell's words make us ask: To what degree is the homage of imitation mere parroting of another's words rather than their transfiguration into fresh claims upon our attention? Are such echoes of Emerson and Wittgenstein what Jesus calls "vain repetitions," or are they a way of acquiring a voice of one's own?[14]

Cavell first broaches his interest in *The Winter's Tale* as a transitional thought on the way to more sustained reflection upon *Othello.* In the beginning of "Othello and the Stake of the Other," he notes the kinship between Hermione's fate and that of Desdemona: in one sense or another, both are turned to stone. Skepticism, manifested as jealousy in both their cases, demonstrates a capacity literally to astonish its victims, Leontes and Othello; and their vindictive recoil against such petrifying doubt leads them to visit their fate upon significant others, Hermione and Desdemona. In their efforts to exorcise their most intimate fears and avoid a necessary reckoning with themselves, both Leontes and Othello harden their suspicions against their wives. Hermione's ultimate reappearance as a statue tellingly signals Leontes' mental disposition, as do

Othello's words in admiration of the sleeping Desdemona's body, "that whiter skin of hers than snow,/And smooth as monumental alabaster." Thus, in discussing "the body's fate under skepticism," Cavell is very much revealing the mind's panicked flight from its habitation in the body and the world.

The very dualism of such formulations points to their further consequences. In arriving at evidence for his own existence via the mind alone, the Cartesian skeptic is stuck with the insurmountable challenge of knowing others for sure only through the warranty of their minds. However, he is barred access there because of the essential otherness of another's mind. God can serve as a guarantor of the external world because He would not play such a malicious trick upon the Cartesian skeptic as to deceive him completely about the world's existence. But this doubter, like his counterparts in Shakespeare, Leontes and Othello, can at best know other persons' minds only by analogy but never with clarity and distinctness and, thus, never with unqualified certainty. Moreover, when Descartes seeks to ascertain whether or not he is alone in the universe, it is to God Whom he turns, not to another finite human being like himself. Christian convictions about the double nature of Christ as the God-man further influence the lines of thought available to such a skeptic. As Cavell notes, this sort of thinker does not even have access to the argument from analogy; for, "[a]fter all, the body has essentially nothing to do with the soul!"[15] Cavell, therefore, wishes "to understand how the other bears the weight of God" as a consequence of the Cartesian turn toward God to solve the problem of the skeptical individual's aloneness in the universe.[16] Similarly, in tragic cases like Othello's, because he is unable to bear his skepticism about other minds, Othello puts Desdemona in the place of God, where she inevitably fails him. Unable to bear the loss of the world that such another's alleged failure entails, the Cartesian skeptic in Shakespearean tragedy takes revenge by destroying this apotheosis, and the world too, as it is constituted for him by such another's place or, really, misplacement, in it. In these patterns of thought and feeling we can discern an oscillation between the extremes of idolatry and iconoclasm in which no middle ground seems tenable to the tragic agonist who suffers such an ordeal of skepticism.

So far as he is a skeptic, Leontes undergoes such an ordeal ostensibly because of his disappointment in the agreements over criteria that allow us to know anything and especially in their inability to provide certain knowledge in the matter of paternity. The ways that we know things, if they can be known at all, entail (often implicitly) certain standards or premises. As classical skepticism demonstrates, we can always ask what are the criteria of our criteria and be led into a potentially infinite regress. However, we usually forbear from such relentless questioning, and explanations do come to an end somewhere. Leontes, however, yields to this interrogative mood; and he uses it as a cover for his own misgivings about fatherhood and the ambiguities of his intimate involvement with various others.[17] As doubt overtakes him, it rapidly spreads from concerns about the unborn child in Hermione's womb to concerns about Mamillius, and it undermines Leontes' confidence in this regard as well.

> Leo.   How now you wanton calf,
>   Art thou my calf?
> Mam. Yes, if you will, my lord.
> Leo. Thou wants a rough pash, and the shoots that I have
>   To be full like me; yet they say we are
>   Almost as like as eggs—women say so,
>   That will say almost anything. (1.2.126–30)

Leontes' acceptance of the idea that he is a cuckold contains none of the mitigating humor characteristic of men's ironic acquiescence to such a fate that pervades the circle of his counterparts in *Much Ado About Nothing,* Benedick and Claudio. Benedick's mock consent to the wearing of horns helps to appease anxieties that arise from the ultimate indeterminacy of fatherhood before the science of DNA could decisively resolve such questions. He demonstrates a willingness to live his skepticism by pretending to accept the worst possible of cases in regard to Beatrice's fidelity. Leontes, however, presses for further proof via proverbial wisdom and argument from analogy by citing a commonplace term of comparison, the likeness among eggs that makes them virtually indistinguishable one from another. In Shakespeare's literary culture, Erasmus and Montaigne both give word to this traditional comparison, and interestingly enough, both manage a reckoning with skepticism before it can unleash its ultimately destructive powers.[18] But Leontes succumbs to the force of doubt, Cavell argues, not only by making a choice to reject the limited kinds of knowledge and assurance available in his situation. He also seeks proof of something for which there is no unshakably conclusive evidence: that Mamillius *is* his son.

This avoidance of the limits of knowledge is willful, and it is utterly Cartesian in the numerical precision upon which it fixes in its demand for self-justification. What Cavell calls being "engulfed by economic terms" in reading *The Winter's Tale* bears a kinship to Descartes's mathematical orientation and his esteem for the precision with which such calculations can be performed.[19] But Leontes' demand for absolute certainty is unappeasable *not* because it arises in a world that lacks the exact methods of DNA testing. Once such methods become necessary, they can resolve the legal issue of child support, but they cannot credibly inspire remarriage. In Shakespeare's play the Delphic oracle functions as such an ultimate authority, and Leontes notably rejects its truth until Mamillius dies. Only then can Leontes confess, "I have too much believed mine own suspicion" (3.2.148). About this confession Cavell rightly asks this apposite question: How much would be enough? This rhetorical question aptly provokes a felt understanding of how suspicion consumes belief, as we have witnessed in Leontes' case. Hereafter Leontes exactly plays the protagonist's part in the sad kind of tale that's best for winter, as Mamillius has already glossed Shakespeare's tragicomedy from within its second act. Leontes virtually dwells by the churchyard for the next sixteen years, during which he makes daily visits to the graves of his dead wife and child. His despair evolves into long-suffering resignation, but he abandons all hope for a second chance at marriage. Indeed, he consigns any choice in that matter entirely to Paulina, who clearly thinks that no worthy replacement of Hermione is conceivable.

In Cavell's film criticism *The Winter's Tale* serves as a primary model for what he calls the Hollywood comedy of remarriage. But it better exemplifies a structure characteristic of this genre—in which the central pair get *back* together, or get together *again,* rather than for the first time—than it corresponds to the happy endings that such Hollywood couples achieve in the face of internal obstacles and external incomprehension. The element of resurrection in Shakespeare's play typifies the dying into love's reanimation exemplified by such a definitive instance of this genre as *The Philadelphia Story.* In this film Tracy Lord (Katharine Hepburn) explicitly announces her own death after an early morning swim in the pool where, the day before, her statuesque body was displayed in the company of human figures of marble and bronze and she was both dressed in a garment, and described in terms, befitting the form of a Greek goddess. Hermione's resurrection could serve as a model for this representation of Tracy's spiritual rebirth, but not for her reawakened love for her ex-husband, Dexter (Cary Grant).

At the close of the first paragraph of "Recounting Gains, Showing Losses," Cavell ominously notes that, at the end of *The Winter's Tale,* a dead seven-year-old boy "remains unaccounted for."[20] He thus signals the haunting of this play or, at least, of the remarriage of its principal couple, by a loss no reckoning can finally enable them to overcome. Cavell then performs the previously quoted tour de force of skeptical interrogation in challenging the unaccountability of Mamillius's death that he initially asserts. Cavell dubs this mode of importunate and, ultimately, insatiable questioning the "skeptical recital," and he occasionally exploits its rhetorical possibilities via overwhelming performances of unappeasable doubt.[21] On this occasion, however, though he rattles off eight successive questions in a relentless effort to undermine his own assertion, the claim still stands unshaken. D. L. Miller's recent book about sacrificial sons and the father's witness, *Dreams of the Burning Child,* seems to account for the death of Mamillius by uncovering the legacy of child sacrifice in patriarchal culture, but even he responds explicitly to Cavell's claim by admitting that he "cannot imagine accounting for such a thing."[22]

Among remarriage comedies, Cavell links Preston Sturges's 1941 comedy, *The Lady Eve,* most immediately with *The Winter's Tale.* His reasons are manifold, but the theme of resurrection, which Cavell often connects with what he calls the creation of the woman, provides an inviting premise for comparative analysis of the two works. This latter formulation also indicates Cavell's use of the Genesis myth of Eve's creation as a prototype for the process of coming into being anew that remarriage entails; and Sturges's comedy positively flaunts its relations to the myth of the Fall, which also permeates Shakespeare's play. But film has particular means of dramatizing the sort of death that skepticism can visit upon the objects of its doubt, and these are means specific to its resources as an artistic medium. As still photography, it has the documentary power to fix things in time as relics of the past, whereas the successiveness of motion pictures can catch us up in kinetic passages of their own time, the temporality both of the stories they relate and of the period of their projection on screen.

Ironically, Cavell cites Shakespeare as a maxim for the conclusion of *The Philadelphia Story* when such resources are being pointedly employed. That movie ends with a shift from motion pictures of its principal stars—Cary Grant, Katharine Hepburn, and James Stewart—to still photographs of them in a wedding album (and perhaps in a *Spy* magazine story as well). Cavell glosses this finale with some of Edmund's last words in *King Lear:* "all three/Now marry in an instant" (5.3.227–28). This seems a rather macabre collocation of comic image and tragic sentiment; but, though it may be voicing a provocative thought about marriage and death that Cavell has expressed before, it also uses the difference between stills and motion pictures to good effect.[23]

Here that effect illustrates an aspect of Cavell's claim that "film was as if meant for philosophy," for such a transition makes unexamined viewing, if not the unexamined life, hard to sustain. As we leave the film, however caught up we have become in its action, it pointedly reminds us that we have been watching a movie. But the fixity of still images in *The Lady Eve* serves a function more congruent with the problem of idolatry so central to Shakespeare's play and to the questions of art's relation to the life of the spirit, whose answers art vies with religion to provide. When Charles Pike (Henry Fonda) shows Jean Harrington (Barbara Stanwyck) the picture that identifies her as a con artist who preys on gullible victims, by way of a response she asks him, "Rotten likeness, isn't it?" However undeniably it is a picture of her, it is *not* her, at least not now, she seems to be saying; and he should not mistake it as such.

As Cavell puts this in *The World Viewed,* "The reality in a photograph is present to me while I am not present to it; and a world I know, and see, but to which I am nevertheless not present (through no fault of my subjectivity) is a world past."[24] Whatever truth this still photo reveals about Jean is no longer true; that is, it is not true now. Given the photographic basis of motion pictures, the projections they screen are also past. To experience them as present requires a yielding to the effect of presentness that they can achieve, especially via contrast with still photos in the same picture on screen. "Magic," indeed, is a good word for this effect, and it is notable that, in the "magic world" of Harry Potter, newspaper photos are motion pictures. Cavell uses this word to describe the automatic or mechanical means of production of both photos and movies, and "magic," of course, is what Leontes fears may be unlawful in the lifelikeness of Giulio Romano's statue of Hermione.

As *The Winter's Tale* concludes, it constantly reminds us of its mere fictionality by repeatedly voiced comparisons between the play's plot and the incredible wonders that typify romance as a narrative genre. The discovery of Perdita's true identity as the Sicilian princess who has long been presumed dead elicits exclamations of wonder and disbelief that consign the miracle of her reappearance to the realm of storybook fantasy. It is "like an old tale" (5.2.28, 60). But these distancing effects actually prepare the audience for the ultimate closing of the gap between art and nature. This occurs when Hermione's statue turns out to be *not* a likeness of Hermione, but Hermione herself; or, as we're perhaps supposed to believe, the likeness turns into Hermione herself.

Cavell makes more of an issue of the indirect presentation of Perdita's previously inconceivable return to Sicilia than it perhaps warrants. He is seeking to sharpen the contrast between what can be said, or recounted, and what can only be shown. His essay's title, "Recounting Gains, Showing Losses," highlights this difference, which clearly distinguishes between kinds of representation in the last two scenes of the play. As Paulina puts it, by now almost repeating a refrain, when she affirms Hermione's return to life, "That she is living,/Were it but told you, should be hooted at/Like an old tale" (5.3.115–17). But the story of Perdita's rescue from certain death and her upbringing as a shepherdess, etc., however surprising it may be to the Sicilians, is actually quite familiar to the play's audience. For, unlike the Sicilians, we have already seen key episodes of this story, so what we hear about Perdita truly amounts to a recounting, a twice-told tale that we actually witness the first time around. The play is emphatically soliciting our empathy with the Sicilian lords, for whom this is all wondrous news, and it is getting us in the mood for the ultimate wonder of Hermione's resurrection. That truly is an unspeakable event, which you must see to believe.

The coming to life of the statue of Hermione does raise a perennial question: Has she been alive all along? This strikes me as a basically uninteresting question because, whether we like it or not, the play has led us to believe she is dead, not just "transcendentally lost," as Cavell puts it, but in the ground, dead and buried. However ingenious they may be, explanations of how she has been secretly kept alive thus seem beside the point. What the play wants us to experience is a miracle that coincides with our desire for a happy ending, and it harps on the incredibility of Perdita's reappearance to whet our appetite for such an outcome in the case of Hermione. In her case the play defiantly flirts further with heresy and flaunts the theatre's powerful capacity to influence the human soul. Jacobean Protestants would vehemently bridle at the spectacle of kneeling before a statue, as Perdita does before Hermione's alleged likeness; and Paulina's apparent necromancy would also give such believers compelling cause for anxiety, though, in *The Tempest,* Prospero acknowledges the practice of this forbidden art in a context less fraught with immediate religious implications.

I realize that such an expression as "the human soul" raises all sorts of interesting problems. For example, do human beings have souls and, if they do, are Jacobean souls different from twenty-first-century American souls? Cavell, it seems, believes human beings do have souls because he speaks of the kind of philosophical writing he does as competing with poetry in its aspiration to "[make] things happen to the soul."[25] Moreover, he cites Emerson's claim about literary experience in which historical differences become temporarily irrelevant: "[w]hen a thought of Plato becomes a thought to me,—when a truth that fired the soul of Pindar fires mine, time is no more." Such a claim is not idle romanticism because it does not seek to transcend history. Rather, it seeks to find ways to begin history anew, ways in which we can become part of the story as it proceeds. As Emerson's great inheritor, Friedrich Nietzsche, would argue, "when the past speaks it always speaks as an oracle: only if you are an architect of the future and know the present will you understand it."[26]

Of course, the statue of Hermione is a monument, and it notably records the effects of time that sixteen years would have impressed upon her body. The awestruck credulity that it elicits from those who view it thus risks the charge of idolatry. The lifelikeness of this sculpture tempts them to believe that its creator, "that rare Italian master Giulio Romano," could perform the work of the Creator. The possibility of such "superstition" only increases when Paulina informs the viewers, "It is required/You do awake your faith." Leontes shows himself on the brink of such heresy when he asks in admiration of the statue, "What fine chisel/Could ever yet cut breath?" (5.2.95; 5.3.94–95, 78–79).

Breath, of course, is air, and breathing is the respiratory process. As D. L. Miller finely observes, the line-ending between the verses that contain Leontes' query marks a pause that precisely mimes a cutting of the breath, or a caesura, as such a pause is called when it occurs within the line itself.[27] Thus, in its mimetic power, Shakespeare's art here warrants the sort of tribute already ascribed to the verisimilitude of Giulio Romano's statue of Hermione. But even the "small Latin" that Shakespeare supposedly possessed can instruct us that "breath" is also spirit, or "spiritus" in Latin, and "[cutting] breath" may not only indicate the formal work of a caesura or a line-ending in a verse of poetry. It may also indicate the formative work that poetry in general aspires to perform. It aims, in Cavell's words, "to make things happen to the soul," and so far as Cavell's perfectionist philosophy shares that ambition, it stands in competition with poetry as an effort to achieve similar results by means of a rival pursuit.

At this moment, if we go along with it, Shakespeare's theatre overcomes our skepticism and fulfills our wish for the satisfaction of a happy ending. It awakens our faith by satisfying a longing whose appeasement, the play has gone well out of its way to inform us, warrants our fullest suspicion. Thus, we experience the impulse to believe in good fortune, or what the play repeatedly, from its opening scenes, calls "grace"; and we have that experience full in the face of our skepticism. In this regard, we witness our own inclination to do what the play warns against in its first scene, to "pay too much for what is given freely" (1.1.16–17). More importantly, whether we have learned this lesson seems quite beside the point. The play does not instruct us in this manner, even though much of its dialogue and action clearly pertains to such matters of theology and aesthetics. Rather, it makes something happen to us, from which, of course, we may choose to take immediate flight into sage and serious deliberations about the canons of mimetic realism or the mechanics of collective desire or other matters that will keep at bay an acknowledgment of our longings and the possible transformation of our selves in the process of imaginatively experiencing the fulfillment of those longings. Leontes obviously struggles with the challenges of such a choice, which he has come to wish he can finally make in favor of a happy ending. In the last scene, the optative mood overtakes his preoccupation with limiting conditions when he exclaims,

> O, she's warm!
> If this be magic, let it be an art
> Lawful as eating (5.3.109–11).

Eric Rohmer's *Conte d'hiver* meditates upon Shakespeare's play in many of its dimensions, but these lines provide an inviting point of entry. The movie's English title contains all of the canonical French title for Shakespeare's play in translation except the initial definite article, *Le.* For this reason, its English title uses the indefinite article, and it is called *A Tale of Winter.* Moreover, Rohmer's film contains a stage performance of the last scene of Shakespeare's play, which occasions some clarifying reflections about the film's central problem. *Conte d'hiver* centers upon the relationship between two lovers, Felicie and Charles, and it explores this matter exclusively from the woman's perspective. These two are quite literally estranged, inasmuch as they have inadvertently, but completely, lost contact with one another. During this period of estrangement, and entirely unbeknownst to Charles, Felicie has borne and reared the child of their summer love over five years ago. The film's main concern is Felicie's stubborn conviction that Charles returns her love despite the apparent evidence to the contrary of their long separation.

These lovers are a beautician and a cook. The French would call Felicie *une esthéticienne,* and she shears hair as Perdita's companions shear sheep. She also traffics in an art very close to cosmetics or "painting," which Perdita singles out for emphatic disapproval in *The Winter's Tale* (4.4.99–103). As a cook, Charles practices something very close to "an art as lawful as eating." Indeed, the reunion with Felicie and their daughter provides this cook with the welcome opportunity not only to fill his role as father and lover but also to offer the beautician a new and better job. Together with their daughter, she can come away with him and join him at the restaurant where he will soon be the chef and she may be the cashier or the manager. Meanwhile, he will cook the New Year's dinner for Felicie and her side of what is now becoming his new family.

Charles's sudden reappearance in *Conte d'hiver* reprises Hermione's return to life in *The Winter's Tale* and offers a parallel between the plots of these two works that suggestively revises the sex, if not the gender, of the skeptical part in their kindred stories. It is the woman who undergoes the ordeal of doubt in *Conte d'hiver*. Cavell first raises the question of the gendering of skepticism in relation to *The Winter's Tale* and another film of Eric Rohmer's, *The Marquise von O———*, when he observes that "in that text of Shakespeare's the entire drift of things is that it is the man, and not the woman, who doubts."[28] What the husband doubts is his role in the parentage of their children, but the wife has no similar uncertainty about her role. Her biological connection to her offspring is undeniable because its embodiment makes it self-evident, as does Hermione's pregnancy, which is so prominently featured in the opening of *The Winter's Tale*. However, the man's physical connection to their children is demonstrable only indirectly, if at all, before the relatively recent emergence of the biochemistry of blood types and DNA testing.

Cavell's fascination with Rohmer's film of Heinrich von Kleist's narrative, *Die Marquise von O———*, derives from the unusual circumstances of the title figure's impregnation. Because she is raped while unconscious, she remains unsure of her child's father, but *Conte d'hiver* allows Cavell to return to the Shakespearean context in which this question first emerged, and subsequently evolved, due to Janet Adelman's response to Cavell's skeptical reading.[29] The tenacity with which Felicie clings to her conviction about Charles's reciprocation of her love could qualify her as the sort of skeptic that Cavell (following Kant) calls a fanatic. Among the Shakespearean characters whom he analyzes, Cavell specifically applies this label to Leontes and to Cleopatra. The second of these characters, Cleopatra, manifests skepticism more through her denial of doubt than through doubt itself; and the stubbornness of Felicie's convictions about Charles bears a family resemblance to this kind of skepticism. Ironically,

Rohmer seems to be playing a little Aristotelian joke that would undercut such a characterization of Felicie, for he names the rivals for her affection Loic and Maxence, and he pointedly has their merits discussed as representative of two extremes. In a film full of explicitly philosophical exchanges and reflections upon slips of the tongue, it is hard not to hear in these names, and in the alternatives that they represent, a punning allusion to the golden mean between excess and defect, to "Max" and "Low," if you will.

Loic is the explicitly philosophical voice in the film, and such inclinations occasionally earn him affectionate, but wry, demurrals from Felicie. After her obviously transfiguring experience at *Le conte d'hiver,* Felicie engages in a conversation with Loic in the car on their drive home. This exchange elicits both her firm declaration that she lives in hope regarding her love for Charles and Loic's various friendly attempts to describe her disposition in philosophical terms. At first Pascal's wager seems a good fit, but, as they continue, Loic dubs her a Platonist and attributes to her something he calls "instinctive science."[30] We next cut to Loic's apartment where Felicie hands him a cup of tea and warns him that it's "hot." He is reading to her a passage from the *Phaedo* in which Cebes argues that Socrates, given his theory that we learn by remembering, must believe in something akin to metempsychosis: "Furthermore, Socrates, such is also the case if that theory is true that you are accustomed to mention frequently, that for us learning is no other than recollection. According to this, we must at some previous time have learned what we now recollect. This is possible only if our soul existed somewhere before it took on this human shape. So according to this theory too, the soul is likely to be something immortal (73a)."[31]

Loic's idea of "instinctive science" reminds Cavell of Emerson, who, as we have seen, "denote[s] this primary wisdom Intuition." Loic finds a pretext for such convictions in Plato, and the film itself has already featured a dinner party conversation about Hindu beliefs in the transmigration of souls that foreshadows the passage from Plato that Loic reads out loud. This earlier scene concludes comically with a parting guest wishing Loic and Felicie a "happy karmic New Year," and it is on New Year's Eve that a chance meeting on a bus will bring Felicie and Charles back together again. This confirmation of her intuition provides the film with a happy ending whose power derives in part from the way Rohmer alludes to the ending of *The Winter's Tale.* In their child's bedroom, Felicie has placed a picture of Charles, taken when they were lovers at the beach five years ago. In a playful exchange, Felicie's sister draws attention to it and expresses mild disapproval of the handsome Charles by identifying him as a sort of beefcake. Later, this photograph comes to life, if you will, via the animation that motion pictures add to stills, when Charles appears in the seat on the bus across from the girl and her mother on New Year's Eve. Like the stone-cold immobility of Hermione in Giulio Romano's statue, Charles's frozenness in time past melts into warmth and breath or, at least, projections of them on screen. Such miracles can awaken the capacity for faith in an audience that surely knows, or thinks it knows, the difference between aesthetic experience and the real thing.

But what is the difference? Or, as Emerson puts it, "Where do we find ourselves?" He asks that question at the beginning of "Experience," an essay as haunted by the death of a child as *The Winter's Tale,* despite the ultimately minimal mention of each of these boys in the texts where their deaths are directly registered. Indeed, Cavell thinks he may hear "an allusion to, or interpretation of, *The Winter's Tale*" in this sentence from Emerson's "Experience": "For contact with [reality] we would even pay the costly price of sons and lovers."[32] When Emerson asks, "Where do we find ourselves?" he elaborates his response by reference to what he calls an "old belief" about Genius as the gatekeeper of the underworld. Thence issue freshly oblivious souls, ultimately recyclable from the land of the dead only after they take a draught of Lethe from the hand of Genius. Emerson, I'm sure, inherits this figure from Spenser's *Faerie Queene,* where Genius is the cupbearer who keeps the gate to the Garden of Adonis: "He letteth in, he letteth out to wend,/All that to come into the world desire" (3.6.32.1–2). Spenser, in turn, is drawing upon Platonic doctrines, among which the passage cited above from the *Phaedo* is a commonly accepted source.

Filtered through Emerson, via Cavell, such thoughts bring us to Shakespeare and the movies with a disposition to acknowledge our skepticism in the face of aesthetic experience, like remarriage comedy, that dramatizes the human capacity for change and renewal. Marriage and the domestic serve as a means to represent the everyday, and skepticism threatens to drain the everyday of all resonance and vitality. The routines of language also become vain repetitions. As Emerson puts it, "Man is timid and apologetic; he is no longer upright; he dares not say 'I think,' 'I am,' but quotes some saint or sage."[33] The ironic echo of Descartes slyly belies—or does it enliven?—this melancholy assertion. Or does it show Emerson's slavish reliance upon his philosophical precursors even in an essay called "Self-Reliance," an idea that Emerson himself glosses as an aversion to conformity?[34] More to the point, does remarriage overcome the skepticism that threatens the quotidian routines of domestic relations? Since Cavell chose *The Winter's Tale* as a primary representative of the deep structure of the genre he names remarriage comedy, the questionable satisfactions of its ending leave this query wide open to a persistence in skepticism.

Remarriage Comedy and the Myth of the Fall

The myth of the Fall is a major theme in *The Winter's Tale,* and it also pervades Cavell's writing, not only in essays on Shakespeare and on the movies, but elsewhere as well. For example, in his first Beckman lecture, "The Philosopher in American Life," Cavell makes an indirect allusion to that mythical event in the beginning of human experience. As we have seen, he posits a connection between ordinary language philosophers and American transcendentalists when he subtly evokes the idea of "paradise lost."[35]

In this regard, Cavell summons the Genesis story in "Recounting Gains, Showing Losses" to read it somewhat against the grain. He asserts, conventionally, that this story presents "the origin of marriage . . . as the creation of the woman from the man" and that this is "how they are one flesh." But Cavell then presses this matter further and emphasizes that "this ceremony of union takes the form of a ceremony of separation, thus declaring that the question of two becoming one is just half the problem; the other half is how one becomes two."[36] The puzzle of Hermione's silence toward Leontes at the end of *The Winter's Tale* and the residual mystery of revenge or forgiveness that consequently hovers about the play's conclusion pertain directly to this problem. Cavell sees the forgiveness of Leontes ultimately residing in his own disposition to accept such a kindness, just as he sees his fall into unappeasable jealousy and hyperbolic skepticism as a choice but not a necessity, a possible frame of mind into which Leontes lets himself slip.

Another of Cavell's reflections on the Fall in the Beckman lectures can deepen our understanding of Leontes' fateful choice to insist upon his suspicion of Hermione's infidelity. For Cavell concludes his reading of "The Ancient Mariner" by interpreting the Fall as an allegory. Moreover, he specifies the gist of that allegory as "any spiritual transgression in which the first step is casual, as if, to borrow a phrase, always already taken," and he then aligns that transgression with "the craving to speak, in Wittgenstein's phrase, 'outside language games.' "[37] We can sense this transgression occurring when Leontes will brook no resistance from Camillo, who challenges his charges against Hermione. We also hear it quite explicitly from Hermione herself: she declares that Leontes speaks a language that she does not understand, and he responds with uncanny perversity by offering what sounds like an admission of guilt while persisting in arbitrary willfulness (3.2.78–82). Finally, Leontes' precipitous decline into absolute doubt hits its nadir when he summarily dismisses the Delphic oracle's contradiction of his claims against his wife and completely disregards the authority customarily granted to this representative of divine truth. Leontes' "casual" step occasions two "casualties," to borrow Emerson's deadly serious play upon the root connection of that adjective and that noun.[38] Heard that way, those words disclose their revelatory power about our fatedness to expression despite the endless dodges we attempt. Who does *not* see what Leontes is up to, himself not least?

Of course, all of this willful denial also demonstrates Leontes' absolutism in a political sense, inasmuch as he has the power, as Sicilia's king, to get away with the arbitrary imposition of his own fantasies upon others by simply overriding all contrary opinions. But, in mischievously trying to see things Leontes' way, Howard Felperin's exercise in devil's advocacy, despite its own demonstrable craving for speech "outside of language games," also shows how easy it is for the skeptical impulse to change the rules of such games and lead us into extravagances of perverse speculation.[39] For Felperin is certainly right in observing that we can't know "for sure" that Hermione is faithful to her husband and that the Delphic oracle is an unimpeachable source of truth, but it is a rightness that reveals perhaps more about the critic than it does about the text. Still, nobody's convictions in this regard are completely invulnerable to doubts of a certain stubbornly excessive kind. Rather, such convictions are plot premises about which we obligingly suspend disbelief. Cavell describes this (our) condition via the myth of the Fall in this way: "The explicit temptation of Eden is to knowledge, which above all means: to a denial that, as we stand, we know. There was hence from the beginning no Eden, no place in which names are immune to skepticism."[40]

But in the myth of the Fall, as the Genesis story goes, there was an Eden. Our tenure there was simply precarious, given the freedom that we had to choose knowledge over both obedience and, as it turned out, the evanescent innocence that residence there required. Cavell balks at a Christian interpretation of *The Winter's Tale* and prefers to see Shakespearean drama in general as "competing" with religion—competing, I would add, for the souls of their respective audiences. In this line of thought, Cavell follows Northrop Frye, his most constant guide in the interpretation of Shakespearean comedy and romance, especially as they anticipate deep structures that Cavell discerns in the Hollywood comedy of remarriage; but he follows Frye at a considerable distance and very much on his own terms.

In his recent article, "Knowledge and Belief in *The Winter's Tale*," Walter Lim characterizes Cavell's sense of rivalry between religion and theatre in these terms: "For Cavell, Hermione's resurrection obtains its primary significance not in relation to a theological framework, but to the power of the dramatist to bring words to life through art."[41] This characterization seems fair enough, so long as it does not fail to acknowledge that, in Shakespeare's romance, theology and art are involved in a dynamic exchange. The terms of religious discourse, as well as the theology that they adumbrate, do not simply shed one set of meanings and assume another as they come into play in different institutional contexts. Rather, their meanings are appropriated and inflected according to the sites of their deployment, such as the church or the theatre.

Frye elaborates on these issues by claiming that "the world *The Winter's Tale* leaves us with is neither an object of knowledge nor of belief. It would be an object of belief, of course, or symbolize one, if we could feel that *The Winter's Tale* was an allegory. I have been assuming that it is not: that in Shakespeare the meaning of the play is the play, there being nothing to be abstracted from the total experience of the play. Progress in grasping the meaning is a progress, not in seeing more in the play, but in seeing more of it."[42] Such a view bespeaks a certain formalism that has recently been discredited because it tends to seal the plays off from the world in which they first came into being. Cavell's version of these relations as competition between religion and theatre by no means involves an extensive "historicization" of *The Winter's Tale* in the context of Reformation controversy and anti-theatrical polemics, but it does provide a perspective that can bring institutional rivalry between church and stage dynamically into our consciousness.

Significant references to the Fall appear strategically at the opening of *The Winter's Tale,* and they are embedded in a context where allusions to grace notably abound. Moreover, such allusions are repeatedly associated with Hermione, and they recur at later moments throughout the play. Paulina, of course, bears a name that blatantly evokes a particular line of Christian theology, and her exhortation to the visitors in her gallery to "awake their faith" suits the play's central mystery over which she presides. For, inasmuch as Saint Paul defines faith as the evidence of things unseen, he characterizes an attitude that might not only appease our curiosity about how Hermione was "preserved" so she could come to see her lost daughter, Perdita, again, it might even help us to understand how Leontes recovers his lost soul, or *anima perdita*. Whether Hermione has simply been hiding out or she is miraculously resurrected, we can never know for sure, because the play provides contradictory evidence in this regard; but another aspect of Pauline theology bears directly upon the play's thematics of the Fall and our recovery from its consequences. Doctrinally, Christ's sacrifice and resurrection answer for the Fall of man in Genesis, according to Saint Paul, who is far more than the nominal prototype of Paulina in *The Winter's Tale*. "For since by man came death, by a man came also the resurrection of the dead. For as in Adam all die, even so in Christ shall all be made alive" (1 Cor. 15:21–22, AV). Theologically speaking, this is the "grace" that Hermione so harps upon in the play's second scene (1.2.79, 99, 104). By its action we are redeemed from original sin, "the imposition cleared/Hereditary ours" in the words of Polixenes (1.2.73). Despite the Sicilian propensity to strive for its attainment, grace is an unearned bonus. Ironically, Leontes' chief courtier, Camillo, specifically describes this Sicilian fallibility at the beginning of the play, when he chides Archidamus, his counterpart in the retinue of Polixenes: "You pay a great deal too dear for what is freely given" (1.1.16–17).

Moreover, in this regard we can see the competition between religion and theatre with particular clarity. When Hermione departs for prison, where Leontes has summarily consigned her, she speaks some lines that have occasioned considerable uncertainty and multiple interpretations. In particular the following words of self-description have elicited various explanations: "this action I now go on/Is for my better grace" (2.1.121–22). The word "action" has especially given rise to a range of glosses that Orgel itemizes in some detail, and they ascribe three different sorts of meaning to the word "action"—legal, military, and dramatic. All of these readings fail to satisfy completely because there is no record for the expression "to go on an action" in any of these senses. Finally, Orgel concludes on a more general note: "Action, in any case, has a wide range of meanings; and there is no reason to assume that Hermione's metaphor cannot be, like so many others in the play, a mixed one."[43]

This flexible response leaves the matter invitingly open, and I would like to suggest a more pervasive theme that these words bring into play at this juncture. Why not read the problematic word "action" as directly in tension with one of the keynotes of *The Winter's Tale,* "grace," which is here struck again? Such a reading places this passage directly in the context of the Reformation debate over faith and works, which pervades this play in such basic contrasts as Sicilia and Bohemia, art and nature, etc. As Robert N. Watson has convincingly shown, these antinomies constitute deep structures of the play that complement each other and establish fundamental arguments pursued via multiple perspectives throughout *The Winter's Tale.*[44] The oscillation between idolatry and iconoclasm, noted previously as central to Cavell's thought, readily maps onto these pairs of alternatives to reinforce a sense of their pertinence to the play's basic thematic design.

In the immediate context of Hermione's speech, she counsels herself to cultivate patience: "There's some ill planet reigns./ I must be patient till the heavens look/With an aspect more favorable" (2.1.105–7). In the English Bible, the root meaning of this word, "suffering," appears most remarkably in the argumentative Job's Christian reputation for patience (James 5.11, AV and 1602 Geneva); for, in the Old Testament account of his experience, Job mightily protests his lot in life. He even wishes to acquit himself of any suspicion that he deserves such affliction by taking God to court. He is unwilling to sit still for what strikes him as unjust suffering. Ironically, James's Epistle represents the canonical tradition that transforms the Christian sense of Job's heroism into the virtue of patience, which ultimately comes in part to mean long-suffering acceptance of what can be quite unfair treatment (*pace* Job!). Moreover, James's Epistle itself stands at the center of the Reformation controversy over faith and works. Because it offers an extreme statement of the importance of works—"Even so faith, if it hath not works, is dead, being alone" (2.17)—Luther deemed it, quite simply, unbiblical. "I therefore refuse [James] a place among the writers of the true canon of my Bible," he concluded in his preface to this epistle.

This doctrinal issue echoed in debates throughout Shakespeare's England, so allusions to its dominant concerns would resonate in the theatre even if they did not awaken a purely theological interest. Indeed, the very impurity of touching obliquely upon such controversial religious matters on the public stage may impart to them the sort of transgressive excitement often associated with the forbidden fruit of taboo topics and sensitive issues. Hermione's resolute advice to her attendants thus carries such provocative overtones:

> Do not weep, good fools,
> There is no cause. When you shall know your mistress

> Has deserved prison, then abound in tears
> As I come out; this action that I now go on
> Is for my better grace. Adieu, my lord (2.1.118–22).

The matter of "desert," like that of "patience," stands at the center of debates over faith and works; but the particularly operative words in this passage are "action" and "grace," which constitute a kind of paradox. Grace requires no more (and perhaps even less) than a disposition to receive, an openness to blessings unearned. The action of grace is not something one performs; it is something one suffers or undergoes. Hermione, moreover, is going to prison, where her only labor will be the ordeal of childbirth. Paulina, a notable activist, will champion her cause, and like Saint Paul, question the "[lawfulness]" of an "express commandment" (2.2.8–10); but for her part, Hermione will ultimately assume the immobility of stone. If she is "preserved" in life, she becomes a kind of performance artist with an uncanny ability for motionless posing.

Her posture expresses another sort of grace, artistic and/or natural beauty, which is also basic to that word's Jacobean meanings and more immediately pertinent to customary theatrical usage. Moreover, such grace raises further questions of idolatry and iconoclasm that typified early modern protestant attacks on stage plays and their allegedly maleficent powers. It has a remarkable precedent in *Antony and Cleopatra,* as we shall see in the next chapter. In this context, however, remember that Cavell links Hemione's stunned immobility with the anatomy of human likeness that Shylock's anguish prompts him to elaborate vindictively to his Venetian tormentors and with the monumental appearance of the sleeping Desdemona under the gaze of Othello's murderous jealousy. For Cavell, who is fully conscious of Wittgenstein's claim that the body is the best picture of the human soul, these dramatic moments represent what Cavell calls "the body's fate under skepticism."[45] The petrification of Hermione, her "astonishment" at the hands of Leontes' murderous accusations, bears witness to the soul-killing consequences of his aggressive distrust of his wife. When he tauntingly claims that her actions are his dreams (3.2.8), we can recognize the fully psychotic image of her that he has fashioned and enforced. Because he is the king, he can make it stick; but, as a product of his imagination, it also reveals the psychopathology that went into the creation of this "diseased opinion" (1.2.294). The cure for this malady takes a long time to come, though, given the severity of the offense, it is a miracle that it should come at all. Moreover, there lingers in mind irrepressibly the death of Mamillius, who, even at the end, remains unaccounted for.

157

The power of art provides a cure by imitating nature, but in that process, the line between mimesis and the reality it would imitate becomes impossible to locate decisively once and for all. Before the statue of Hermione moves and descends from its pedestal, the harsh realism of the artist's hand is fully registered in Leontes' surprise at seeing the wrinkles in her face (5.3.27–29). Time has not stood still; it never does, despite our natural yearnings that it do so. As Florizel rhapsodizes to his beloved Perdita:

> What you do
> Still betters what is done. When you speak, sweet,
> I'ld have you do it ever; when you sing,
> I'ld have you buy and sell so; so give alms;
> Pray so; and for the ord'ring of your affairs,
> To sing them too. When you do dance, I wish you
> A wave o' th' sea, that you might ever do
> Nothing but that; move still, still so,
> And own no other function (4.4.135–42).

It's not so much that Florizel is his father's son, but one of Adam's. Florizel is not abnormally frightened at the power of time to cause change, just frightened enough to take flight in impossible fantasies of permanence. And it is love that makes him fearful.

Normally, the aging process makes its mark little by little. But when we see close friends, or family members, whom we have not seen in years, the effects of time upon them bring us up short. We have undergone a similar process of aging in the meantime, but we have noted its gradual occurrence on a more regular basis. It does not suddenly dawn upon us after a wide gap of time with no intermediate stages of development. Unless special circumstances make it apparent, we are not caught off guard by "the unimaginable touch of time," as Wordsworth memorably put it. But Leontes has been out of sync since the play's beginning, caught up in a mad rush to what his warped mind considers justice.[46] The destruction thus wreaked upon his world then requires of him sixteen long years of slow penance. When that penitential reformation of his spirit finally seems at an end, he remains (perhaps inevitably) unaware of the full cost of the time he has wasted. Hermione's wrinkles bring home the impact of the lost years he can never completely redeem. The statue, before it moves, helps Leontes to a fresh appreciation of human finitude, and it brings us along with him if we are open to the kind of work the play aims to perform upon us.

And what is this skepticism that so afflicts Leontes? What insight or understanding does he lack? In his situation, neither the wisdom of Solomon nor the knowledge of Descartes adequately applies. Though Solomon could not have known who was the disputed child's *real* mother in the case presented to him, he could discern who was the *true* mother. She was the one who, regardless of biological relation, demonstrated genuinely maternal feeling in putting the child's well-being ahead of satisfying her desire to have the child as her own. Love prevailed over possession for her, but not for her rival; and we can fairly say that that is all that Solomon learned through his shrewd ploy.

For Descartes, knowledge must meet the criteria of clarity and distinctness to make convincing judgments in specific cases. In Leontes' situation no such criteria obtain even though the mathematical exactness of the measurement of time in Polixenes' opening speech sounds something like a convincing note of precision. "Nine changes of the watery star" (1.2.1) equals nine months, which *clearly* is not only the period of Polixenes' visit to Leontes; it is also the time it would take for a child to come to term. Can this be merely a coincidence? Perhaps not to someone in Leontes' frame of mind, but it could be no more than that to anyone else.

Nowadays, however, we have taken the direction of Descartes much further, so we can be far more sure about a child's paternity than was foreseeable in Shakespeare's time. Decoding the genetic composition of flesh and blood answers such questions decisively, but the frame of mind in which they are asked is, in Emerson's phrase, "not whimsical but fatal." Answering them with certainty, as we now can, will decide who should pay child support. It will not credibly inspire a loving reunion. Skepticism has gone too far.

How far would have been far enough? How do we know when to stop the flow of questions? Once they have begun to pour, can we stop them, or is it always already too late? Must skepticism consume belief?

Or perhaps Solomon and Descartes are the wrong exemplars since neither has such a personal stake in the matter? Perhaps Joseph's "misdeeming thoughts" about Mary are more pertinent to Leontes' situation? Perhaps such a situation requires nothing less than angelic intervention. Or perhaps that's just the way of saying it requires a change of heart, even for the king. As Perdita puts it,

The self-same sun that shines upon his court
Hides not his visage from our cottage, but

Looks on all alike (4.4.442–46).

In today's idiom Leontes is not exactly a "deadbeat dad," but there is a burden of responsibility that he seeks to shirk. He substitutes knowledge for understanding in the suggestive picture of the latter word's meaning offered by taking it part by part, "standing under" a burden, supporting the weight of uncertainty that such a posture requires. Intellectual limitations make patience and trust and acceptance necessary virtues despite the mind's urgent insistence: its demand for certainty or its claim of certainty in dubious circumstances, which are both familiar ways of covering up avoidance and flight from responsibility to others.

Phrases like "action of grace" sound from a human perspective—and what other perspective is there for us? *In*human? Divine?—like descriptions of some sort of spiritual exercise. They specify a fault line between passion and action that often divided opposing sides in Reformation debates over Christian theology, but they also suggest a recurrent theme in Cavell's reflections upon the myth of the Fall, especially as they arise in response to Emerson's essay "Experience." For Cavell, this essay, along with "Self-Reliance," marks a turning point where Emerson begins to realize, very much like Cavell in the final section of *The Claim of Reason,* that he must *live* his skepticism rather than try to solve it. He thus reconceives the challenge of doubt in a manner that accepts the diminishment of reason's role in response to this trial. The synthetic powers of argument and the grasping of ideas become hazards rather than resources in abiding such uncertainties as we inevitably face due to the problem of other minds, the unconscious depths of sexual feelings, and unavoidable human finitude.

In his groping meditations upon the death of his five-year-old son, Waldo—nearly the age of Mamillius, who reminds Leontes so vividly of himself "unbreeched" (1.2.154)—Emerson comes to inhabit consciously this dimension of his experience, and he formulates it unforgettably: "I take this evanescence and lubricity of all objects, which lets them slip through our fingers then when we clutch hardest, to be the most unhandsome part of our condition."[47] The pun in "unhandsome" nicely sharpens this sketch of the mind's ham-handed fumbling as it persists along lines of thought that lead ever further away from the objects it seeks. Leontes, moreover, epitomizes this kind of intellectual fanaticism that cannot let go of its own desperate convictions until they wreak havoc and destruction upon all who oppose them, however mildly or diplomatically they express their resistance. Both Hermione and Camillo are among the prime victims of this self-will run riot at the court of Sicilia, and their encounters with Leontes dramatize both his relentless dogmatism and the vanity of mind that tempts him to self-congratulation as he proceeds along his course of skeptical annihilation.

Undeniably, political power and patriarchal entitlement expedite Leontes' fanaticism in the world of this play and render it virtually irresistible. Shakespeare began his career during the reign of a monarch, Elizabeth I, whose father, Henry VIII, had executed her mother, Anne Boleyn, on trumped up charges of adultery; and he composed *The Winter's Tale* during the reign of a monarch, James I, whose claim to the throne derived from the failure of such arbitrary violence to achieve its desired end. Cavell's tendency to overlook such issues in reading *The Winter's Tale* may reveal both the limits of his approach to this play and his disengagement from current trends in Shakespeare studies. However, one of the features of having an approach, *any* approach, is the acceptance of limits; and, as I have noted, expert readers of *The Winter's Tale* have recently found Cavell's approach especially provocative and engaging.

Moreover, he has not neglected such challenges in embracing Emerson's ideas. For example, in *Conditions Handsome and Unhandsome,* he takes as his point of departure the question whether Emersonian perfectionism is inherently elitist; and his response to that challenge has inspired persuasive defenses, not only of Emerson, but also of Nietzsche, against such charges.[48] But Cavell also addressed a version of this challenge decades ago when he turned his attention to remarriage comedy and rejected the dismissive notion that these Hollywood movies were no more than fairy tales for the Depression. To explain their "settings of unmistakable wealth" and "the people in them who have the leisure to talk about human happiness, hence the time to deprive themselves of it unnecessarily"—this latter phrase being an uncannily exact characterization of Leontes as Cavell views him—he cites the following passage from Emerson's "History": "It is remarkable that involuntarily we always read as superior beings. . . . We honor the rich because they have externally the freedom, power, and grace which we feel proper to man, proper to us. So all that is said of the wise man by Stoic or Oriental or modern essayist, describes his unattained but attainable self."[49]

The Lady Eve

At the start of her commentary on *The Lady Eve,* Marian Keane asserts that the genre of remarriage comedy is about the Fall, and she offers the opening credit sequence of this Preston Sturges movie as evidence of this claim. Its caricature of key elements of the myth of Eden—the apple, the serpent, and the name of Eve—reveals its relation to such themes of the Genesis story as the human awakening to mortality and the mutual dependence of male and female. "Their wish for knowledge is tied up with their wish for love," Keane avers, "and love binds them together."[50]

In claiming a strong affinity between the genre of this film and the Bible's account of humankind's initial experience, Keane is following Stanley Cavell. In *Pursuits of Happiness,* however, Cavell makes this connection most explicitly via Milton's *Doctrine and Discipline of Divorce.* Indeed, Cavell does not directly explore the biblical analogue in any depth until the introduction to *Contesting Tears,* where he reads the Genesis story as a gloss upon relations between the sexes. He finds a warrant for this procedure in *Adam, Eve, and the Serpent* by Elaine Pagels. She explains how biblical commentary, rather than a more direct approach to explicit issues, served early Jews and Christians as a means of discussing such vital topics as marriage, divorce, and gender.[51]

However, Cavell initially finds "a precedent for the structure of remarriage in Shakespearean romance, and centrally in *The Winter's Tale.*"[52] A number of decisive features of that structure link the film genre with Shakespearean romance, but the central example offered by Cavell also shows noteworthy affinities to the myth of the Fall. *The Winter's Tale* is a story about the loss of a world or, from the perspective of Leontes, who suffers that loss, it is a story about losing *the* world. Seasonally, winter brings death into the world. Figuratively, it brings what Milton calls "all our woe." Leontes's story is about a "loss of Eden" and the indelible acquaintance with mortality that such a loss occasions.

In its opening act Shakespeare's play makes explicit reference to the myth of the Fall (1.2.66ff.), and in its final lines, it figuratively alludes to the Genesis account of the occasion when "first/We were disseuered" (5.3.154–55). Early in Act 2, the play also tells us that tales of winter are about mortality. Mamillius begins such a tale and sets its scene beside "a churchyard," a place where graves are customarily located (2.1.30). This boy himself will prove the most promptly mortal of the characters in the drama. Although his name signals that he is the least fallen and most innocent among them, nominally a nursling yet to be weaned from breast-feeding, Mamillius will be the first to die, and his death undeniably haunts the play ever after. No matter what happiness its ending ostensibly achieves, Hermione's silence during her ultimate reunion with her husband, Leontes, measures the distance likely to remain between them, despite his repentance and her virtual resurrection.

Mamillius's death raises a vexing question of theodicy inherent in the myth of the Fall: why do apparently innocent victims suffer indistinguishably along with the guilty? Adam and Eve, the perpetrators of the original offense, were forewarned, so it makes sense that they must face some consequence for their disobedience. But what about us, their descendents? What about the presumption of our guilt, before any misdeed of our own actually demonstrates it? This seems patently unjust; and anxiety or outrage over this injustice in a founding myth of the Judeo-Christian tradition has prompted an unceasing flow of commentary. However, this problem notably occurs at the fault line between different kinds of narration.

As a myth about the human condition, the Genesis story seeks to communicate an essential truth about human nature, something built into our very being before time had a start. In Hebrew, Adam's name itself, which means "man" or "human being," signals allegorically his representative function in this sort of narration. This genre transpires in a time before time when the foundations of our existence first were established. As a story, it unfolds sequentially and thus suggests the logic of cause and effect: one thing leads to another as we move from the beginning to the end in a temporal ordering of events equally as familiar in historical writing as it is in myth or any other narrative genre. As a myth, however, this kind of narration claims absolute priority, a kind of transcendence of time, the very element through which it exists as a story.

Cavell clearly wants to bring that dimension of this story into play when he first hints at its relevance to comedies of remarriage in the introduction to *Pursuits of Happiness*. He characterizes the central couple of such films "as having known one another forever, that is from the beginning, not just in the past but in a period before there was a past, before history." Their discovery of sexuality together coincides with their entry into society, their assumption of publicly recognizable roles as adults. "This is the beginning of history, an unending quarrel," Cavell claims. "The joining of the sexual and the social is called marriage. Something evidently internal to the task of marriage causes trouble in paradise."[53]

Cavell's reading of the Hollywood comedy of remarriage as a genre whose deep structure maps tellingly onto the Genesis story of human beginnings has occasioned thoughtful disagreement. For example, its myth of Eve's secondary creation from Adam's rib has recently given rise to notable dissent from Maria DiBattista in *Fast-Talking Dames*. In her essay on *The Lady Eve,* DiBattista takes issue with Cavell's use of this myth as a heuristic device because it confines him to the limits of the Genesis story's explanatory powers. In a sense it cuts him off from the reality of what actually happens in this film, if we may speak thus para-doxically of a celluloid fiction's "reality." It imposes the false understand-ing of a stereotype upon this movie's eponymous protagonist.

In this case, of course, the film's title itself is responsible for this impo-sition, but Cavell's insistence upon the creation of the woman from the man is the fundamental issue in DiBattista's objection to his reading of *The Lady Eve.* Moreover, she also counters Cavell's similar claim about the father's role in remarriage comedy. In this Hollywood genre Cavell sees this role as significantly different from his function in Shakespearean comedies such as *A Midsummer Night's Dream* and *The Merchant of Venice,* where the father is a blocking figure whose will must be defied and overcome to produce a happy ending. Fathers in remarriage comedy are allies and friends of their daughters' desires, which they facilitate rather than obstruct. They participate significantly in the creation of women and thus make that process (*pace* DiBattista) very much "the business of men," as Cavell describes it to her dismay.[54]

Obviously, both of these arguments—one derived from Genesis and the other from Shakespeare (pointedly revised)—assert the primacy of male influence upon female identity; and DiBattista, like Naomi Sche-man before her, balks at this notion.[55] Taking her cue from Emerson, DiBattista ultimately claims that such characters as Barbara Stanwyck portrays in *The Lady Eve* are self-created.[56] The ideas of selfhood that she is invoking derive from a source with which Cavell is not merely conver-sant. He has also elaborated upon these Emersonian ideas as precedents for his own thought on this topic and sought thereby to come into pos-session of them as his own. But there is incoherence in the way DiBattista presents her argument for the self-creation of this Stanwyck character. Unless she means to indicate only Jean Harrington's successful imperson-ation of an English aristocrat, which seems no more than a self-evident plot point, she undercuts her own claim for the Emersonian self-creation of this fast-talking dame. In her chapter on *The Lady Eve,* DiBattista clearly acknowledges Jean's indebtedness to her father's instructive exam-ple. On two occasions—once before and once after she has asserted that "Jean's primal hubris is that she dares to create herself. She gives birth to Lady Eve Sidwich"[57]—DiBattista acknowledges that the inspiration for Jean's independent sense of herself derives from her father's instruction.

First, she writes about Jean that the "uncommon woman, the artful Eve, is practiced in the worldly sport of double-dealing, having herself been taught by the subtlest beast of the field." Then, she later pays tribute to this evidently satanic proxy for his "successful parenting" since he has transmitted to his daughter "the family tradition of artful seduction" that enables her to take full control of the ongoing action of this comedy.[58] At his most exhilaratingly willful, Emerson would fully concur: "if I am the Devil's child," he defiantly proclaims, "I will then live from the Devil."[59] Moreover, this rebellious embrace of complete independence, despite the worst possible consequences, occurs in an essay which also advocates shunning all family ties in the process of self-realization.[60] Thus, Jean would seem to fit DiBattista's description of another such "female Pygmalion" as "self-reliant in the approved Emersonian way."[61]

But the glibness with which DiBattista invokes "the approved Emersonian way" betrays the condescension to Emerson's thought that Cavell decries. The phrase indicates something known beforehand and already in place. Thus, DiBattista will not bother to look further in the direction she has pointed because she thinks she already knows what is there. Emerson is the voice of self-assertion and non-conformity, not intuition and obedience. She indicates no awareness of the philosophical power of passiveness that Cavell claims for Emerson, and this blinds her to the mutuality of remarriage as it is represented in *The Lady Eve*. Jean Harrington's misgivings and the surprises of feeling that she undergoes become intelligible through a perspective that centrally includes susceptibility as well as assertiveness in any concept of self-reliance pertinent to the film under discussion. Fortunately, Jean does not always have complete control of either the action or her responses to her own experience, try as she may. DiBattista seems oblivious to this dimension of Emerson's thought and Jean's experience, which Cavell has made essential not only to his inheritance of Emerson but to any responsible reading of "Self-Reliance."

Perhaps what DiBattista aims to do in this chapter is to separate the revised Shakespearean precedent for the father's role in these remarriage comedies from the Genesis precedent for the husband, Adam, whose rib serves as the makings of his wife, Eve. DiBattista expresses her acceptance of Cavell's heuristic use of Shakespeare with regard to these films, which, as Cavell notes, pointedly reverse the Shakespearean dynamic by transforming the patriarch from an obstacle into an ally. Thus, DiBattista may think she has no quarrel with this revised version of family relations, because she fails to note how it undercuts her claim for female self-creation. But she does find Cavell's "mythic analysis" questionable. With its over-reliance upon "archetypal association," such an approach is unsuitable for "Sturges's use of the myth of Eden," which "is more parodic and suspicious, more radical in its account of this misogynist myth of sexual relationships."[62]

Here DiBattista's general complaint about Cavell's treatment of *The Lady Eve* amounts to a judgment about the decorum with which he approaches Sturges's comedy. Ironically, Cavell's alleged indecorum derives from the seriousness with which he brings the Genesis myth to bear upon the wild parody of Sturges's allusions to our lapse from Eden. Cavell is too grave and should lighten up. Decorum, of course, entails the idea of propriety in the sense of suitability or aptness to the occasion at hand. One can be too solemn as well as too light-hearted. This sort of impertinence, whether due to seriousness or levity, comprehends a whole spectrum of ways in which one's response can fail to fit the moment that elicits it.

Cavell occasionally indicates his awareness of this kind of problem, but in his film criticism, he initially seems to worry about it from, so to speak, the other side. He wonders, for example, whether he is courting outrageousness by beginning his essay on *It Happened One Night* with a sustained exposition of some of Kant and Wittgenstein's ideas about skepticism. Annexing this account of their ideas to his essay on a popular Hollywood comedy runs the risk of trivializing such major thinkers. Yet Cavell concludes this essay by claiming that *It Happened One Night* provides a solution to the problem of other minds, the very concern that occupies the last and longest section of *The Claim of Reason,* which itself concludes with a reading of *Othello.*[63]

Perhaps we can see how far we have come in this regard by listening carefully to this simple, apparently untroubled, sentence from an interesting essay in a recent collection on philosophy and popular culture: "I hope that discussing [Wittgenstein's] *Philosophical Investigations* will make discussing *Seinfeld* easier."[64] Frankly, I imagine most discussions of popular TV sitcoms would never get off the ground if Wittgenstein's later philosophy were the explicitly designated point of departure. There may be manifold ironies involved in this critic's deadpan expression of such a hope, but it also suggests that the boundaries between high and low, or elite and popular, culture have become hazier and leakier than was conceivable two or three decades ago. Our sense of decorum about the differences between these realms of culture and about interchanges between them has significantly altered. Indeed, the pleasures of transgression have often proved irresistible because the very existence of such distinctions can feel like pedantic fastidiousness.

For example, questions of decorum constantly arise with regard to philosophy's professionalization, and the ironies that they can generate become vivid even in the careers of the earliest philosophers. Socrates unforgettably embodies and exploits the contradictions between amateurism and expert authority, as does the ordinary language philosophy of Austin and Wittgenstein, upon which Cavell has founded his career as a philosopher. Moreover, Cavell's writings on Emerson and Thoreau amount to a recognizable continuation of his early work on those European thinkers because of the preoccupation with the near, the common, and the low characteristic of these definitive American transcendentalists. Yet Cavell often notes how their writings rarely count as philosophy in most versions of that discipline as a profession in institutions of higher education nowadays.

As we have seen earlier in this chapter, Cavell's reflections with regard to the myth of the Fall center decisively on a particular passage from Emerson's "Experience," a somewhat later essay composed in the aftermath of the death of his five-year-old son, Waldo.[65] The skepticism voiced in such a passage maps tellingly onto the experience of Charles "Hopsie" Pike (Henry Fonda) and his efforts to discern the identity, if not the essence, of Jean Harrington/Eve Sidwich (Barbara Stanwyck) in *The Lady Eve*—her being *so* or *being* so, as Cavell distinguishes between these two challenges to human perception. The camera's blurred focus gives a vivid picture of the initial "cockeyedness" of Pike's infatuated gaze, which Emerson might prompt us aptly to call his "subject lenses." Clear photographic evidence subsequently occasions his first opportunity to acquire the knowledge of good and evil, and a still photo helps to indicate a drastic change in his mood. He inhabits a world where, in Emerson's phrase, the "creative power" of personal perception is centrally on display. During the traumatic moment of Pike's initial disenchantment, Jean offers him the sort of knowledge supposedly available from the taste of such a fruit as the bitten apple with which she first "conks" him on the head as he boards the ocean liner: "You don't know very much about girls, Hopsie. The best ones aren't as good as you probably think they are, and the bad ones aren't as bad, not nearly as bad."[66]

Unfortunately, Pike doesn't get it. At the film's end, however, when he and Jean reunite in the same setting, Pike is willing to forgo the sort of knowledge he once valued and thought he could rely on. At that stage, you might say, he has acquired knowledge of a different kind, which he originally could not apprehend because it is unavailable to those of an exclusively scientific or, in Pike's case, ophiological, cast of mind. In doing so, he has accepted his own fallenness when, in Emersonian terms, he allows the partiality of his own inclination to override his quest for certainty in crucial matters of the heart: "I don't want to understand. I don't want to know. Whatever it is, keep it to yourself. All I know is that I adore you, that I'll never leave you again. We'll work it out somehow."[67]

Despite his Emersonian affinity for the myth of the Fall as indicative of our uncertain epistemic condition, Cavell's feminist critics Naomi Scheman and Ann Kaplan have deemed him what you might call prelapsarian. Scheman's preferred term is "innocent," and Kaplan's would aptly be "naïve."[68] Kaplan's attribution of naïveté centers upon her allegation that Cavell treats movie characters as if they were real people.[69] It doesn't directly pertain to issues here under discussion, but it bears notably upon Scheman's pointed efforts both to renounce the pleasure she experiences in viewing remarriage comedy and to cultivate a guarded view of such films. Scheman, on the other hand, follows Kaplan in her discussion of missing mothers and film melodrama in order to address the same issue raised by DiBattista: the "creation of the woman" as the "business of men" and the various entailments of this process (such as the absence of mothers and the woman's forgoing of motherhood) as characteristic features of remarriage comedy.[70]

Scheman offers a subtle and interesting argument about certain Freudian ideas about gender that Cavell employs in discussing remarriage comedy. Nonetheless, she fundamentally depends on a stark opposition between, on one hand, the pre-Oedipal mother and the loving attachment of relations between her and her child, and, on the other, the castrating father of the Oedipus complex and the resultant autonomy that derives from successful negotiation of this crisis by shifting to an identification with this figure. According to Scheman, the costs of this transition from attachment to the mother to independence, via identification with the father, are too high.

Such a conviction, however, need not put her irreparably at odds with Cavell, for she is offering a false alternative and a misdescription of human strengths often acquired, though not without tears, at these different stages of development in early childhood. When the options are starkly presented as an either-or choice between connection or autonomy, the tragic view unduly monopolizes the mythic space of human origins. Call it Eden or early childhood, what transpires there is subject to interpretation, both by those who respond to accounts of such dramas and by children and grownups who participate in these ordeals and survive them, sometimes quite handsomely. In her resistance to "patriarchal control and compulsory heterosexuality," Scheman overlooks aspects of human potential demonstrably present both in children and in the myth of Eden as it has been construed over the centuries.

Indeed, if we return to it briefly, Elaine Pagels's *Adam, Eve, and the Serpent* can help us by doing more than informing us that Jewish and Christian cultures in late antiquity used exegesis of the Genesis story to discuss such vital topics as marriage, divorce, and gender. That is the cue that Cavell takes from Pagels to license his own foray into biblical interpretation vis-à-vis Hollywood movies. But Pagels's primary purpose is to excavate pre-Augustinian readings of human beginnings, early interpretations whose emphasis upon human possibilities was subsequently overshadowed by the doctrine of original sin. The robust tradition of early Christian resistance to the oppression of personal liberty found sanction in ideas of human dignity read out of this myth, whose traumatic story nonetheless includes our creation in the image of God and the assumption of our moral autonomy. In the tradition that Pagels seeks to revive, Christian baptism recovers our divine inheritance. Similarly, when Cavell describes remarriage as the transformation of festival into daily festivity, of holiday into a heightening of the everyday, he appeals to Luther's conviction that "all our experience of life should be baptismal in character."[71]

Although Cavell's thought frequently engages ideas of conversion or transformation, the mingling of painful separation into discrete selfhood and the claiming of that selfhood in relation to others repeatedly characterize his philosophy of the human person. We mourn our separateness, or sometimes, like Leontes in *The Winter's Tale*, we tragically resist it until a time too late both to own *and* to overcome it through honest reckoning and responsiveness. In a romance like *The Winter's Tale*, the next generation can reclaim life-giving attachment despite the time when "first/[w]e were dissevered." Perhaps this is an analogue for a best-case scenario of feminist modifications of Freudian theory, and the polarity between attachment and autonomy need not be an insuperable opposition. But, even so, recovery from the ruin of Leontes' patriarchal tyranny and self-will run riot requires the next generation and "that wide gap" of time during which younger strengths can mature.

The stages along life's way, however, need not be viewed, or experienced, as mutually exclusive steps in human development. Cavell implicitly endorses this view when he characterizes youth as a dimension of the self, not necessarily accessible only to the young.[72] Moreover, Charles Pike, even though he's not a poet but an ophiologist, intuits the basis of such a view. On the deck of the ocean liner he begins to articulate this view when he says to Jean, "Every time I've looked at you here on the boat it wasn't only here I saw you. You seemed to go way back. I know that isn't clear but I saw you here and at the same time further away, and then still further away, and then very small."[73]

The flagrant hypocrisy (or complete obliviousness) with which Pike later recites this same speech to Eve during a horseback ride on his family estate suggests the capacity for forgiveness that Jean will have to summon once she overcomes her desire for revenge against him. The analogy here with *The Winter's Tale* continues to be revealing, as do its differences from *The Lady Eve*. For Hermione's final silence toward her husband, Leontes, expresses the perhaps unbridgeable gap between them, just as the blessing she solicits for her daughter, Perdita, indicates what is the significant reunion that Shakespeare is staging here. This reunion is not confined to the limits of one generation, as is the happiness of the childless couples who get back together in remarriage comedy. But whether all of the couples from these films of the 1930s and '40s were predestined to *remain* childless is a question Cavell can prompt us to ask about the ideal of a "marriage of equality" that they seem to embody. Moreover, that question remains a challenge for that ideal nowadays, and it hardly seems "naïve" or "innocent" to approach it skeptically—yet without altogether giving over the resources of idealism. In this regard Cavell routinely omits a relevant modern distinction about the genre of Shakespeare's late comedies. In 1623 the first folio placed the plays in three generic categories—tragedy, history, and comedy—and it listed *The Winter's Tale* among the comedies. In the past century, however, these late comedies have come most frequently to be called romances, thanks initially to Edward Dowden and subsequently to Northrop Frye, Cavell's primary guide in such matters of dramatic form. In part, this label indicates the willful reliance upon wonder in these plays, regardless of whether it strains credibility, but they also depend consistently upon children to hold out the promise of time's redemption and "make old hearts fresh" (1.1.38). As they become of marriageable age, the younger generation repairs the rifts that have tragically sundered families and friendships, states and alliances. These plays could not achieve comic endings without the presence and promise of children who have become young adults and offer the opportunity of reconciliation and beginning anew.

More importantly, the wonders upon which their plots customarily turn require more than willing suspension of disbelief. They tap into collective desires and express the fulfillment of wishes that the plays themselves openly acknowledge and blatantly encourage. In the return to life of Hermione, *The Winter's Tale* notoriously stages a miracle of apparent resurrection that defies credibility and thus elicits negative criticism or anxious rationalization. This final *coup de théâtre* comes in the wake of conspicuously astonished reports of the prior wonder (repeatedly so-called) of Perdita's arrival home sixteen years after assurance of her death was the common opinion in Sicilia. These manifold protestations of wonder flag a key feature of romance while they prepare the court to expect, or at least accept, the unpredictable and miraculous. Still, the extravagance of Shakespeare's breathtaking showmanship has the power to catch an audience by surprise even though they are fully forewarned of the miracle to come. "It is required/You do awake your faith," the aptly named Paulina instructs the courtly company on stage and, of course, the audience as well (5.3.94–95).

Perhaps readiness to accept such instruction and believe simply betokens a Jacobean version of the naïveté and innocence that Cavell's critics have discerned in his response to merely cinematic fictions like Hollywood remarriage comedies and their melodramatic counterparts. But perhaps not. "It is impossible to say," as Binx Bolling, the moviegoing stockbrocker in New Orleans, sums up his final uncertainty about how to take such an occasion that arises from his own wondering about it in the penultimate scene of Walker Percy's *The Moviegoer*.[74] As this story about one subtly transformative week of Binx's "thirtieth year to heaven" unfolds, we gradually realize that he has gone through some major changes despite the low key of the narrator's voice. His restraint here produces a telling silence fraught with unspoken significance at the same moment that it summons us into that silence. We do not have to enter. We can remain outside, aloof; and we can insist upon the insignificance of such a silence. Silence will not contradict us in Percy, nor will it in Shakespeare, once the last words are spoken and the curtain falls at the close of *The Winter's Tale*.[75]

6

CAVELL'S ROME

or Cavell, Shakespeare's late Roman plays, *Antony and Cleopatra* and *Coriolanus,* evoke a world where the fatefulness of moods and the existential challenges of human finitude and the social contract decisively take the spirit's measure. The agons of these characters also put into question the genre of tragedy as an occasion that plumbs the depths of the human spirit or reveals its absence of any such depths. Cleopatra rises to such an occasion; indeed, she may transcend it. Coriolanus, however, falls significantly short and thus fails, in the process, to elicit pathos. Despite his alleged limitations, Emerson again serves Cavell as a resource in reading these plays. As the inventor of what Cavell calls the "tragic essay," he possesses a sensibility that can help us understand the ordeals of such figures; and his detractors, who condescendingly deem him wanting in a sense of evil or tragedy and deny him the name of philosopher, need seriously to reconsider these received opinions.[1] For Emerson paradoxically reveals a literary and philosophical capacity adequate to respond both to the loss of a child, in "Experience," and to the national tragedy of slavery (and its original inscription in our American social contract), in "Fate." Despite such tragic understanding or, rather, because of its acknowledgment, he can also encourage us onward to the realization of an eventual community worthy of our visionary hours, however transitory they may be.

Similarly, Emerson's champions, the pragmatists who would enlist him as their forerunner, need to reflect upon perhaps nothing less than their idea of human nature.[2] In the title of a much discussed essay, Cavell asks this provocative question, "What's the use of calling Emerson a pragmatist?" Cavell's brief against pragmatism basically amounts to the

172

claim that it sometimes provides solutions to human problems that require more work, or work of a different kind, than pragmatism deems
necessary. Cavell succinctly indicates the problems that pragmatism mis-
recognizes either as more easily solvable than they actually are or as simply avoidable. He calls them skepticism and tragedy. They often travel in
tandem, especially in Shakespearean drama, and the sort of work they
usually require is like that of mourning, which takes patience and depends upon change within. Mourning can lead, in Thoreau's play upon
that word, to morning; but this redescription of our condition involves
a process more painstaking and hazardous than the verbal mastery that a
pragmatist such as Richard Rorty so enthusiastically celebrates in, for
example, his chapter on "The Contingency of the Self" in his *Contingency, Irony, and Solidarity*.[3]

While philosophers and students of American literature, like Russell
Goodman and James Albrecht, have responded to Cavell's defiant question, its emphasis on tragedy and skepticism warrants attention from
Shakespeare scholars as well.[4] Among that group, Lars Engle has written
a book, *Shakespearean Pragmatism,* inspired in good part by the thought
of Richard Rorty and the line of American philosophy that he represents.
However, as we shall see, Engle's arguments against Cavell are unpersuasive, and he later seems to abandon them altogether.

Cavell's collection of essays on Shakespeare first appeared in 1987,
almost a decade after he initially acknowledged his failure to see Emerson
on his horizon as an unavoidable and necessary American thinker. He
had previously fallen for a false alternative—either Thoreau or Emerson,
but not both—and he chose to correct that mistake in a 1979 paper,
"Thinking of Emerson," by embracing the sage of Concord as an epistemologist of moods. According to Cavell, this idea of Emerson makes him
a legitimate inheritor of the Kantian critical enterprise, though Cavell
balks at Kant's distinction between subject and object, and emphasizes
the succession of moods and objects that constitutes consciousness for
Emerson. This "succession, this onwardness, means that you can think
of [experience] as at once a succession of moods (inner matters) and a
succession of objects (outer matters). This very evanescence of the world
proves its existence to me; it *is* what vanishes from me."[5] This idea of
Emerson also construes his thought in ways entirely amenable to phenomenology's effort to overcome epistemology, as Charles Taylor perceives this project in two philosophers of great consequence for Cavell,
Heidegger and the later Wittgenstein.[6] In that regard, however, we
should note that the operative sense of "proof" here is empirical or,

rather, existential, not formal, as in agreement with some logical procedure. To "prove" means to test or essay some claim by the evidence of our own experience of the world.

Cavell's belated embrace of Emerson thus occurs at a moment when he is composing his second essay on Shakespeare, the reading of *Othello* that serves as the conclusion to *The Claim of Reason;* and he is yet to compose all of the rest of his writings on Shakespeare that will appear in the two editions of *Disowning Knowledge* and other later books of his. (Indeed, Cavell continues his practice of concluding his books with an essay on Shakespeare in his recent collections, *Emerson's Transcendental Etudes* and *Cities of Words*.) At this moment when Emerson claims Cavell's attention, he is also in the early stages of his writings about Hollywood movies that will subsequently appear in *Pursuits of Happiness* and *Contesting Tears*. These books, which make frequent reference both to matters of genre and to specific characters and plays in the Shakespearean corpus, abound in explicitly Emersonian reflections. Thus, the confluence of these three dominant currents of Cavell's later thought—Shakespeare, Emerson, and Hollywood movies—pervades his publications of the last quarter century.

Antony and Cleopatra: The Withdrawal of the World

Besides Cavell's merger of Wittgenstein and Emerson that we have noted in the introduction to *Disowning Knowledge,* he also performs an Emersonian interpretation of *Antony and Cleopatra*. Under the sign of "mood," he addresses the issues of genre that have traditionally engaged interpreters of this play, and he particularly emphasizes what he calls "the withdrawal of the world" as the experience of tragedy suffered by both protagonists in this play. Citing Emerson's assertion in "Circles" that our moods do not believe in each other, Cavell dwells upon the lines of skepticism and romanticism that he discerns in the play. If skepticism threatens us with the tragedy of loss and abandonment, then imagination and the powers of representation can respond to this threat by recreating a world to which our allegiance makes redemptive sense. Dissolution into doubt does not preclude recovery and affirmation; rather, our oscillation between everyday versions of these extremes may be a fundamental rhythm of the human condition in the modern era.

Cavell's emphasis on mood, both as it figures in the analysis of character development within this play and as it figures in a spectator's experience of the play itself, sets him decisively apart from major trends in contemporary Shakespeare criticism that stress political perspectives to the drastic diminishment, if not complete exclusion, of personal experience as an illusory domain that exists mainly, if not entirely, through self-deception. Linda Charnes alludes to Tina Turner's hard-boiled hit song in defiantly entitling her interpretation of *Antony and Cleopatra,* "What's Love Got to Do with It?" On Cavell's reading, that challenge would be (not so) simply answered, "Everything," though he carefully avoids direct employment of the totalizing rhetoric that Charnes so skillfully exploits. The confrontational bluntness of Turner's question, "Who needs a heart if a heart can be broken?" might elicit the response that feelings—or let us say moods—however radically they may differ from person to person and culture to culture, are not an option on any human model, as Macbeth and his wife instruct us in their monstrous efforts to prove otherwise.[7] Thus, "inevitably does the universe wear our color," as Emerson puts it, in "Experience"; and in "Self-Reliance," he characterizes our perceptions, colored as they are by our moods, as "not whimsical but fatal."[8]

Lars Engle, another notable recent interpreter of *Antony and Cleopatra,* concludes his chapter on the play by preemptively reclaiming his reading from the slightest hint of any Christian spiritual significance, which his penultimate assertion initially suggests: "The play renders unto Caesar what is Caesar's. But what remains remains political." To his credit, Engle does not say *always and only* political, but he apparently lacks a language, or even a motive, for saying what else the "increasing pressure of transcendence claims" in the play's final acts could signify other than "moves in a contingent politics of self-advancement."[9] In the face of obviously imminent death, it is hard to imagine what ultimate lack of advancement could inspire such entirely political maneuvering. Rendering Caesar "an ass unpolicied" defeats him in his own terms, but "playing til doomsday" allows "a lass unparalleled" more freedom of expression than such an exclusively strategic triumph employs.

Though he does admit that Cleopatra may be hallucinating her ecstatic finale, Cavell, on the other hand, stresses the play's Christian overtones and suggestions that its action may signify something beyond merely recording another chapter in political history and the behavior characteristic of such accounts. He seeks in this way to bring out the relevance of the view from within that both his reading and his mode of interpretation find inescapable. He summons Hegel's claim that the advent of Christianity entails the discovery of a new subjectivity to situate the play's Roman story in the larger religious narrative that accommodates pagan poems like Virgil's Fourth Eclogue and changes its prophetic note into messianic pronouncement. "The time of universal peace" that is at hand after Caesar subdues his last major rival becomes, in this perspective, the long-awaited moment when the savior is born. Concurrently with this spiritual impact of the development from pagan to Christian experience, there occurs within the latter the break away from Catholicism to Protestantism, with its stress on the individual believer's unmediated relations with God. In his essay on *King Lear* almost two decades earlier, Cavell had provocatively observed that Machiavelli and Luther saw the same thing at the same time, but Luther saw it "from inside."[10] In Engle's reading of Cleopatra's final agon, we seem stuck with Machiavelli's perspective alone, despite our awareness of the early Protestant culture that helped to form the sensibilities of Shakespeare and his contemporaries. This spiritual change is part of the relevant history for Cavell's reading, which would thus be more open to associating Cleopatra's "strong toil of grace" with the Reformation theology of grace and works that it readily evokes from a perspective that is not so eager to rule out completely the least hint of its pertinence as does Engle: "Again, this is not to suggest that *Antony and Cleopatra* covertly endorses Christianity. Cleopatra's strong toil of grace is not identifiable with Christ's."[11] Though Christianity may be unendorsed and Cleopatra's ordeal unidentifiable (in its absolute sense) with that of Christ, we still need a language that can at least acknowledge the aspects of human experience whose pertinence such a phrase suggests once we pause to wonder about it.

As we have seen, Shakespeare would soon explore manifold ramifications of the idea of grace in *The Winter's Tale,* where its courtly, theatrical, and theological implications resonate pervasively. At the conclusion of *Antony and Cleopatra,* theatricality is an undeniably prominent theme, so the self-conscious grace of a stage performance is immediately pertinent. Shakespeare, however, is also exploiting the tension between grace and works here, in this far unlikelier context. It is well recognized that Cleopatra transforms her notoriety for Epicurean excess into the surprising dignity of Stoic autonomy by her willful embrace of death on her own terms in the face of defeat and impending degradation at the hands of Caesar. Thus, she truly becomes "a lass unparalleled" by a grand gesture "in the high Roman fashion" that leaves the victorious Caesar truly "an ass unpolicied" (5.2.315; 4.16.89; 5.2.306–7). The precedent for this Shakespearean presentation of Cleopatra triumphant in her death derives from Horace's Ode 1.37, and it may have another source in Montaigne's essay "Of Cruelty," which cites that ode's description of Cleopatra as all the more ferocious for having chosen death (*deliberata morte ferocior*). But listen to these lines from none other than Caesar during that play's final moment:

> O noble weakness!
> If they had swallowed poison, 'twould appear
> By the external swellings; but she looks like sleep,
> As she would catch another Antony
> In her strong toil of grace (5.2.343–47).[12]

The paradox of "noble weakness" aptly expresses the manner of Cleopatra's unanticipated transcendence, in the face of imminent humiliation and ultimate death, of both her straitened circumstances and her cornered self. Moreover, Caesar's diagnostic concern for "external swellings" suggests a register of pertinent meaning beyond merely clinical observation of her symptoms as signs of the cause of her death. This austere tactician has already registered his contempt for the pomp of Egypt's political pageantry and the role that Antony has agreed to play in such ceremonies; but here he notes nothing puffed up, which, taken figuratively, suggests no show of pride and outward display. Shakespeare's sonnet had previously put "external grace" in its place, so to speak, via contrast with "constant heart" (5.3.13–14). Cleopatra follows a similar trajectory from "infinite variety" to "marble constan[cy]" (2.2.246; 5.2.238), but this amounts to a breathtaking surprise.

Caesar's final observation in this speech emphasizes the appearance in Cleopatra of utter passivity—"She looks like sleep"—and as the next comparison turns into the activity of "catching," we perhaps recall the several occasions on which fishing has actually or figuratively come into play. Successful angling, of course, requires patience, and the ostensibly dormant forces of Cleopatra's sleeplike appearance signify, if nothing else, an evident absence of restlessness. But such tranquility gives way to the banked forces of "her strong toil of grace," and we hear again in this formulation the central binary of Reformation theology, concisely reduced to a paradox. "[T]oil," of course, is a net; and if we probe the word's origins in this sense, "toile," the French word for linen, we may even speculate about the material composition of Cleopatra's net. But the modern sense of "work," as labor or effort, is fully available in Jacobean English as a meaning of "toil." The ecclesiastical sense of "work," as sacrament, is the central concern of much of the Reformation controversy about faith and works, and it does not come into play in the word "toil." But the semantic field covered by "work" was an ever-expanding one in that debate. Thus, it is no strain to hear Shakespeare's competitive transformation of mainstream theological language into triumphantly theatrical expression during the death of Cleopatra, just as we can hear it in Hermione's parting words on her way to prison: "this action I now go on/Is for my better grace" (2.1.121–22). Their "grace" is the expressive power of the actor who played them and the beauty of the character whom he portrays. The performer's struggle to achieve such expression warrants acknowledgment, even though it may almost disappear from our consciousness under the spell of the best of performances.

Cavell finds a language for such claims in Emerson, and he borrows not only Emerson's emphasis upon the existentially decisive role of moods in human consciousness and our experience of the world. He also evokes Emerson's hortatory lyricism in "Give All to Love," close though it may be to the sermonizing tones that initially put Cavell off this thinker and made him feel that Thoreau alone among these founders (or finders) of American thought seemed inheritable. The world recedes from Antony into formlessness devoid of meaning. His sad captains desert him, as does his bluff and manly confidant, Enobarbus. What Heidegger calls "the worldhood of the world" (which Cavell appositely illustrates elsewhere via reference to a scene in Buster Keaton's *The General*)[13] becomes apparent by its absence in the desolation of Antony, a premonition of which Shakespeare offers in the eerie scene of Antony's apparent abandonment by the god Hercules. This alleged sign of divine leave-taking invites an allusion to Emerson precisely because Cavell has put into play the Christian overtones audible at numerous turns in *Antony and Cleopatra* that Engle acknowledges but hastens to exclude from pertinence.

Though neither Emerson's poem nor Cavell's interpretation of Shakespeare confines us to an exclusively Christian reading, both enable us to see "transcendence claims" as potentially far more than self-deception or only "moves in a contingent politics of self-advancement." They help sustain Cleopatra's compelling fantasy of a marriage in heaven and a reunion with her beloved "husband" that he initially projects both with his assertion that "Dido and her Aeneas shall want troops" upon his and Cleopatra's arrival in the afterworld and with his intention to "be/A bridegroom in his death, and rush into't/As to a lover's bed." They demonstrate that love has got a great deal to do with Antony and Cleopatra despite arbitrary attempts to rule it out. Indeed, we should recall that Dido and Aeneas already "want troops" in the Virgilian underground that Antony evokes. Because of Dido's unforgettably disdainful shunning of her inconstant lover, they do not even have a reunion. Antony's grand rhetoric of love's transcendence of the grave thus anticipates Shakespeare's critique of epic heroism, which Cavell discerns in *Coriolanus* (as we shall soon see), by claiming another sort of accomplishment far worthier of celebration. Moreover, that love is not exclusively transcendent in its appeals to the imagination for a satisfying conclusion of Antony and Cleopatra's career as a peerless pair in the annals of love. In this play with manifold puns upon the sexual sense of death and dying as terms for female orgasm, Cavell construes Cleopatra's exclamation, "Husband, I come!" as an acknowledgement of her otherwise unknowable satisfaction. He also takes Antony's assertion of their love's peerlessness democratically, as a sign of a world without Peers of the Realm, an area of experience where rank can be irrelevant and happiness more open for all to pursue.

Cavell observes of Antony's desertion by his tutelary deity that, "[b]eing soldiers, [his men] feel the change in their godlike commander as a loss of power. But we are free to wonder whether spirits or half gods leave except on the appearance or invocation of a greater god."[14] The terms of this genuinely philosophical reflection—for what is philosophy if not the exercise of one's freedom to wonder?—derive from the final stanza of Emerson's "Give All to Love":

> Though thou loved her as thyself,
> As a self of purer clay,
> Though her parting dims the day,
> Stealing grace from all alive;
> Heartily know,
> When half-gods go,
> The gods arrive.[15]

Through his openness to the play's more easily questionable claims, Cavell keeps skepticism alive rather than solving it or the problems it raises. He thus makes an imaginatively inhabitable world out of the words of this play rather than foreclosing their rich possibilities. As he puts it in an apposite analogy, "Caesar has violently occupied the world, but that is not the same as dwelling in it. So-called solutions to skepticism would be such an occupation."[16] Dogmatism is one such solution.

Current and Source

It is as a philosopher of transformation that Emerson comes primarily to sponsor Cavell's understanding of himself as a perfectionist thinker; and an unsoldierly understanding of a loss of power, a willingness to yield responsively to action *upon* oneself, to accept unavoidable suffering with patience rather than take arms against it, leaves the self open for change in ways that resistance forecloses. This perfectionist mode of thought increasingly makes itself felt in Cavell's criticism of Shakespeare and Hollywood film during the last quarter of a century. These currents of thought pervade his writing, and their currency matters most because transformation counts for little if it is not a present possibility. The onwardness of the self, which the evanescence of the world makes palpable to our present consciousness, requires a readiness to respond to inevitable shifts of circumstance and perspective that only death can finally bring to a stop. It requires what Cavell aptly dubs "presence of mind" in exploring the qualities that can keep a marriage alive.[17]

Though Cavell refers to Shakespeare's primary source, Plutarch's "Life of Antony," in his reading of *Antony and Cleopatra,* two other likely sources, Horace's "Cleopatra Ode" (1.37) and Montaigne's essay "Of Cruelty," complement Cavell's interpretation. They fortify its differences from contemporary readings that do not centrally explore the transformations of character in both the dramatis personae and the spectator but rather emphasize political affairs virtually to the exclusion of personal matters as key features in reading this play. Indeed, by seeing this formulation, the personal and the political, as a false binary opposition, critics have been tempted not so much to collapse it or, in Engle's words for pragmatism's stated ambition, to seek to "[convert] binary oppositions into continua," as to overemphasize what they deem the neglected half of the pair, the political.

Horace's famous "Cleopatra Ode" celebrates the defeat of the Egyptian forces at the battle of Actium and thus deftly turns a civil war into a foreign affair. Previous critics have seen this poem as a likely source for Shakespeare's play, and its surprising revaluation of the Egyptian queen in its final quatrains mirrors the changes that Cleopatra undergoes in Shakespeare's last act.[18] The emotional course that this ode runs from delight to wisdom, to borrow Robert Frost's precisely apposite description of the figure a poem makes, also represents a dramatic change in the mood of its speaker and the attitude toward Cleopatra that initially makes itself felt in the words of this poem. Just as we witness an astonishing transformation in Shakespeare's Cleopatra from "infinite variety" to "marble [constancy]," an attentive reader of Horace's ode must experience a surprising shift from triumphal rejoicing and contempt to sober admiration of an enemy who becomes a sort of stoic role model, an

exemplar of heroic dignity in the Roman mode that she seemed to contradict utterly by every aspect of her previous behavior. Indeed, "infinite
variety" initially appears as the best face the play puts upon her mercurial
nature, her impulsiveness and instability, and it comes from the unlike-
liest of voices, the stoic and skeptical Enobarbus, whose "inconstancy"
finally leads him to suffer what one might characterize as the most unqualified tragedy of the entire play, the first of the play's concluding
series of suicides. These enormous changes at the last moment in the
protagonists of *Antony and Cleopatra* undermine the settled values of
complacent victors just as Philip Larkin's engagement of Sidney's sonnet
in "Sad Steps," which we examined earlier, shakes the very foundations
of this poem's easy contempt for what it initially presumes it is talking
about. But to appreciate this experience, or simply to have it, whether
in Horace or Larkin, one must be willing to enter it openly, unguarded
by preconceived notions. Or as Cavell puts this, following Luther, we
must believe before we can understand.[19]

Ideological critique, like deconstruction, would deem such an approach a fool's errand, since it apparently abandons suspicion unre-
servedly rather than seeking to disenchant our false consciousness with a
cold dash of realism. Cavell's conditional openness to such skeptical projects bespeaks his own career-long preoccupation with philosophies of
doubt, but it is also well to attend to his reservations about them. "If
deconstruction . . . is to disillusion us," Cavell writes, "it is a noble
promise and to be given welcome. Disillusion is what fits us for reality
. . . But then we must be assured this promise is based on a true knowledge of what our illusions are."[20] Horace's ode is embedded in Augustan
ideology and construes Cleopatra as a crazed barbarian or demonized and
ultimately inhuman other (a *monstrum*) along familiar Roman lines that
celebrate the civilizing effects of imperial dominion. At least that's how
it starts out. The poem seems not only to know what its illusions are; it
seems to believe them. However, it turns upon itself with some surprise,
as the other turns into an heroic version of herself, masterfully in charge
of her own destiny despite the apparently absolute constraint of her final
moment in Roman captivity. This reversal of fortunes turns, not from
good to ill, as Aristotle says tragedy usually runs its course, but from ill
to a reconception of the good under present circumstances. It charts a
palpable change of course, if we are open to the surprises it holds in store
for us; and its record of a dramatic shift in emotional trajectory, or what
Emerson calls mood, suggests a change of heart in the speaker whose
voice the poem represents. This palpable suggestion can also provoke a

version of such a change in responsive readers, who may become willingly, if not unguardedly, caught up in the surprising figure made by this poem.

In Horace's Cleopatra ode, this line describes the Egyptian queen's Roman resolve on a death of her own choosing, within the narrow margins of choice that remain for her in her final hours: "Deliberata morte ferocior" (fiercer now she has resolved on death, 1.37.29). Her stoic exemplarity resurfaces remarkably, some sixteen hundred years later, in Montaigne's "Of Cruelty," a text to which Shakespeare may have had access even before its publication in 1603 through his occasional patron and friend, the earl of Southampton, who also patronized John Florio, the Elizabethan translator of Montaigne into English. In that essay the line cited from Horace describes the soul of an exemplary Roman hero, Cato the Younger, as part of Montaigne's quest to understand the true nature of virtue. Like Cavell, Montaigne more often gives accounts of processes of thought than he makes rigorous philosophical arguments, and thus the course that this essay seeks to chart matters as much as any specific proposition that it seeks to demonstrate. That course includes Montaigne's questioning of the grimmer quality of willfulness that Stoicism seems to entail in order to affirm both the love of virtue that, according to Montaigne, must motivate real heroes (like Socrates and Cato the Younger) and the consequent pleasure that they must take in doing good and noble deeds. This emphasis on love and pleasure adds a distinctly Epicurean element to the idea of true virtue that Montaigne is developing, and this idea is also suggestively set off by Montaigne's self-descriptions of his own tender-hearted and easy-going nature that frame the essay. He even bridles at the violence and bloodshed in hunting animals, an activity sanctioned by social convention among his compatriots and peers. But Montaigne's paradox of an exemplary Stoic possessing a Cleopatra-like soul and acting like an infamous Egyptian Epicure (in the moralistic misconstruction of that term against which Montaigne himself warns his readers) points to the complications of character and inwardness that resided within the tradition of representation that Shakespeare stood in the way of inheriting in the process of creating his own paradoxical version of that particular scion of the Ptolemies.

What's the Use of Calling Shakespeare a Pragmatist?

All of these reflections, of course, are about character. Moreover, they are given voice by a writer whose own character seems embodied in every sentence he writes. Emerson, for whom "[c]haracter is higher than intellect," remarked about those sentences by his beloved Montaigne, "Cut these words, and they would bleed," an Emersonian formulation that nearly cites (and likely echoes) Shylock's passionate appeal for the acknowledgment of his own humanity in *The Merchant of Venice:* "If you prick us do we not bleed?" (3.1.58).[21] Cavell cites this entire speech at the crucial turn to Shakespeare near the end of *The Claim of Reason,* which leads, via Shylock and also Leontes in *The Winter's Tale,* into his essay about *Othello,* which concludes the book.[22] That essay finds in that tragedy an expression of what philosophy calls the problem of other minds. In Cavell's exploration of skepticism, it is not our doubts about the existence of the world that can haunt us relentlessly; it is our doubts about others that we must learn (and relearn), not only to live with, but to live.

The idea that skepticism may amount to an inevitable struggle that all persons must face in one form or another makes Richard Rorty take issue with Cavell. Furthermore, Rorty explicitly seeks to erase from current usage such traditional formulations of the kinds of skepticism as the Problem of the External World and the Problem of Other Minds. He deems them symptoms of "professional deformation" among philosophers and hopes teachers someday "will stop trying to sucker freshmen into taking an interest in [them]."[23] Cavell's own appeal to Pascal's pithy dictum that "[c]ustom is our nature" reveals that he has long been wary of the hazards of essentialism without feeling obliged to abandon pertinent efforts at generalization.[24] Moreover, his turn to Shakespeare's Othello, via Shylock and Leontes, indicates his refusal to accept the confines of philosophical argument as the sole means of entertaining questions raised by inquiry and reflection, activities from which amateur status affords no one an exemption (though dullness can take its toll!). Cavell's turn to Othello definitely took place in the company of a large number of freshmen, since *Othello* ultimately appeared on the syllabus to his undergraduate lecture course as a replacement for *King Lear* in the late seventies. But I doubt he was trying to sucker those freshmen into anything. Rather, he was succumbing happily to philosophy's need of literature in its effort to make itself understood, just as he was using philosophy to make Othello's ordeal understandable and more available to his audience. He had done this memorably before, as "The Avoidance of Love: A Reading of *King Lear*" amply testifies.

Rorty's wishing away of the problem of others resembles a similar gesture that Cavell muses over in Freud's essay on the uncanny. The

E.T.A. Hoffmann story that Freud there interprets, "The Sandman," includes a beautiful automaton, and Freud denies that the question posed by this ambiguous presence about the "uncertainty whether an object is alive or inanimate" gives rise to the uncanniness of this tale. Rather, he insists that "the uncanny in Hoffmann's tale is directly attached to the idea of being robbed of one's eyes, and hence, given [Freud's] earlier findings, to the castration complex." For Cavell, Freud's insistence on his interpretation and the flat denial of an alternative that it entails bespeaks "the denial that philosophy persists within psychoanalysis."[25]

Rorty's impatience with the elevation of a particular expression of a philosophical problem into an unavoidable rite of intellectual passage perhaps simply indicates his refusal to be stuck with words and ways of seeing that needlessly confine us to worn out routines. And who wouldn't sympathize with such a feeling? Rorty's passion for redescription as a means of fresh and creative apprehension can helpfully serve to renew ideas and perceptions whose force is otherwise spent by the vain mantra-like repetitions that professional training sometimes seems to require. Cavell's resistance to philosophy's professionalization indicates his sympathy in this regard, as does the use to which Toril Moi puts Cavell's work and that of ordinary language philosophy in general in her critique of psychoanalysis's overuse and misapplication of the idea of castration anxiety.[26] What Moi feels that psychoanalysis leaves out due to this particular mistake of emphasis is precisely the problem of others as well as that of human finitude. These are aspects of the self's experience that require acknowledgement, and hasty diagnosis and confident deployment of the idea of castration anxiety ignore them in a reductive distortion.

Thus, it is pertinent to note that, in more detailed engagements with literary texts, Rorty's redescriptions can also reveal a kindred lack of imagination, if not simply denial, in this regard. In his chapter on "The Contingency of Selfhood" in *Contingency, Irony, and Solidarity*, Rorty excerpts three quatrains from Philip Larkin's "Continuing to Live" in order to make his point about the utility of psychoanalysis. Rorty omits the poem's title and opening two stanzas, and Larkin's verses become specimens of a host of curable ills that Rorty seeks to redescribe therapeutically. They are taken as examples of the misbegotten desire to generalize about such things as the human condition or human nature, which Freud freed us from by his revelations about the idiosyncratic nature of human identity. The decisive influence of early childhood experience does not exert an unfathomable power or make what Larkin describes as a "blind impress" upon our character. Analysis can render the particularity of such experiences intelligible, and we can embrace them as our own in an idiom of our own creation. Rorty's merely instrumental reading of Larkin's poem takes it as an occasion for advancing this position while correcting Larkin's mistakes in this regard. Even so, Rorty retains an interest in the pathos of finitude for which he has no quick fix to offer. The intelligibility of the idiom we create for our selves, however, diminishes the anguish of individual isolation that Larkin's poem needlessly laments as though it were an inevitable human dilemma.

As we have previously seen, Cavell's brief against pragmatism basically amounts to the claim that it sometimes provides solutions to problems that require more work, or work of a different kind, than pragmatism deems necessary. Since Cavell specifies tragedy and skepticism as the human dilemmas that pragmatism fails adequately to acknowledge and fully to address, simply conceiving of such daunting challenges as "problems" may itself give rise to the tone of exasperation in Cavell's title. He first delivered the paper so-called at a conference in New York generally dedicated to the acknowledgment, if not the celebration, of the revival of pragmatism, so the note Cavell struck was by no means in the dominant chord of the proceedings. (Perhaps we should also recall that this event occurred on the weekend that Yitzak Rabin met his tragic end by assassination.)

Cavell's interest in recovering the fullness of Emerson's philosophical voice derives in good part from an unwillingness to shrink "before a description of the very possibility [philosophy] undertakes to refute, so it can never know of itself whether it has turned its nemesis."[27] Cavell is discussing Descartes and Emerson. He is distinguishing between philosophy and literature in the process of demonstrating both the limits of argument and inference and Descartes's need for a literary response to express the possibility of his own non-existence that he sets about pondering—to express, in other words, where skepticism leads him and where tragedies routinely end. In this essay Cavell is also discussing what he calls "transcendental" relations "as they have so far shown themselves" and Emerson's "grammatical answer" to "Descartes's question." We have, in other words, a situation here, a human predicament with determining constraints, whether, as Larkin puts it in the images Rorty consigns without hesitation to oblivion, we are playing chess or poker, whether providence or chance prevails. The ordeal of individuation requires the truest words that we can find, but it also requires all the patience we can muster to bear the significance of whatever straits we happen to find ourselves in.

In "Sad Steps," Larkin's poem that evokes a sonnet of Sidney's, we can witness this poet's engagement of a prior text that begins in glib mastery and evolves into chastened wisdom via the discovery of human limitation or what Rorty calls the pathos of finitude. This poem is more accepting of human isolation and difference than the generalizations that Rorty deems misconceived at the close of "Continuing to Live." If one takes the latter poem as representative of Larkin's position, Rorty's point carries some conviction; and if "truth is a mobile army of marching metaphors," then, figuratively speaking, Rorty is due a triumph, like Caesar after the battle of Actium, for his successful redescription of Larkin's lyric. So much of the poetry has been lost in the process, however, that we must celebrate a decidedly Pyrrhic victory.

But a poem like "Sad Steps" charts a course that makes the distinction between discovery and creation, which Rorty insists upon in his characterization of selfhood, inadequate to describe both the poetic process and the experience of reading. And Horace's "Cleopatra Ode" follows an equally surprising path of discovery, although it does not begin as an exercise in something we might call redescription. Robert Frost claimed that he never knew how his poems would end, and he compared writing poems with foreknown destinations, with their endings already composed, to backing a car into the garage. We have learned to distrust Robert Frost, like everyone else, but that does not mean that we know he was simply lying or overstating his claim. A charitable interpretation that automatically gives him the benefit of the doubt might seem foolhardy, but manuscript research could help make us sure whether he ever violated this principle. However, it also would undoubtedly remind us that the composition of poems is a process, and often a long one, in which discovery plays a frequent part even when that experience is transformed into a further creation.

This tension between creation and discovery comes fully into play in Cavell's "Finding as Founding: Taking Steps in Emerson's 'Experience,'" which notably discusses that Emersonian essay as a commentary upon its own composition. As his title reveals, Cavell is concerned with the problem of foundations and the groundlessness that threatens post-Cartesian thought, a danger he deems foreseen in Shakespearean tragedy. Emerson's essay poses an opening question that suggests, in the very terms of its formulation, the need for an answer that must preserve the tension between creation and discovery that conceiving of Emerson as a pragmatist according to Rorty's view rules out. "Where do we find ourselves?" Emerson asks at the start of his essay, and he then proceeds in a manner that makes any decisive answer to that question an over-reaching gesture that is destined to fumble what it seeks firmly to grasp. Where we find ourselves is not just here, or just there, but on the way and in between the start and the finish. When a moment of fuller discovery dawns, it occasions an outburst of paradoxical excitement that reveals the onwardness of the journey under way. Where we find ourselves, Emerson calls "this new yet unapproachable America." It is new because its inhabitation requires a change in us. It is unapproachable because we are already there. But our presence frequently feels like an absence since we are often numb to the necessary transformation that dwelling in such a place requires. When we awake to that need, we find ourselves and our true country, whence we proceed ever onward. It is our openness to that process that we may come to call home.

Lars Engle's *Shakespearean Pragmatism* tries to demonstrate the inadequacy of Cavell's readings of Shakespeare by taking his emphasis on Cartesian skepticism as symptomatic of a pervasive misconception about the plays. This book defines one of the strengths of its own pragmatic approach, which it offers as an alternative to Cavell's, as "the redescription of fixed structures as economies"; and it characterizes one of the "central intellectual moves" of that approach as "the conversion of binary oppositions into continua." However, when it comes to redescribing Cavell's Shakespeare, we are given drastically reductive accounts that basically rely upon a binarism: either Montaigne or Descartes, but never the twain shall meet. Cavell, Engle writes, "goes too far in making Shakespeare into Descartes"; he "[sees] Shakespeare as Descartes." Such claims do not lack some evidence; but, while they extol the virtues of complexity, they oversimplify. Engle cites Stephen Toulmin as his guide against Cavell's Cartesian extremes; but, ironically, Toulmin describes the very project that Engle finds exemplary and uses to contrast with the undesirable Cartesian extremism of Cavell in terms that could as well be accurately applied to Cavell. Toulmin describes our current dilemma as "our need to reappropriate the wisdom of the 16th-century humanists, and develop a point of view that combines the abstract rigor and exactitude of the 17th-century 'new philosophy' with a practical concern for human life in its concrete detail." I would assume that the *combination* of abstract rigor and practical concern that Toulmin here commends would amount to the sort of *continuum* that Engle seeks in his pragmatic redescriptions, though he insists upon an either-or in representing Cavell's approach—either Montaigne or Descartes, either theory or practical philosophy.

Toulmin's account stresses the decisiveness of a turn toward Descartes and other certainty projects together with a turn away from Montaigne's tolerance for ambiguity and his emphasis on *la condition humaine* with all its tangle of entailments. It is this phrase of Montaigne's that Erich Auerbach singles out to make, among other points, this important claim: "the tragic is not yet to be found in Montaigne's work; he shuns it."[28] So, for Toulmin and Engle, there is a break or rupture that characterizes the advent of modernity, as there is for Cavell. For Toulmin and Engle, Cartesian philosophy typifies the modern side of that schism while Renaissance humanism, which includes Montaigne and Shakespeare, distinguishes the world we have lost and need to recover at least in part, the part that features practical philosophy and expresses impatience with abstraction and pure theory. If Engle's wish for continua were not merely recuperative, he could have turned to other philosophers, such as Alasdair MacIntyre and Charles Taylor, whose redescriptions of the advent of modernity see this transition less drastically.[29] MacIntyre, moreover, uses Shakespearean tragedy as a handy means of illustrating what it feels like to live through a "paradigm shift" of such proportions, though he stresses continuities that lessen the shock rather than make opposite sides of the divide incommensurable.

Cavell's argument, like Auerbach's, claims that Montaigne lacks a capacity for the tragic; but Cavell finds in Shakespearean tragedy the extremes of Cartesian doubt, the abyss of ungroundedness that becomes a constant threat in the modern age. Also, while he believes there is no going back, our onwardness in this regard does not render Montaigne useless or irrelevant, as becomes apparent through Cavell's affiliation with the Montaigne-like Emerson. Emerson's alertness to the succession of moods and objects that distinguishes human experience and constitutes for us a world made his philosophy resonate tellingly with Cavell and provided a means of reading *Antony and Cleopatra*. This aspect of Montaigne's writing, what we might follow Emerson and call its "March weather," also informs Emerson's recognition of this condition of human consciousness which refuses to split the difference between subject and object. Moreover, moods straddle this divide between subject and object in a way analogous to the reading of a text, where what the reader brings to that experience becomes a decisive part of what's there to get out of it. A spectator's experience of a play similarly informs his interpretation of the action, and it becomes a resource for understanding the agons on stage.

Seven years after the publication of *Shakespearean Pragmatism,* Engle seeks to characterize Shakespearean skepticism by singling out features that make it precisely fit Rorty's version of pragmatism: "perspectival thinking" and "an appetite for competitive redescription." However, when he turns to the matter of genre, Engle basically restates Cavell's argument about skepticism and Shakespearean tragedy as a step in his own process of thought. Thence he proceeds to elaborate upon a "more comic skepticism" in the so-called Problem Plays, where he finds "pervasive skepticism or pragmatism."[30] Cavell's argument does not separate tragedy from extreme skepticism in Shakespeare. Rather, it claims that they map onto one another closely enough to be symptomatic of kindred crises. As we have seen, Ellen Spolsky tries to make tragedy, as a dramatic form, the cause of any drastic skepticism that Shakespeare communicates.[31] The playwright himself remains a Pyrrhonist even though his plays explore attitudes and experiences that such a philosophy cannot begin to address adequately. In a way Cavell's discontent with pragmatism derives from a similar sense of pragmatism's shortcomings in the face of tragedy. It tries to solve what we must suffer, and that pretense of a solution bespeaks an evasion that shrinks from an experience we must undergo.

Emerson records one of his own head-on encounters with grief in "Experience," an essay in which his inadequacy in the face of the death of his beloved young son, Waldo, makes him feel detached, adrift, and befogged—incapable, precisely, of a head-on encounter with such a loss. However, this helpless evasion, if that's the right word, is unintentional; and it only compounds the pain of loss, just as surely as it communicates the ordeal of that pain more feelingly because Emerson acknowledges the experience of numbness and insensibility that his condition occasions. Because this essay closes with the claim that "the true romance which the world exists to realize will be the transformation of genius into practical power," its finale may be construed as a ringing endorsement of pragmatism, an affirmation of a philosophy that sometimes just looks the other way or conveniently changes the subject when one gets bogged down in the sort of anguish with which Emerson struggles so fully to reckon.[32] But that claim requires obliviousness to the abysses of loss that he has sounded on the way to that hopeful envoi, and it overlooks the "[p]atience and patience" that Emerson repeatedly recommends, using a term memorably applied to Job, not because of his restraint and forbearance, but because of his unrelieved suffering during the vast majority of his story, its tragic part.

Cornel West celebrates the evasion of epistemology that American thought has achieved. Since it is sometimes averred that there is no such thing as American philosophy, West understandably refers to the American evasion of *philosophy* to describe this turning away from such problems of knowledge and criteria of certainty as have preoccupied European thought since the early modern period and have, refreshingly, posed no great challenge to pragmatism. A kindred evasion appears in Engle's account of Shakespearean pragmatism by virtue of what plays he chooses to discuss and how he conducts that discussion; and probably for this reason, Cavell's basic ideas about Shakespearean tragedy remain completely intact in Engle's subsequent essay despite his flawed attempt to dismiss them earlier, in his book. Although Engle fails to acknowledge this feature of his work, his book addresses only one of the four Bradleyan tragedies, so-called because of A. C. Bradley's famous book *Shakespearean Tragedy,* which most decisively defined that genre for the twentieth century. Moreover, it discusses that one Bradleyan tragedy, *Hamlet,* from the angle of its protagonist's theatrical strategies and problem-solving. These are undeniably interesting aspects of the play, and they are perfectly suited for a pragmatic approach. However, they are hardly the ideal point of departure or focus for a consideration of tragic experience as it is represented in this play. Though Engle does discuss *Antony and Cleopatra* and *Coriolanus,* as did Bradley in essay-length lectures delivered after the publication of *Shakespearean Tragedy,* both are plays where problems of genre loom especially large in their reception, and these problems are often connected to questions of character and its representation. Both plays are more readily construed in exclusively political terms, and the challenges of character analysis that they raise are usually deemed less complex.

Coriolanus and Sidney's Poetics

Cavell's idea of Rome in Shakespeare's late tragedies emphasizes this particular city as the place in the West where Christian history is inaugurated and whence it spreads. Thus, just as Cavell sees messianic prophecy as relevant to understanding Shakespeare's larger vision in *Antony and Cleopatra,* so he sees *Coriolanus* in terms of sacrifice and the transformation of community that enables a society to sustain itself for the common good. Even as he acknowledges the general superiority of psychological approaches to this play, and Janet Adelman's example of such a reading in particular, Cavell is beginning to develop an alternative reading of the play that is as much a religious interpretation as it is an exercise in political science. Arguments about the formation of civil society and the creation of a social contract figure prominently in Cavell's work from the first part of *The Claim of Reason* through his readings of *His Girl Friday* and *Now, Voyager;* and the idea of consent pervades his writings of the last quarter century.[33] However, the language of blood and nourishment that recurs in *Coriolanus* leads Cavell to considerations of cannibalism and communion that emphasize speech itself as another kind of food that passes in and out of our mouths and requires our willingness to share (and be shared) as the unavoidable price of participating in a community. "There is no world elsewhere," as Cavell sums up his sense of the constraints of both language and civil society while he demonstrates Coriolanus's inaptitude for sharing in both.[34]

Cavell poses the question of this play's genre via the overlap between Sir Philip Sidney's *Defence of Poesy* and *Coriolanus* in their use of Menenius's fable of the belly. Cavell construes this "pretty tale" as an example of how a Shakespearean play works and ultimately uses it to pose the question, "What is a Shakespearean play?"[35] Cavell's exercise of his freedom to wonder in asking such fundamental and capacious questions sets him apart from many academic critics whose entry into the plays usually comes by way of established arguments in the scholarly reception of these works. While clearing the way by detailing the paths of those who have gone before them in the same direction, such scholars usually situate their approach in relation to many another. Though Cavell sometimes employs this sort of approach as well, he also more readily steps back to achieve perspectives that make such basic questions once again audible and engaging.

Sidney describes Menenius's tale as "notorious" because it smacks of sophistry, though his main purpose is to show the "alteration" that it works upon Menenius's initially rebellious audience by bringing about "a perfect reconcilement."[36] Sidney is intent on illustrating the transformative power of poetry, its therapeutic effect in a moment of crisis that could otherwise have had a disastrous outcome. It is precisely this power that perfectionist philosophy competes with poetry to exercise in its own way, as Cavell has acknowledged in the process of consolidating his own identity as just such a philosopher. The success of Menenius's tale, however, glosses over the possibility that the plebeians may have a case whose just claims are rendered inaudible in the interests of avoiding conflict. The adjacent example in Sidney's *Defence* thus becomes pertinent because it shows a similar use of fable to transform an alert audience, but the change thus wrought bespeaks justice and truth more unambiguously than Menenius's tale. It is the story of Nathan the prophet who confronts King David in court about his murderous adultery with the wife of Uriah the Hittite, Bathsheba. Through his parable of the rich man's selfish appropriation of the poor man's only ewe, Nathan awakens David's conscience, initially to the injustice of the rapacious rich man, but ultimately to the wickedness of his own behavior with Bathsheba. Thanks to poetry, moral philosophy hits home, though it would be hard at such a juncture to distinguish between them decisively. Is the parable poetry and David's interpretation philosophy? His passionate response certainly exceeds the usual "claim of reason" and raises the sort of questions Cavell asked to conclude his book of that title: "[C]an philosophy become literature and still know itself?"

Pragmatism, of course, prides itself on evading philosophy, but it wishes to include literature within the purview of "cultural criticism," a phrase both Rorty and West use to define the ambitions of pragmatism. However, it also wants to be prophetic, at least as West represents that American line of thought in the process of making Emerson pragmatism's progenitor. Yet it is hard to imagine a vocation that would more quickly give rise to the sorts of epistemological questions in which philosophy allegedly has foundered since skepticism reemerged in the early modern period than the prophet's calling. What, for example, is the basis of prophetic authority? In the Judeo-Christian tradition that West articulates with such passion and conviction, a prophet was no mere seer who foretold the future. He spoke on God's behalf here on earth, as the so-called messenger formula that is attached to much prophetic speech in the Hebrew Bible attests: "Thus says the Lord." In early modern Europe, when skepticism emerges, it initially is enlisted more readily in the defense of religion than in its subversion, as the phenomenon of fideism often attributed to Montaigne among others amply demonstrates. Subsequently, however, it signifies, with greater and greater specificity, disbelief in the realm of religion although Emerson employs a notable variation on this argument. Skepticism serves him as a means of belief, an approach to faith; but it does so by enabling him to give the lie to false forms of belief and the passionate conviction they seek to enforce. Comparing the confident adherents of such doctrines with "dreaming beggars," he asserts that "they assume to speak and act as if these values were already substantiated."[37]

Cavell's argument about Shakespearean tragedy begins by focusing on the network of verbal relations that ordinary language philosophy understands as the bonds of familial and civil attachment holding people together in forms of life that enable mutual intelligibility and meaningful interaction. However, Cavell is alert from the beginning to the threat of

God's disappearance that can sunder those bonds. Cavell's Cartesian reading of *Othello* makes this explicit in the aftermath of the refutation of Kant's claim about the necessity of the soul's immortality for life to make moral sense in Cavell's reading of *King Lear*.[38] The visions of groundlessness that Cavell finds in Shakespearean tragedy entail aspects of human experience from which pragmatists such as Rorty routinely turn away and which West's religious faith makes less immediately threatening than Cavell's sense of skepticism's devastating potential in such tragedies will allow. Lars Engle clearly indicates that he is following the pragmatism of Rorty rather than West, and this choice involves a general avoidance of tragedy, not only as Cavell understands that genre in Shakespeare, but also as it is exemplified in most of the prime instances of such plays by Shakespeare.

The Emerson with whom Cavell seeks to affiliate his philosophy also differs significantly from the proto-pragmatist whom others posit as the chief source of this line in American thought. There is plenty of room for disagreement about these different accounts of Emerson, but the intimacy with which Cavell responds to Emerson's writings warrants note because it distinctly reveals the philosophical ambitions that his readings seek to realize. In Cavell's interpretation of Emerson, Cavell's philosophy is as much at stake as Emerson's, and thus we might rightly use a favorite term of Emerson's and call those readings resolutely partial. Cavell wants to demonstrate the presence of an Emerson to whom others have condescended or whom they have simply ruled out: an Emerson well aware of the power of evil, the potential of tragedy, and the full weight of skepticism; an Emerson as receptive as he is assertive and fully aware of what Cavell calls "the philosophical power of passiveness."[39] Thus, Cavell intervenes in discussions where Emerson might seem, at most, indirectly relevant and where Nietzsche or Heidegger appears to be more clearly the central topic. Cavell finds such an occasion in John Rawls's consideration of the principle of perfection in *A Theory of Justice*. There Nietzsche is singled out to exemplify a kind of elitism that Cavell discerns he could only have inherited from Emerson. The work of Nietzsche, "Schopenhauer as Educator," that Rawls selects to illustrate the liabilities of perfectionism as a moral theory contains pervasive transcriptions from Emerson. Emerson thus requires a defense, which Cavell provides, and he also saves Nietzsche's text from Rawls's misreading in the process.

Similarly, the debate over Heidegger's politics under the Nazi regime becomes an occasion for Cavell to raise the question of the politics of race in Emerson's writings. Barbara Packer expresses some impatience about this aspect of Cavell's second essay on Emerson's "Fate," "Emerson's Constitutional Amending," when she declares "surely the relationship here is not one of reverse filiation but of analogy."[40] By "reverse filiation" Packer construes Cavell's meaning this way: Heidegger, who, as a later writer, stands in the filial position, somehow has the capacity to taint the earlier writer by an association mediated through an intervening writer, Nietzsche, who comes between Emerson and Heidegger and transmits Emerson's thought to Heidegger. Packer questions this idea, which seems to write the history of influence backwards, and she suggests that the idea of analogy better characterizes the similarity between the situations in which these philosophers did their relevant work. Both lived during politically treacherous times and faced kindred challenges: slavery for Emerson and Nazism for Heidegger. But Cavell believes that, if the earlier writing has some disease, like racism or anti-Semitism or elitism, it can infect its descendents. Thus, we must carefully analyze the etiology of such ills to avoid false attribution and test the soundness of all the writings in such a line of succession.

The pragmatist version of Emerson occludes, at the least, another side of this writer, which constitutes a precious legacy for the perfectionism that Cavell seeks to advance. Rorty speculates thus, in a passage that Engle cites, "Had Bacon—the prophet of self-assertion, as opposed to self-grounding—been taken more seriously, we might not have been [stuck] with a canon of 'great modern philosophers' who took 'subjectivity' as their theme."[41] But if one listens for Bacon in "Self-Reliance," one hears, surprisingly, this turn on one of his most famous aphorisms: "Who has more obedience than I, masters me, though he should not raise a finger." And why is this so surprising? Elsewhere in the same essay, Emerson writes, "We lie in the lap of immense intelligence, which makes us receivers of its truth and organs of its activity. When we discern justice, when we discern truth, we do nothing of ourselves, but allow a passage to its beams." Our surprise at such sentences comes from having accepted an idea of Emerson as himself a later prophet of self-assertion, a proto-pragmatist, despite the fact that "reliance" suggests dependence and the self upon which we rely—"the aboriginal Self upon which a universal reliance may be grounded"—becomes available as a gift, not a possession, which we receive through acceptance, not assertion. We may then act upon the receipt of such an unsought endowment as our yielding brings us to. "We denote this primary wisdom as Intuition," as Emerson expresses this interplay of passion and action, "whilst all later teachings are tuitions."[42]

Cavell characterizes his Shakespeare criticism as such tuitions, which follow out the intuitions that prompt them.[43] He discerns in *Coriolanus* a failed tragedy, and the specific nature of this failure becomes apparent through putting Shakespeare's play into conversation with Sir Philip Sidney's theory of literature, initially via their mutual reprises of a classical topos, Menenius's fable of the belly. The transformation of the angry crowd into more conversible citizens shows in little how a play works, or rather, the work that a play does when it succeeds. It brings about change in those who are susceptible to its representation of human actions and the worlds in which they transpire. But Coriolanus is the least conversible of citizens, and thus, when he appears in the wake of Menenius's rhetorical success, he offers curses instead of persuasion and undoes the work that Menenius has accomplished.

Cavell then extends the conversation between Sidney and Shakespeare into an argument about the kinds of literature and their relative efficacy. Sidney's defense of what he calls poesy (and what we have come to call imaginative literature) as the best of teachers corresponds in telling ways to the continual dialogue between philosophy and literature in Cavell's writings. Philosophical exposition craves examples precisely because of the shortcomings of precepts. In their abstractness, such formulations are understood only by experts, by philosophers, who may thus have no further need of instruction; but they leave the rest of us cold, unmoved, and unenlightened. We may, however, find satisfaction in fables—in Hollywood movies and Shakespearean drama—as Cavell does in his quest to make his philosophy more immediately available or in his discovery that it already is available in such works of art. But Cavell posits an argument between Sidney and Shakespeare in *Coriolanus* about the comparative efficacy of tragedy and heroic literature, and he reads Shakespeare's play as a failed tragedy precisely because it has the wrong kind of hero, an interloper from the realm of epic, who thus offers a critique of Sidney's poetics.

According to Sidney, it is the work of poetry not only to instruct us in virtue, but to move us to virtuous action. A pragmatist might call such action "consequences."[44] Heroic poetry best effects this ambition because it inspires us more than any other genre; it moves us most, and the consequence of such inspiration will be virtuous actions of our own for the public good. Shakespearean tragedy frequently features a protagonist whose ostensible virtues have their most fitting home in epic (Othello, Macbeth, Antony) and romance (Othello), the two genres whose merger constituted the heroic poetry typical of Shakespeare's age.

As these figures cross the threshold into love and domestic relations, however, their military excellence faces the sorts of challenges that reveal its limits. The ordeals they thus undergo become the stuff of tragedy. In his broader scheme, what Cavell sees emerging in such plays is a new kind of privacy, which contrasts painfully with the public excellence and accomplishments of these valorous soldiers. In one sense they all find themselves in the wrong kind of play, though Ellen Spolsky's Pyrrhonist solution to that discovery misses its point, as would pragmatist self-assertion. Of course, they would do better if martial heroism was called for alone, without the ambiguities of personal relations, of sorting things out in fraught conversation with others, and without the anguish of individual decision-making; but instead something is required of them like the "patience" of Job, who, we may recall, complained loud and long, refused "comfort," and, crucially, suffered. As their ordeals crack these figures open, we are exposed to the passions undergone by such agonists, whose expressive powers (thanks to Shakespeare) move us to participate in their suffering if we are at all responsive to tragic experience.

The failure of *Coriolanus* as a tragedy derives from its protagonist's unyielding temperament, which gives no quarter to human weakness and becomes monstrous in the process. Coriolanus's inhuman lack of susceptibility holds fast until the final act, when his resistance at last breaks during his interview with his mother and other family members. On the brink of vindictive revenge against Rome, Coriolanus succumbs in a scene he himself deems unnatural and laughable. He acknowledges what, following Lady Macbeth, we may call his "human kind*ness*" (emphasis added):

> O mother, mother!
> What have you done? Behold, the heavens do ope,
> The gods look down, and this unnatural scene
> They laugh at. O my mother, mother, O!
> You have won a happy victory to Rome;
> But for your son, believe it, O believe it,
> Most dangerously you have with him prevailed,
> If not most mortal to him. But let it come (5.3.183–90).[45]

Where pathos should obtain, laughter threatens, while this "thing of battle" belatedly recognizes its or, finally, *his* own mortality, becoming human only (and perhaps in order) to die. But for Cavell (and in this he again follows Janet Adelman's suggestive reading of this play), Coriolanus's numbness to the humanity of others in all its frailty and limitation offers us further instruction about our experience of theatre. The audience's need for openness to the ordeals of tragic agonists is a central part of what Hamlet calls "the purpose of playing." Coriolanus's unyielding nature exemplifies the premature rigor mortis of a sensibility that cannot recognize aspects of itself in compelling drama, and in return, we withhold our sympathy at this unnatural spectacle of his final submission. Cavell further emphasizes that Shakespeare's play shows the nourishment a community might receive from the blood of such a sacrifice, especially because it takes place near Rome. Though Christianity still lies far in the future, it will ultimately find its Western home there.

Fred Astaire and Racial Differences

This refusal of acknowledgment runs throughout Cavell's writing as a central theme. It is symptomatic of skepticism, which turns disappointment with what criteria of knowledge we have into destructive denial of what we cannot fail somehow to know. Cavell finds its tragic consequences in Shakespearean drama and Hollywood melodrama, and he finds its overcoming in Hollywood comedies of remarriage. Emerson articulates the receptiveness necessary for such overcoming, but he is well aware of our tragic fallibility in this regard. Moreover, a ready heart too easily trusted entails its own risks. Cavell seeks to dramatize the most obvious hazards of such a disposition at its most dim-witted by relating the anecdote of the credulous yokel who rushes on stage to rescue Desdemona from the black man's murderous grip.[46] This Southern gull has forgotten the difference between art and life, and Cavell's critics have also accused him of obliviousness in this regard. Michael Bristol takes particular issue with precisely that anecdote by locating it in a nineteenth-century context where taboos against miscegenation could turn *Othello* into a cautionary tale against interracial marriage and those who violated such taboos could face mortal consequences.[47] The play's operative instruction in such settings had become thoroughly racialized. The yokel in question would still not know the difference between life and art, but his behavior would be symptomatic of a social reality that exploited fear of the alleged violence of black men, and the consequent fear of mixed marriage, to maintain inequalities between the races as the status quo.

Cavell's alleged shortcomings in this regard appear most controversially in his repeated engagement with the figure of Fred Astaire in *The Band Wagon* (1953). Cavell first touches upon this film anonymously in

The World Viewed, and I will quote the paragraph in full. Though it is only the middle, or fourth, sentence that evokes this film, the context is relevant. It is meditation upon human finitude.

> The nostalgia of old photographs is the perception that mortality is at some point to be stopped in its tracks. The figures in them seem so vulnerable, so unknowing of what we know about them, of the knowledge in store for them. We could know this about ourselves, if we could turn the force of nostalgia toward an anticipation of the fact that every moment is always stopped from every other. In the very vulnerability of that embarrassed laugh, in the tilt of the hat, in the way the foot is turned, in the dust that lies on the shoe or in its hopeful shine, in the crook of the arm where the baby nods, the knowledge of mortality has room to live, even jauntily. There is no better place for the knowledge. The roundness of clocks is convenient, but it naturally misleads us about something clocks tell, because its hands repossess their old positions every day and every night. The reels on a projector, like the bulbs of an hourglass, repeat something else: that as the past fills up, the future thins; and that the end, already there against the axle, when the time comes for its running, seems to pick up speed.[48]

The endorsement of jauntiness in the face of our potential knowledge of human finitude—what we "*could* know . . . about ourselves" (emphasis added)—bespeaks the liveliness that epitomizes so much of Cavell's work, even in his forthright engagement of the grimmer aspects of experience. As William Rothman and Marian Keane explain, the possibility of such knowledge offers no guarantee that we will seek it, and the gist of Cavell's thought exposes our habits of willful denial. Indeed, "what we could know is not something we simply fail to know, but something so obvious we cannot simply fail to know it, something we keep ourselves from knowing."[49]

The artful quality of Cavell's *contemplatio mortis* may give us pause and make us wonder if the pleasures of such writing come at a hidden cost. The intensity of the figurative language, especially in the final two sentences, may raise the suspicion of self-indulgence, a charge soon to come against Cavell's philosophical writing in *The Claim of Reason.* But I feel gratitude for the experimental nature of this entire project. The writing of *The World Viewed* required daring in taking film as a subject worthy of philosophical reflection, and its ambition to make such reflection immediately engaging in its own terms handsomely pays off. More than a quarter of a century ago, the academic study of film was in its infancy; and such writing about movies as had staying power, like James Agee's, deployed literary craft with open enthusiasm and emulation for the enviable vitality that film itself so compellingly possesses. As Rothman and Keane amply demonstrate, Cavell skillfully makes his words count in these sentences in ways that repay our closest attention. To borrow a phrase of Cavell's in this chapter, those words can cut their knowledge into an alert reader unforgettably.

Cavell returns to the opening scenes of *The Band Wagon* over a quarter of a century later, first in his presidential address at the annual meeting of the Eastern Division of the American Philosophical Association in December of 1996 and then in his 1998 Spinoza Lectures.[50] Cavell's account of the first two numbers in this musical represents Astaire's progress from melancholy, as a sign of skepticism, in the first of them, "By Myself," to its ecstatic overcoming in the second, "A Shine on Your Shoes." It is a progress from a ghostly haunting of the world to a recovery of the ground beneath his feet and the habitation of his body. The film as a whole tells a story "about making a comeback" or "going back to beginnings," as Cavell describes some of the films he mentions in the chapter of *The World Viewed* which includes his reflections on how the nostalgia of old photographs can instruct us about mortality and how we can live with that knowledge "even jauntily," like Fred Astaire. Cavell's most recent accounts of *The Band Wagon* have met with cogent criticism from Robert Gooding-Williams.[51]

Gooding-Williams explores the two opening routines in telling detail of the sort that distinguishes Cavell's readings of film from the beginning, and he thus challenges Cavell at one of his strongest points as an interpreter of film, his meticulous examination of particular cases. Gooding-Williams's careful attention to the ways in which the film racializes the crucial moods of melancholy and ecstatic recovery reveals a color-coding that Cavell does not touch upon in the first routine. In Cavell's treatment of the second routine, "A Shine on Your Shoes," Gooding-Williams notes that Cavell's return to this number in his first Spinoza lecture "presents criticism of the second routine that declares a ground for finding pleasure in it and praising it *notwithstanding* the conditions of injustice (of white America's unjust appropriation of black culture) it depicts. That judgment and that ground, [Cavell] tells us, is that Astaire's dance of praise, because it affords a 'glimpse of Utopia' that contests the unjust conditions it depicts, is not itself vain."[52]

Cavell's characterizes this glimpse of Utopia as traumatic, and that characterization is of a piece with his mention of the film's depiction of unjust conditions. Gooding-Williams's emphatic "notwithstanding" indicates prominently the daunting odds against which Cavell must make his admittedly rebukeable claim. Moreover, Cavell argues that the second routine intentionally risks its own undoing by the boldly self-conscious way in which "A Shine on Your Shoes" openly deploys the word "shine," a hateful term for a person of color. Cavell is thus recounting a fresh version of his original argument about acknowledgment and avoidance, which, in different ways, also figures in his meditation upon mortality in his earliest reference to *The Band Wagon,* in *The World Viewed,* and in his earliest essay on Shakespeare, "The Avoidance of Love: A Reading of *King Lear.*" The possibility of living with the knowledge of mortality, and even living jauntily, requires first of all our clear acknowledgment of this unsettling aspect of our condition, which we otherwise flee and thus deny. Similarly, in *The Band Wagon,* the acknowledgment of suffering and tragedy serves as a precondition for Astaire's recovery of the motive for dance.

Gooding-Williams argues that Astaire's recovery of his feet and his body, his reincarnation after a ghostly interlude of haunting his life, depends upon reductive and distorting myths of black masculinity and their strategic deployment by the director of *The Band Wagon,* Vincent Minelli. Minelli embeds Astaire's performance within a semiotics of racial difference that includes both the melodrama of *King Kong,* the black beast who threatens a white woman with violence, and the comedy of channeling that force, via the minstrelsy of blackface or a shine on your shoes, into the happy ending of recovered vitality after a spell of suspended animation. Thus, Astaire's initial comeback or return to origins depends upon racial stereotypes that ultimately underwrite an act of cultural "identity theft." His recovery depends upon an appropriation of the art of tap-dancing as it was practiced and perfected by African Americans who are superficially and prejudicially represented in the opening scenes of *The Band Wagon.*

Cavell has a great deal at stake in this response to his reading of Fred Astaire's performance, which, as Gooding-Williams also shows, includes a scene of perfectionist instruction. The revitalized dancer becomes a model for a boy who finds himself drawn to the lively antics of Fred Astaire in the arcade and keeps reappearing to gaze with rapt interest upon this engaging man. As such an exemplar, he would serve to lead the boy on the next leg of his journey to his unattained but attainable self, a self, which, given the terms of Astaire's reanimation, offers "the promise of a white manhood redeemed through the appropriation of black masculinity, a promise that is as dated as America's antebellum tradition of blackface minstrelsy."[53] Since Cavell's explicit embrace of perfectionism initially seeks to justify it as a legitimate form of critique within a democracy, this debased form of that philosophical practice may seem to threaten its acceptability; but Cavell has previously acknowledged the existence of manifold instances of debased forms of perfectionism, especially in American advertising, whose presence does not undermine the validity of this mode of moral response altogether.[54]

Much of Cavell's argument hangs upon the difference between an homage and an appropriation, and Gooding-Williams's reading of this particular case seeks to demonstrate the degree to which the opening routines in *The Band Wagon* resist Cavell's vision of them as an homage. However, the ostentatious and extraneous etymologizing ("'dis-seminate'") with which Gooding-Williams makes his apparently strongest point suggests a forced touch of moral triumphalism. The word he highlights with quotation marks and Latinizing hyphenization appears nowhere in *The Band Wagon* or in Cavell's writings about that movie. Tracing the origins of its entry into Gooding-Williams's argument would lead us back (at least) to Derrida, and it would be quite another and quite a different story from the one we behold on screen (perhaps something like the story of the Trojan Horse). Ostensibly, Gooding-Williams's importation of this word and his special emphasis upon its constituent parts serve to heighten our awareness of a sexual aspect in the alleged unworthiness of Astaire's appropriation of African American dancing, which Gooding-Williams seeks to expose. Perhaps anxiety about taking sides in a political argument about the pervasiveness of racism hobbles our confidence in ordinary language, if not common sense, and we cannot help accepting such a reductive judgment despite what it overlooks. Figuratively, Gooding-Williams's argument seems to claim that Leroy Daniels ejaculates on ("seminates") Fred Astaire's shoes, and this sexual deposit engenders a little man ("homunculus"), the new Fred Astaire/ Tony Hunter. A procreative fantasy of single-sex miscegenation on the shoeshine stand gives rise to a freshly animated hoofer who can now dance with both passion and aplomb, a talent that this particular man has demonstrated in previous films but seems to have lost as *The Band Wagon* opens. And he now can do so with an African American partner. His recovery, Gooding-Williams suggests, solely derives from this African American incubus in the Forty-second Street arcade.

But pervasiveness is not absoluteness, as the "dis" in "disseminate" indicates by signifying the dispersal or widespread sowing of seed. Even directorial racism is subject to the conditions of the medium it seeks to manipulate and control. Film can record more than Minelli meant. The moving pictures of these two individuals on this unique occasion record what Cavell experiences and persuasively describes as a breakthrough moment, a brief but ecstatic connection between one person and another, a person of color and a white man, before the world as we customarily know it reappears to keep them apart. Such a moment puts in its place the context of its occurrence as ultimately *not* the absolute determinant of whatever goes on between these two dancers. Such a moment happens in time, but it also can alter time and the pressure of history as we routinely understand their import. Such a moment does not necessarily trick us into ignoring the mortifying history of American racism or this film's collusion with that potentially death-dealing legacy. Rather, Cavell argues, it precisely acknowledges that history, and daringly so. Then it moves on. Cavell thus hopes against hope that such a moment can help us to begin *our* history anew in a way that includes, rather than leaves out, the truth about the past, as well as another possible "truth": the promise of change for the better in the future as it is now unfolding. But we must first believe in that possibility before we can understand it, as with other recognitions of hope and of despair that works of art can enable us to experience.

Gooding-Williams's reading also contains some minor features, evident in the footnotes rather than the body of the text, that warrant notice in regard to Cavell's concern with doing philosophy in a democracy, because they clearly reveal his characteristic openness to conversation even when it attacks his own position. Cavell honors the importance of the friend in perfectionist dialogue by hearing him out and responding, and thus he accepts the friend as a "beautiful enemy," the role in which Emerson casts him.[55] Gooding-Williams's essay itself depends upon his possession of Cavell's then unpublished Spinoza lecture, "Praise as Identification: At Moments in Henry James and Fred Astaire," and he graciously acknowledges Cavell's generosity in giving it to him. Gooding-Williams also attributes a point he makes about the incest motif in *The Band Wagon* to Cavell's drawing his attention to this phenomenon in that film via an email communication. Thus, Gooding-Williams's somewhat compelling rebuke depends in good part on Cavell's actively inviting that response, which Cavell himself makes clear through the Kantian terminology of aesthetic judgment that he uses to articulate the status of the claims he is entering about this movie.

The Oldest Profession

"To philosophize is to learn how to die." So runs the ancient dictum that Cavell has evoked on occasion. You might call it philosophy's oldest profession and the call to begin philosophy ever anew. It can rouse us from dogmatic slumbers and save us from distractions whose illusory urgency can rob us of the time of our lives. Cavell's preoccupation with the "pathos of the autonomous private subject," for whom awareness of personal finitude generates just such emotions, has given rise to criticism, as though this concern with individuals precludes alertness to political issues and reveals Cavell's blindness in this regard.[56] His advocates have sought to demonstrate otherwise, as has Cavell in his engagement with the question of elitism and the suitability of perfectionism as a democratic mode of thought.[57]

With the help of Fred Astaire, Cavell has undertaken the spiritual exercise of meditating upon the end of life in a context other than that of *The Band Wagon*'s opening routine.[58] However, his account of "Let's Face the Music and Dance" in *Follow the Fleet* (1936) repeats a pattern of thought discernible in his readings of Astaire's transformation in the passage from melancholy to ecstasy that he undergoes from "By Myself" to "A Shine on Your Shoes" in the 1953 movie. According to Cavell the later film's second song and dance "faces the music," or acknowledges the harsh reality of racism, by coming down hard on the word "shine." It means to emphasize the worst, not to exorcise it. That would be a happy outcome, but Cavell does not claim such powers either for the film or for philosophy. However, this emphasis at least acknowledges the legacy of injustice that Cavell's "traumatic glimpse of Utopia" seeks to offer some hope of overcoming. It also celebrates the human capacity to dance and the ecstasy that it represents, despite the undeniably tragic elements of our experience—to dance *not* by turning obliviously away from tragedy but by acknowledging it and finding the grace to move along, even jauntily.

Sometimes, despite larger ambitions and more utopian dreams, the best we can do may be to avoid whistling in the dark by acknowledging the evils that lurk in a world where we still mean to pursue happiness. Keeping those dreams alive in the face of despair, hoping against hope, is a part of the scholar's calling that Cavell seeks honestly to inherit from Emerson. But, if it is the office of the scholar to raise and to cheer, it is certainly not the only office of such a calling. That office also requires the ability to distinguish between "a cheerfulness that genuinely cheers" and false versions of that sort of sentimental education.[59] The Jeremiad rarely suits Cavell's mode or mood as a writer, however; for polemics shut down philosophical exchange and the benefits it can offer. Cavell seeks conversation in the conviction that philosophy can bring us peace. Gooding-Williams points out significant details that Cavell overlooks in reading *The Band Wagon,* and he thus hobbles somewhat Cavell's hopeful claims about "A Shine on Your Shoes." Those hopes, however, can be included in a city of words whose powers of provocation constitute a way of participating in politics.[60] They can and should become part of a conversation in which we better envision a just city where all can pursue happiness without fetters of any kind.

I can remember (a phrase that the pathos of finitude prompts us all to use increasingly as time goes by) sitting in the backyard of Steven Affeldt's pleasant summer rental in Sante Fe, New Mexico, on the evening of July 31, 2003, with a group of colleagues from the NEH Emerson Institute that Russell Goodman and Steven organized at St. John's College that summer. Most of us had met there on Thursday evenings during that month to discuss Cavell's essays on Emerson. Russell and Steven were there, as were about ten others, including our special guest at that time, Cornel West. We were talking about Cavell's second essay on Emerson's "Fate," to which Gooding-Williams turns his attention at the close of his essay on Cavell on Astaire. As Gooding-Williams notes, Cavell's essay questions Emerson's worrisome silence on the issue of slavery in "Fate" and expresses his fear that Emerson's critics, like John Updike and Harold Bloom, may find here some evidence for their view that Emerson "gave up hope on democracy." Despite Cavell's effort "to follow out the consequences of finding in Emerson the founding of American thinking—the consequence, for example, that his thought is repressed in the culture he founded—the irony of discovering that this repressed thinking has given up on the hope and demand for a nation of the self-governing" would be "harder than [Cavell] could digest."[61]

Cavell answers the question of Emerson's silence by stressing his desire to "preserve philosophy in the face of conditions that negate philosophy," and those are the conditions that give rise to the particular kind of writing that Emerson refuses to practice in "Fate," the polemic. In Santa Fe, during our discussion of this essay and of Cavell's essay about it, some expressed impatience with Emerson—and with Cavell—for the silence and for its defense, respectively; and they expressed their desire for a more robust political intervention from both of the philosophers under discussion. As the conversation took this turn, I mentioned my own awareness of the active role that Cavell had played in attempting (unsuccessfully) to introduce a thorough and rigorous program in film studies at Harvard and in supporting (successfully) the creation of a program in women's studies there. The film scholar William Rothman readily affirmed the first part of my contention before Cornel West made this addendum to my examples of efforts on Cavell's part to open up philosophical conversations and make them more inclusive of neglected voices, "If it wasn't for Stanley Cavell, there would never have been African American Studies at Harvard." Thus, when Gooding-Williams claims that he is less interested in the question of Emerson's silence and more concerned with another question, which he asks in this way—"What would it mean to expand the horizon of consequences that Cavell follows out to include a hearkening to African American voices in tracing out the significance of Emerson's philosophical legacy?"—I think I know that Cavell would gladly support his quest for such an expansion of the horizon and greater inclusiveness of other voices.

While Cavell has frankly (and humorously) expressed his little relish in "conducting his education in public" he has, at the same time, acknowledged his greater dislike of "the alternatives [he has seen]."[62] Would that more of us had the courage and good will to do so! When he reissued his early books of the seventies—that decisive decade during which his thought turned in the direction of Emerson and Hollywood movies and he also wrote his essay on *Othello*—Cavell sought to correct several errors of memory and a significant misjudgment. In the enlarged edition of *The World Viewed* he returned to his wish *not* "to disguise the liabilities of the spirit in which the work was written" and rehearsed the mistaken recollections that appear in his accounts of *Mr. Smith Goes to Washington, The Philadelphia Story,* and *His Girl Friday,* and the "more galling error . . . in [his] reading of the final frames of *Rules of the Game.*"[63] This catalogue of documentable errors teaches us not only that formal academic film study was just then beginning and VCRs, DVDs, etc. were still in the future but also that Cavell is interested in knowledge as it relates to human minds, like yours or mine or his, not the quest for certainty that omits the human subject from the process of knowing. In his first essay on Emerson, which appears in the expanded edition of *The Senses of Walden,* Cavell confessed some embarrassment because of the way he had dismissed Emerson in that book and his fresh realization that Emerson too was interested in that sort of knowledge where the difference between subject and object does not decisively obtain and an epistemology of moods underwrites our claims and propositions.

Cavell's steady effort to engage in conversations that further the mutual intelligibility of our shareable, if not common, culture, may have its lapses, as he would readily acknowledge and has often sought to correct. From some perspectives, whose honest expression necessarily imparts their inevitable partiality, it may also produce what seems "an economy of the same" such as occasions Gooding-Williams's dismay. Thus, his intention "to include a hearkening to African American voices in tracing out the significance of Emerson's philosophical legacy" could beneficially alter Cavell's Emersonian project. That project itself remains challenging, if not highly questionable, as Lawrence Buell indicates, via the interrogative mood of a chapter title in his compendious *Emerson,* "Emerson as a Philosopher?" In this regard, Stephen Mulhall goes even further when he writes about "the case for Emerson as a serious philosopher" in a review of *Emerson's Transcendental Etudes.* Though Mulhall is very much in sympathy with Cavell's project, he initially remarks that "[it] is hard to say whether [Cavell's] claim will seem more obviously ludicrous in the United States or in Europe."[64] This idea of Emerson as a philosopher clearly makes people wonder about its aptness as a characterization. Is he a philosopher or did he open a path for Americans to avoid philosophy altogether and thus overcome the doldrums of epistemology, if not tragedy? The open exercise of our freedom to wonder about such issues strikes me as the best of examples of what philosophy in a democracy can, and should, do. Wherever the frontier may lie between an economy of the same and one of difference, the charting of that territory nowadays will do well to hearken to Stanley Cavell and the manifold ways in which he has made philosophy available as a resource in the democratic consideration of such important matters.

Also, this notion of "an economy of the same" does require the assumption of a rather standoffish perspective that emphasizes the otherness of the point of view taken. Call it "Africanist," as does Gooding-Williams, or "feminist," as does Kelly Oliver, whom he is following; but it still amounts to standing outside and labeling all those others within that economy as assimilated, if not simply *the same.* They are made the same by yielding to the pressure of this economy within which they find themselves and outside which Gooding-Williams and Oliver stand as aloof and disapproving spectators. In a way Cavell has already addressed the traumatic nature of this process of assimilation in his reading of *Stella Dallas,* an interpretation that goes against the grain of feminist views of this film and the undiscerning sameness of the stories of victimization that they routinely tell. Cavell, however, finds in Stella a strong sentiment of resistance and he grounds that refusal to comply on her Emersonian claiming of her own existence. Thus, it is well to recall that such a claim, honestly made, will discover (if *any* claim will), through its partiality and insistence upon the particularity of individual cases, the grounds of mutual intelligibility and recognition of shared identity.

In the completeness of Gooding-Williams's rejection of Astaire's dance with the black shoeshine man (Leroy Daniels) in *The Band Wagon,* Cavell discerns nothing less than a denial of Astaire's right to exist, a threat not so much to his being as to his having unforeseeably become what he is by claiming his existence in that very dance with that particular man on that specific occasion. As Emerson warns us, "This one fact the world hates, that the soul *becomes,*" and unless we can overcome that way of the world (in ourselves first of all), we resist this becoming because it unsettles our sense of control whether we are directing or watching this film.[65] The absoluteness of Gooding-Williams's refusal of this moment's accomplishment in this movie leaves no room, none at all, for what Cavell perceives as a "breakthrough" such as can occur on film despite the most minutely organized intentions to the contrary of the director, Vincent Minnelli, or a host of others exerting an influence on what we see on screen in that film. These two men, Astaire and Daniels, dance in the face of the camera, and what happens is unforeseeable. The film tells us this dance cannot yet continue outside the arcade in the "proud land" of which Forty-second Street is a well known part; we cannot now realize *this* "new yet unapproachable America." But, if you have eyes to see, it does happen briefly and it does happen here; and the soul claps hands to behold this "traumatic glimpse of utopia," a "small 'we,'" momentarily discovered and preserved on film to be projected and rediscovered in the eye of the beholder who admits its occurrence and lets it stand for our humanity despite the tragic legacy that haunts any such vision and should not be denied.

In writing about *It Happened One Night* over a quarter of a century ago, Cavell felt obliged to acknowledge his awareness that he may seem to be courting outrageousness by using the thought of Kant and Wittgenstein on skepticism to discuss a popular Hollywood movie. When Gooding-Williams simply asserts that, "*The Band Wagon*'s depiction of a melancholy song-and-dance man very clearly echoes Nietzsche's portrait of the sublime hero," he shows how far we have come in discussing film and philosophy from the felt need for preoccupations such as Cavell's in reading *It Happened One Night.* Is this a good thing? Edward Rothstein expresses doubts about the nature of this whole project in his *New York*

Times review of Cavell's *Cities of Words* without even acknowledging the struggles Cavell himself has often entered over this issue.[66] Is Gooding-Williams, as quoted above, an unconscious inheritor of ways of thinking that he owes in good part to such efforts by Cavell, whose writing about *The Band Wagon* he is setting out to criticize for its misinterpretation of two particular scenes? If we pursue this line of inquiry, is it at all relevant to ask whether Vincente Minnelli or Fred Astaire had been reading *Thus Spoke Zarathustra* in the early fifties? Probably not, though we are free to wonder. But it is to the point to remember that, in discussing Capra's classic, Cavell was using Wittgenstein to talk about our being held captive by a picture and Kant to discuss the problem of representing the noumenal realm and, specifically, the kingdom of ends. Kant deems its representation impossible, and Cavell disagrees because he saw it in re-marriage comedy, though he wants to add a condition to his claim. Yes, it can be represented, but its representation instructs us that we cannot get there alone. The meet and happy conversation among equals in such films as *It Happened One Night* is a sign of a world we can share with mutual regard for the well being of one another. In a democratic philosophy, however, we may do well *not* to call that world a kingdom or a realm, but rather a community, an eventual community, worthy of our highest aspirations and our best efforts to achieve it. Momentarily and traumatically, Cavell catches a glimpse of that utopia in *The Band Wagon,* and it is an adequate cause for singing and dancing, the other side of our suffering and the promised reward of our patience and persistence.

Emerson may sometimes stress polarity, but he does not diagnose an incurably pathological bipolarity in which the emphasis falls upon separateness to the exclusion of the possibility of reunion. Cavell finds a figure for that reunion in what he calls remarriage and in the dance of Astaire and Daniels in *The Band Wagon.* Likewise, Cavell's meditations upon tragedy stress the traumatic force with which an awareness of separateness and isolation can dawn upon the protagonists of such dramas despite their proneness to disown such knowledge. But his most utopian rebuke of American failures to achieve a "more perfect union" envisions that achievement as a process of getting *back* together or getting together *again* after a painful break in which differences are of necessity acknowledged and rehearsed. There is no guarantee of this outcome, and certainly no guarantee of its permanence, if it occurs at all. Moreover, as Cavell has shown us, the melodrama of the unknown woman is a Hollywood genre that specifically, indeed necessarily, explores the failure to achieve such a happy ending. Cavell's desire to raise and cheer us with the prospect of such a reunion may partially impair his overall view of the context in which "A Shine on Your Shoes" takes place in *The Band Wagon*. Gooding-Williams thus has good reason to challenge that view. But Cavell's response to Gooding-Williams's rebuke of his reading of the second scene in *The Band Wagon* memorably takes its measure and exposes its absoluteness with regard to his key perception.

"Perception," as Emerson remarks, "is not whimsical but fatal";[67] and Cavell has duly followed out his perception in his exchange with Gooding-Williams, providing a further tuition for his prior intuition about the dance of Astaire and Daniels in *The Band Wagon*. Their exchange can be taken as an exemplary hearkening to African American voices and an early installment in a further conversation about Emerson that fully includes such voices, as both parties to this present exchange clearly wish. Cavell's recuperation of Emerson as an occasion for such democratic conversations should assure us that we not only have much to discuss, we also have the means to continue such discussions productively. "To hazard a contradiction," Emerson wrote during the gathering storm of sectional division and the debate over slavery, "freedom is necessary."[68] It is a virtual bumper sticker for abolition in an essay where the hope for civil conversation is struggling to stay alive and resist the absoluteness of polemics and, ultimately, the violence of war. Philosophy thus seeks to speak truth and bring peace even in the verbal combat zone where the strife of argument threatens to explode into physical conflict and bloodshed. Not surprisingly, Emerson's philosophy turns to literature and becomes a poetry of ideas, as it remains in memorable stretches of Cavell's writing almost a century and a half later.

They are too numerous to count, but what counts is the turn and the need for it in Cavell's effort to make as clear as possible what he feels called upon to say. When Cavell uses Emerson in his effort to discuss Hollywood comedy, he acknowledges that he discerns in Kierkegaard a kindred spirit in what he calls "the perception of the sublime in the everyday."[69] Early in his writing career, when Walker Percy was publishing philosophical articles in academic journals, he also felt this need for literature and turned to writing fiction. Moreover, he responded precisely to this same sense of affinity with Kierkegaard's "perception of the sublime in the everyday." *The Moviegoer* was the first harvestable fruit of that turn in the form of a novel. When it is reaching a conclusion, as we saw at the end of the last chapter, the narrator and protagonist, Binx Bolling, arrives at the limits of his capacity to say what he cannot help wondering about: the presence of an African American man at the church near his basement apartment in Gentilly. Listen to this fuller excerpt of that moment in Percy's prose:

> It is impossible to say why he is here. Is it part and parcel of the complex business of coming up in the world? Or is it because he believes that God himself is present here at the corner of Elysian Fields and Bons Enfants? Or is he here for both reasons: through some dim dazzling trick of grace: coming for the one and receiving the other as God's own importunate bonus?
>
> It is impossible to say.[70]

Binx is looking at what came to be called, with greater and greater emphasis, a black man, in the decade following the publication of *The Moviegoer* and the rise of the "black power" movement. Thus, you might say, he is a man like Leroy Daniels, if that is what you want to single out about them. And why shouldn't it be? Certainly Binx is attending to that fact about him, his color, and the problem of perception that it raises: whether he has received the ashes in the church he has just emerged from on that day, Ash Wednesday, when the novel completes its week-long stretch of narrative time. Then, in its few remaining pages, the novel turns to another problem, the same problem it began with: the death of a brother or, if you will, the pathos of finitude.

What Cavell is saying about Fred Astaire and Leroy Daniels can serve as an answer to Binx's skeptical questions. It is what Binx stops short of saying, which, minus the Godtalk, is, "Yes," and again, "Yes," to all three questions; and it has everything to do with finitude, the evanescent moments of our lives, and the possibilities of community within them. Of course, there is plenty of room for disagreement about this, but in the meantime we know where Cavell stands.

NOTES

Notes to Introduction: Beyond Adaptation

1. Stanley Cavell, "Foreword: An Audience for Philosophy," in *Must We Mean What We Say?* (Cambridge: Cambridge University Press, 1976), xvii–xxix.

2. Ralph Waldo Emerson, "Self-Reliance," in *Emerson: Essays and Poems,* ed. Joel Porte, college ed. (New York: Library of America, 1996), 259–82, 262, 261.

3. Henry David Thoreau, *Walden and Resistance to Civil Government,* 2d ed., Norton Critical Ed. (New York: Norton, 1992), 216.

4. Stanley Cavell, *Disowning Knowledge in Seven Plays of Shakespeare,* updated ed. (Cambridge: Cambridge University Press, 2003), x.

5. Ralph Ellison, *Shadow and Act* (New York: Random House, 1964), 152, xii–xiii, 7.

6. The best of these books include Timothy Gould, *Hearing Things: Voice and Method in the Writing of Stanley Cavell* (Chicago: University of Chicago Press, 1998); Richard Eldridge, ed., *Stanley Cavell* (Cambridge: Cambridge University Press, 2003); Michael Fischer, *Stanley Cavell and Literary Skepticism* (Chicago: University of Chicago Press, 1989); Russell Goodman, ed., *Contending with Stanley Cavell* (Oxford: Oxford University Press, 2005); Stephen Mulhall, *Stanley Cavell: Philosophy's Recounting of the Ordinary* (Oxford: Clarendon Press, 1994).

7. The lectures for this course are collected in Stanley Cavell, *Cities of Words: Pedagogical Letters on a Register of the Moral Life* (Cambridge: Harvard University Press, 2004). See also Stanley Cavell, "Staying the Course," Introduction to *Conditions Handsome and Unhandsome: The Constitution of Emersonian Perfectionism* (Chicago: University of Chicago Press, 1990), 1–32.

8. Cavell, *Cities of Words,* 421–43.

9. The Harvard Archives at Pusey Library contain syllabi, exams, correspondence, and many other documents relevant to Cavell's teaching in both the Program in General Education and the Core Curriculum at Harvard.

10. Harry Berger, *Making Trifles of Terrors: Redistributing Complicities in Shake-speare* (Stanford: Stanford University Press, 1997), xii; Richard P. Wheeler, "Acknowledging Shakespeare: Cavell and the Claim of the Human," in *The Senses of Stanley Cavell,* ed. Richard Fleming and Michael Payne (Lewisburg, Pa.: Bucknell University Press, 1989), 132–60.

11. David Lee Miller, *Dreams of the Burning Child: Sacrificial Sons and the Father's Witness* (Ithaca: Cornell University Press, 2003), 95–98; Stephen Orgel, introduction to *The Winter's Tale,* by William Shakespeare (Oxford: Oxford University Press, 1996), 1–83, 32–34.

12. Cavell, *Disowning Knowledge,* xiv.

13. John Joughin, ed., "Philosophical Shakespeares: An Introduction," in *Philosophical Shakespeares* (London: Routledge, 2000), 1–17.

14. See Garrett Stewart, "The Avoidance of Cavell," in *Contending with Stanley Cavell,* 140–56.

15. Tania Modleski, *Critical Inquiry* 16 (autumn 1990): 237–38. Diane Stevenson is working on an essay about the feminist reception of Cavell's work in film studies, parts of which she has presented at conferences in Tallahassee, Florida, and Columbia, South Carolina. She shared a version of it with me that abounds in comparable examples.

16. Richard Halpern, *Shakespeare Among the Moderns* (Ithaca: Cornell University Press, 1997), 107 n. 123.

17. Stanley Cavell, "The Philosopher in American Life," in *Emerson's Transcendental Etudes,* ed. David Justin Hodge (Stanford: Stanford University Press, 2003), 33–58.

18. Fischer, *Stanley Cavell and Literary Skepticism,* 3–4, 144–45 n. 6.

19. Richard Rorty, *Truth and Progress: Philosophical Papers* (Cambridge: Cambridge University Press, 1997), 3:46–47. In summarizing what ultimately matters about his reluctance to find in Emerson an unambiguous precursor to American pragmatism, Cavell suggests, "It may come to a difference [between Cavell and those who unhesitatingly deem Emerson a protopragmatist] no less deep than how one thinks of human nature." Further, Cavell raises this question: "What would be lost in America's knowledge of itself if it lost the acuity of hearing its transcendental voice?" See *Contending with Stanley Cavell,* 171.

20. See Robert Frost, "The Gift Outright," in *The Complete Poems of Robert Frost* (New York: Holt, Rinehart and Winston, 1949), 467.

21. Cavell, *Must We Mean What We Say?* 238–66.

22. Stephen Greenblatt, *Shakespearean Negotiations* (Oxford: Clarendon Press, 1988), 20.

23. Cavell, *Disowning Knowledge,* 244.

24. Emerson, "Shakespeare; or, the Poet," in *Essays and Poems,* 710–26, 715.

25. Emerson, "Montaigne; or, The Skeptic," in *Essays and Poems,* 690–709, 697.

26. It is ironic, in this regard, that feminist critic Toril Moi, in her recent reflections upon Simone de Beauvoir's career as a philosopher, has taken inspiration from Cavell's work to understand how de Beauvoir could speak, as a woman, with universality and necessity—and, of course, with the possibility of being wrong and making mistakes. The legacy of Kantian morality abides in these contested concepts—universality and necessity—which Emerson sometimes voices as features of the moral sentiment, the meaning Cavell gives to the Emersonian notion of genius. See Moi, *What Is a Woman? and Other Essays* (Oxford: Oxford University Press, 1999).

27. Cavell, *Disowning Knowledge,* 238.

28. Ibid., 223.

29. Stanley Cavell, *Contesting Tears: The Hollywood Melodrama of the Unknown Woman* (Chicago: University of Chicago Press, 1996), 69.

30. Though initially published two years apart, these essays derive from virtually the same moment. I remember hearing Cavell's *Macbeth* essay as the Bluestone lecture at the University of Massachusetts (Boston) in the spring of 1988, the year the *Gaslight* essay originally appeared. Indeed, Cavell refers to the *Macbeth* essay directly on two occasions in the introduction to *Contesting Tears* (14, 27) and thus makes clear the congruent angles of vision that characterize both of these projects.

31. Cavell, *Contesting Tears,* 14.

32. Stephen Greenblatt, ed., introduction to *Macbeth,* in *The Norton Shakespeare* (New York: Norton, 2000), 2558.

33. Cavell, *Contesting Tears,* 60.

34. Ibid., vii.

35. Cavell, "The Philosopher in American Life," in *Emerson's Transcendental Etudes,* 33–58, 45.

36. The influence of Michel Foucault on early modern studies has especially underwritten such arguments, where power overwhelms the sense of individual identity. Foucault's influence on Stephen Greenblatt's *Renaissance Self-Fashioning: From More to Shakespeare* (Chicago: University of Chicago Press, 1983) is a prominent example of this development. Greenblatt's renewed interest in biography indicates his turn away from such lines of thought, as does the emphasis on "care of the self" in the later Foucault. That aspect of Foucault's thought bears pertinent resemblances to moral perfectionism in both Emerson and Cavell.

37. Cavell, *Contesting Tears,* 51.

38. Nowhere is this more pervasively apparent than in a long letter Cavell wrote in 1981 in response to the initial rejection of his proposal to teach a course in Harvard's recently created Core Curriculum. That course was to include weekly film screenings, and Cavell felt especially moved to defend this dimension of his proposed course. Obviously, he was caught off guard by the rejection and thus put on the defensive, so he makes his strongest claims in what he deems their most powerful form. For Cavell, film at its best warrants the esteem granted

to Shakespeare, and it as fully rewards careful study as does Shakespeare. Thus, it has a similar claim upon centrality in an updated curriculum.

39. Cavell, *Cities of Words,* 438.

40. Stanley Cavell, "What Becomes of Things on Film?," in *Themes out of School: Effects and Causes* (San Francisco: North Point Press, 1984), 173–83, 175.

41. Stanley Cavell, *The World Viewed: Reflections on the Ontology of Film,* enl. ed. (Cambridge: Harvard University Press, 1979), 22.

42. Emerson, "Experience," in *Essays and Poems,* 471–92, 479. Cavell finds in Harry Berger, Jr., a kindred critical spirit in this regard. See "Reading Harry Berger," *Shakespeare Studies* 27 (1999): 65–73, 66–67.

43. W. H. Auden, "The Shield of Achilles," in *Collected Shorter Poems, 1927–1957* (London: Faber and Faber Limited, 1966), 294–95.

44. John Milton, "The Doctrine and Discipline of Divorce," in *John Milton: Complete Poems and Major Prose,* ed. Merritt Y. Hughes (Indianapolis: The Odyssey Press, 1957), 700.

45. William Rothman and Marian Keane, *Reading Cavell's* The World Viewed*: A Philosophical Perspective on Film* (Detroit: Wayne State University Press, 2000), 26. In *Disclosure of the Everyday: Undramatic Achievement in Narrative Film* (Trowbridge, Wiltshire, England: Flick Books, 2000), 5 n. 2, Andrew Klevan acknowledges the pervasive presence in his book of Cavell's work on film by making a kindred observation about its lack of recognition by film scholars in Britain.

46. E. Ann Kaplan, review of *Contesting Tears,* by Stanley Cavell, *Film Quarterly* 52.1 (fall 1998): 77–81, 80; Maria DiBattista, *Fast-Talking Dames* (New Haven: Yale University Press, 2001); David R. Shumway, "Mystifying Marriage," in *Modern Love: Romance, Intimacy, and the Marriage Crisis* (New York: New York University Press, 2003), 89–100.

47. Flannery O'Connor, *Wise Blood,* in *Collected Works* (New York: Library of America, 1988), 34.

48. Paul Tillich, *The Courage to Be* (New Haven: Yale University Press, 1952), 9–17. In his recent exposition of what he calls Stanley Cavell's "embrace of the human," Ronald Hall takes particular care to distinguish between Cavell's overcoming of skepticism and stoic resignation. See Hall, *The Human Embrace: The Love of Philosophy and the Philosophy of Love: Kierkegaard, Cavell, Nussbaum* (University Park: Pennsylvania State University Press, 2000), 107.

49. Cavell, *Contesting Tears,* 16–17.

50. Thoreau, *Walden and Resistance to Civil Government,* 91.

51. Samuel Johnson, *Selections from Johnson on Shakespeare,* ed. Bertrand H. Bronson (New Haven: Yale University Press, 1986), 240.

52. Cavell, *Disowning Knowledge,* 80–81.

53. Cavell, *Contesting Tears,* 40.

54. Ibid., 190.

55. Jay Tolson, *Pilgrim in the Ruins: A Life of Walker Percy* (New York: Simon & Schuster, 1992), 277, 315–16.

56. Walker Percy, *The Moviegoer* (New York: Knopf, 1961), 78.

57. Walker Percy, "Stoicism in the South," in *Signposts in a Strange Land* (New York: Farrar, Straus, and Giroux, 1991), 83–88, 85–86.

58. Percy, *The Moviegoer,* 23.

59. Cavell, *Contesting Tears,* 40.

60. Percy, *The Moviegoer,* 13.

61. Wallace Stevens, "The Sense of the Sleight-of-Hand Man," in *The Collected Poems of Wallace Stevens* (New York: Alfred A. Knopf, 1965), 222.

62. Stanley Cavell, *Pursuits of Happiness: The Hollywood Comedy of Remarriage* (Cambridge: Harvard University Press), 14–15. The relevant phrase in Kierkegaard occurs during his discussion of the knight of faith's ability "absolutely to express the sublime in the pedestrian." See Søren Kierkegaard, *Fear and Trembling,* in *Fear and Trembling; Repetition,* trans. Howard V. Hong and Edna H. Hong, Kierkegaard's Writings, no. 6 (Princeton: Princeton University Press, 1983), 41.

63. Walker Percy, letter to Stanley Kauffmann, 11 February 1960, quoted in Tolson, *Pilgrim in the Ruins,* 286.

64. Emerson, "Experience," in *Essays and* Poems, 492.

65. Cited in James Conant, "Cavell and the Concept of America," *Contending with Stanley Cavell,* 55–81, 59. See Johannes Climacus, *Concluding Unscientific Postscript,* ed. S. Kierkegaard, trans. Walter Lowrie (Princeton: Princeton University Press, 1968), 49. "That we humans must decide to be human" is the central theme of Ronald Hall's *The Human Embrace.* See Hall, *The Human Embrace,* 1.

66. Emerson, "The American Scholar," in *Essays and Poems,* 53–71, 60.

67. Ibid., 57–58.

68. Percy, *The Moviegoer,* 238–41. See 216 for the other.

Notes to Chapter 1: Meeting Places

1. Stanley Cavell, *The Claim of Reason: Wittgenstein, Skepticism, Morality, and Tragedy* (New York: Oxford University Press, 1979), 125.

2. Stanley Cavell, *Disowning Knowledge in Seven Plays of Shakespeare,* updated ed. (Cambridge: Cambridge University Press, 2003), 19–20.

3. Ibid., x.

4. Carolyn Heilbrun, *Writing a Woman's Life* (New York: Norton, 1988), 93.

5. Northrop Frye, "The Argument of Comedy," in *English Institute Essays, 1948,* ed. D. A. Robertson, Jr. (New York: Columbia University Press, 1949), 58–73.

6. Stanley Cavell, *Pursuits of Happiness: The Hollywood Comedy of Remarriage* (Cambridge: Harvard University Press, 1981), 79, 87.

7. Stanley Cavell, *Conditions Handsome and Unhandsome: The Constitution of Emersonian Perfectionism* (Chicago: University of Chicago Press, 1990), 6.

8. Cavell, *The Claim of Reason,* 496.

9. John Hollander, "Stanley Cavell and *The Claim of Reason*," *Critical Inquiry* 6.4 (summer 1980): 575–88; Charles Bernstein, "Reading Cavell Reading Wittgenstein," *Boundary 2: A Journal of Postmodern Literature and Culture* 9.2 (winter 1981): 295–306; Jay Cantor, "On Stanley Cavell," *Raritan* 1.1 (summer 1981): 48–67. See Michael Fischer, *Stanley Cavell and Literary Skepticism* (Chicago: University of Chicago Press, 1989), 3–4 and 144–45 n. 6, for an account of rival views of Cavell's literariness.

•10. Cavell, *Disowning Knowledge,* 179.

11. Walker Percy, "From Facts to Fiction," in *Signposts in a Strange Land* (New York: Farrar, Straus, and Giroux, 1991), 186–90, 190.

12. Charles Taylor, *Philosophical Arguments* (Cambridge: Harvard University Press, 1995), 8.

13. Charles Taylor, *The Ethics of Authenticity* (Cambridge: Harvard University Press, 1992), 1–12.

14. Cavell, *Disowning Knowledge,* 93–94.

15. Cavell, "The Philosopher in American Life," in *Emerson's Transcendental Etudes,* ed. David Justin Hodge (Stanford: Stanford University Press, 2003), 36.

16. Walker Percy, "The Man on the Train," in *The Message in the Bottle* (New York: Farrar, Strauss, and Giroux, 1975), 83–100, 83.

17. Stanley Cavell, *Contesting Tears: The Hollywood Melodrama of the Unknown Woman* (Chicago: University of Chicago Press, 1996), 137–38.

18. Ibid., 132.

19. Slavoj Žižek, *Enjoy Your Symptom! Jaques Lacan in Hollywood and Out* (New York: Routledge, 1992), 17.

20. Ibid., 18.

21. Cavell, *Contesting Tears,* 138.

22. Teresa de Lauretis, *The Practice of Love: Lesbian Sexuality and Perverse Desire* (Bloomington: Indiana University Press, 1994), 133, 138.

23. Stanley Cavell, *A Pitch of Philosophy: Autobiographical Exercises* (Cambridge: Harvard University Press, 1994), 187.

24. Ralph Waldo Emerson, "The American Scholar," in *Emerson: Essays and Poems,* ed. Joel Porte, college ed. (New York: Library of America, 1996), 64.

25. Walker Percy, "Stoicism in the South," in *Signposts in a Strange Land,* 83–88, 85.

26. Emerson, "Experience," in *Essays and Poems,* 484–85. See Cavell, *Transcendental Etudes,* 132–33.

27. Cf. William Day, "*Moonstruck,* or How to Ruin Everything," *Philosophy and Literature* 19.2 (1995): 292–307, for a useful discussion of the Emersonian representativeness that film stars can project on screen. This essay persuasively brings together Cavell on film and on Emerson.

28. Adam Phillips, "Psychoanalysis and Idolatry," in *On Kissing, Tickling, and Being Bored* (Cambridge: Harvard University Press, 1993), 109–21, esp. 120–21.

29. Cavell, *Disowning Knowledge,* 96.

30. Cavell, "The Politics of Interpretation (Politics as Opposed to What?)," in *Themes out of School: Effects and Causes* (San Francisco: North Point Press, 1984), 52.

31. Lawrence F. Rhu, "An American Philosopher at the Movies," *Double-Take* 7.2 (spring 2001): 116.

32. Martin Luther, "The Pagan Servitude of the Church," in *Martin Luther: Selections from His Writings,* ed. John Dillenberger (Garden City, N.Y.: Anchor Books, 1961), 328.

33. E. Ann Kaplan, review of *Contesting Tears,* by Stanley Cavell, *Film Quarterly* 52.1 (fall 1998): 77–81, 80.

34. Walker Percy, *The Moviegoer* (New York: Knopf, 1961), 68.

35. Ibid., 226.

36. Ibid., 227.

37. Ibid., 228.

38. Jay Tolson, *Pilgrim in the Ruins: A Life of Walker Percy* (New York: Simon & Schuster, 1992), 269–302.

39. Percy, *The Moviegoer,* 230.

40. Ibid., 15–17.

41. Ibid., 232.

42. Percy, "Stoicism in the South," in *Signposts in a Strange Land,* 85–86.

43. Cavell describes himself as a "moviegoer" in "The Philosopher in American Life (toward Thoreau and Emerson)," an important "essay" (or attempt) at placing himself as a thinker in relation to an American tradition of thought wary of the professionalization of philosophy. See Cavell, *Emerson's Transcendental Etudes,* 33–58, 33.

44. Percy, *The Moviegoer,* 237.

45. Ibid., 109.

46. Emerson, "The American Scholar," in *Essays and Poems,* 67, 68.

47. Cavell, *Pursuits of Happiness,* 14–15. Re Kierkegaard, see 217 n. 62 in this book.

48. Percy, *The Moviegoer,* 79–80.

49. Cavell, "Being Odd, Getting Even (Descartes, Emerson, Poe)," *Emerson's Transcendental Etudes,* 83–109, 86; Stanley Cavell, *Cities of Words: Pedagogical Letters on a Register of the Moral Life* (Cambridge: Harvard University Press, 2004), 190–207, esp. 199ff.

50. Ibid., 63.

51. For some further thoughts in this regard, see Lawrence F. Rhu, *The Genesis of Tasso's Narrative Theory: English Translations of the Early Poetics and a Comparative Study of Their Significance* (Detroit: Wayne State University Press, 1993), 43ff.

52. Percy, *The Moviegoer,* 138.

53. Ibid., 69–70.

54. Stanley Cavell, "Skepticism as Iconoclasm: The Saturation of the Shakespearean Text," in *Shakespeare and the Twentieth Century,* ed. Jonathan Bate, Jill

L. Levenson, and Dieter Mehl (Newark: University of Delaware Press, 1998), 231–47. See "The Interminable Shakespearean Text," in *Philosophy the Day after Tomorrow* (Cambridge: Belknap Press of Harvard University Press, 2005), 7–27 for the revised and expanded version of "Skepticism as Iconoclasm."

55. David Denby, *Great Books: My Adventures with Homer, Rousseau, Woolf, and Other Indestructible Writers of the Western World* (New York: Simon & Schuster, 1996), 305–6.

56. Harold Bloom, *A Map of Misreading* (New York: Oxford University Press, 1975), 32.

57. Stanley Cavell, "Notes after Austin," *The Yale Review* 76.3 (spring 1987): 313–22, 322.

58. Ibid., 314–15.

59. See Stanley Cavell, *The World Viewed: Reflections on the Ontology of Film,* enl. ed. (Cambridge: Harvard University Press, 1979), 14; Cavell, *Contesting Tears,* 12.

60. I am much indebted to James Kugel's discussions of prophetic call narratives in a variety of contexts. See, for example, "The Moment of Confusion," in *The God of Old: Inside the Lost World of the Bible* (New York: The Free Press, 2003), 5–36.

61. Stanley Cavell, *The Senses of Walden,* exp. ed. (San Francisco: North Point Press, 1981), 29.

62. Ibid., 35.

63. Denby, *Great Books,* 261.

64. John Milton, *Of Education,* in *John Milton: Complete Poems and Major Prose,* ed. Merritt Y. Hughes (New York: Macmillan, 1957), 632. Unless otherwise noted, all references to Milton are to this edition and are cited parenthetically in the text.

65. Cf. Michel de Montaigne, "Of the Education of Children," 1.26, in *The Complete Essays of Montaigne,* trans. Donald M. Frame (Stanford: Stanford University Press, 1958), 106–31, esp. 119.

66. Cavell, *Pursuits of Happiness,* 75–80.

67. Cavell, *Themes out of School,* 3–26.

68. Stanley Cavell, *A Pitch of Philosophy* (Cambridge: Harvard University Press, 1994), 3–52, esp. 3–5. Cf. Cavell, *Contesting Tears,* 3, where Cavell refers to "what in [his] work [he] conceive[s] of as the call for philosophy, the right to its arrogation."

69. Cavell, *Pursuits of Happiness,* 58.

70. Milton, *John Milton: Complete Poems and Major Prose,* 706–7.

71. See Stephen Greenblatt, *Marvelous Possessions: The Wonder of the New World* (Berkeley: University of California Press, 1991), 2 and 162 n. 3. On "thick description" see Clifford Geertz, "Thick Description: Toward an Interpretive Theory of Culture," in *The Interpretation of Cultures* (New York: Basic Books, 1973), 3–30.

72. Cavell, *Pursuits of Happiness,* 141–2. Cavell makes a comparable claim in *Disowning Knowledge,* 219.

73. "Always historicize" is the curiously transhistorical form that Frederic Jameson uses to express this injunction in *The Political Unconscious* (Ithaca: Cornell University Press, 1981), 9.

74. Regarding the rejection of some masculinist inferences vis-à-vis *Tetrachordon* and *Paradise Lost,* see John T. Shawcross, *John Milton: The Self and the World* (Lexington, Ky.: University of Kentucky Press, 1993), 7.

75. Stanley Fish, "Why We Can't All Just Get Along," *First Things* 60 (February 1996): 18–26. In *Stanley Cavell and Literary Skepticism* (Chicago: University of Chicago Press, 1989), 119–41, Michael Fischer persuasively demonstrates how Cavell's understanding of skepticism offers an effective resistance to certain arguments typical of deconstruction as they are deployed by Stanley Fish among others. Further, Fischer's exposition of how Cavell "reconceives" (esp. 121–22 and 159 n. 301) the skeptical challenge shares key features of the pragmatist refutation of Fish that Lars Engle offers in *Shakespearean Pragmatism: Market of His Time* (Chicago: University of Chicago Press, 1993), 17–19. Unfortunately, Engle has already dismissed Cavell by playing him off against Stephen Toulmin in their respective accounts of early modern skepticism vis-à-vis Shakespeare. Engle thus misses an inviting opportunity to perceive how the "redescriptions" of fixed structures as economies or of binary oppositions as continua share a profound affinity with Cavell's "reconception" of skeptical interrogations and quests for certainty. I explore this issue in "Shakespeare's Ariostan Skepticism," *Shakespeare Yearbook* 10 (1999): 359–73.

76. Cf. Montaigne, "Apology for Raymond Sebond," 2.12, in *The Complete Essays,* 318–457. E.g., "Wherefore we must conclude that God alone *is*—not at all according to any measure of time, but according to an eternity immutable and immobile, not measured by time or subject to any decline; before whom there is nothing, nor will there be after" (457).

77. Fish, "Why We Can't All Just Get Along," 20.

78. Cavell, *Pursuits of Happiness,* 150–51.

79. Ibid., 150, 147. The phrase belongs to George Kittredge, whose name may contain an allusion to the famous Shakespeare scholar at Harvard, George Lyman Kittredge. See the exchange between Douglas Bruster and David Shumway in *PMLA* 112.3 (May 1997): 438–39. Cavell returns to this phrase in his essay on *North by Northwest:* "I also claim that the remarriage is, using a repeated phrase of [*The Philadelphia Story*], of national importance. My ground is the thought that while America, or any discovered world, can no longer ratify marriage, the achievement of true marriage might ratify something called America as a place in which to seek it. This is a state secret." See Cavell, *Themes out of School,* 172.

80. Cavell, *Pursuits of Happiness,* 79.

81. Cavell, *The Claim of Reason,* 22–25. Cf. the discussion of these pages in "Politics: The Social Contract," chap. 3 of Stephen Mulhall, *Stanley Cavell:*

Philosophy's Recounting of the Ordinary (Oxford: Oxford University Press, 1994), 55–68.

82. In paragraph 101 of his *Second Treatise of Government* (p. 54 of C. B. Macpherson's edition [Indianapolis: Hackett, 1980]) Locke passes up the chance to say that the state of nature is merely an explanatory myth, a useful fiction to help us imagine earlier conditions. Rather he enters upon the issue of the origins of the social contract in a way that makes him vulnerable to Hume's taunting.

83. Cavell, *The Claim of Reason,* 24.

Notes to Chapter 2: On Bloom and Cavell on Shakespeare

1. Harold Bloom, *The Western Canon: The Books and School of the Ages* (New York: Riverhead Books, 1994), 17.

2. Harold Bloom, "Emerson: Power at the Crossing," in *Poetics of Influence: New and Selected Criticism,* ed. John Hollander (New Haven: Henry R. Schwab, 1988), 309–23, 318–21.

3. Stanley Cavell, "The Thought of Movies," in *Themes out of School: Effects and Causes* (San Francisco: North Point Press, 1984), 3–26, 5.

4. Stanley Cavell, *Pursuits of Happiness: The Hollywood Comedy of Remarriage* (Cambridge: Harvard University Press, 1981), 5.

5. Stanley Cavell, "The Philosopher in American Life," in *Emerson's Transcendental Etudes,* ed. David Justin Hodge (Stanford: Stanford University Press, 2003), 33–58, 39.

6. Arnold Davidson, "Beginning Cavell," in *The Senses of Stanley Cavell,* ed. Richard Fleming and Michael Payne (Lewisburg, Pa.: Bucknell University Press, 1989), 230–41, 232.

7. Stanley Fish, *Professional Correctness: Literary Studies and Political Change* (New York: Oxford University Press, 1995), 94.

8. See Paul Alpers, "Giamatti's Spenser," *Aethlon: The Journal of Sport Literature* 14.2 (spring 1997): 91–99, esp. 96–97.

9. Harold Bloom, *Shakespeare: The Invention of the Human* (New York: Riverhead Books, 1998), 280.

10. Personal communication. See Lawrence F. Rhu, "An American Philosopher at the Movies," 115–19 for an account of my visits with Cavell.

11. Stanley Cavell, *Disowning Knowledge in Seven Plays of Shakespeare,* updated ed. (Cambridge: Cambridge University Press, 2003), x.

12. Bloom, *Shakespeare: The Invention of the Human,* 507.

13. Stanley Cavell, *Contesting Tears: The Hollywood Melodrama of the Unknown Woman* (Chicago: University of Chicago Press, 1996), 197–222. Cavell initially published his address as "Skepticism as Iconoclasm." See 219–20 n. 54 (Cambridge: Belknap Press of Harvard University Press, 2005), 7–27 for the revised and expanded version of "Skepticism as Iconoclasm."

14. Harold Bloom, *How to Read and Why* (New York: Scribner, 2000), 19; Bloom, *Shakespeare: The Invention of the Human*, 476.

15. Bloom, *How to Read and Why*, 19.

16. See Stanley Cavell, "Hope Against Hope," in *Emerson's Transcendental Etudes*, 171–82.

17. Bloom, *The Western Canon*, 47.

18. Ralph Waldo Emerson, "Shakespeare; or, the Poet," in *Emerson: Essays and Poems*, ed. Joel Porte, college ed. (New York: Library of America, 1996), 718.

19. Emerson, "Self-Reliance," in *Emerson: Essays and Poems*, ed. Joel Porte, college ed. (New York: Library of America, 1996), 259–82.

20. Henry David Thoreau, *Walden*, ed. William Rossi, 2d ed. (New York: Norton, 1992), 91, 65.

21. See David Denby, *Great Books: My Adventures with Homer, Rousseau, Woolf, and Other Indestructible Writers of the Western World* (New York: Simon and Schuster, 1996), passim, on the teaching of Edward Tayler; e.g., 31: " 'You're not here for political reasons. You're here for very selfish reasons. You're here to build a self.' "

22. Stanley Cavell, *Conditions Handsome and Unhandsome: The Constitution of Emersonian Perfectionism* (Chicago: University of Chicago Press, 1990), 1.

23. Bloom, *How to Read and Why*, 20.

24. The first chapter of *Conditions Handsome and Unhandsome* is entitled "Staying the Course" and elaborates on Cavell's experience teaching Moral Perfectionism in the Moral Reasoning division of Harvard's Core Curriculum, the successor to the Program in General Education.

25. See Cavell, "Finding as Founding: Taking Steps in Emerson's 'Experience,' " in *Emerson's Transcendental Etudes*, 110–40, 137.

26. Cavell, *Conditions Handsome and Unhandsome*, 4–5: "It is not meant to do more than activate the fantasy, perhaps it vanishes early, that there is a place in the mind where the good books are in conversation, among themselves and with other sources of thought and pleasure; what they often talk about, in my hearing, is how they can be, or sound, so much better than the people who compose them, and why, in their goodness, they are not more powerful."

27. See Stanley Cavell, "Film and the University," in *Pursuits of Happiness*, 265–74, and Cavell, "The Thought of Movies," in *Themes out of School*. In 1982 Cavell's proposal to teach a course in the Literature and Arts division of Harvard's Core Curriculum was not accepted. This course, "The Art of Film," was instead offered in the Humanities division in the Program in General Education during the spring of 1983. The uncertain status of Cavell's proposal elicited a lengthy letter from him to the classicist Emily Vermeule, who then chaired the Core Committee. In its thoughtful defense of film as a subject for scholarly study, it is a notable document. Cavell particularly stresses the link between Shakespeare and his work on film as though an invocation of the bard's unquestionable

authority will help his audience overcome any skepticism they might have about film study as a legitimate academic pursuit.

28. John Rawls, *A Theory of Justice* (Cambridge: Harvard University Press, 1971), 325.

29. For a discussion of Nietzsche's transcriptions of Emerson in "Schopenhauer as Educator," see James Conant, "Emerson as Educator," *ESQ* 43.1–4 (1997): 181–206.

30. Friedrich Wilhelm Nietzsche, *Untimely Meditations*, trans. R. J. Hollingdale (Cambridge: Cambridge University Press, 1983), 182–83.

31. Emerson, "Montaigne; or, the Skeptic," in *Essays and Poems*, 702.

32. Rawls, *A Theory of Justice*, 325.

33. Stanley Cavell, "Aversive Thinking: Emersonian Representations in Heidegger and Nietzsche," in *Emerson's Transcendental Etudes*, 160–61.

34. Nietzsche, *Untimely Meditations*, 162–63.

35. Cavell, *Conditions Handsome and Unhandsome*, 8.

36. Emerson, "Self-Reliance," in *Essays and Poems*, 259.

37. See Cavell, "Aversive Thinking," in *Emerson's Transcendental Etudes*, 150–51. Judith Shklar discusses the democratic force of Emerson's term "representative" in "Emerson and the Inhibitions of Democracy," in *Pursuits of Reason: Essays in Honor of Stanley Cavell*, ed. Ted Cohen, Paul Guyer, and Hilary Putnam (Lubbock, Tex.: Texas Tech University Press, 1993), 124–25.

38. Ibid., 121: "This inhibition was not, however, something externally imposed upon [Emerson] against his will or better judgment. He was not giving in to something he could not overcome."

39. Cavell, "Aversive Thinking," in *Emerson's Transcendental Etudes*, 156. See Cavell, *Pursuits of Happiness*, 5.

40. Bloom, "Emerson: Power at the Crossing," in *Poetics of Influence*, 320, 321.

41. Ibid., 318, 321.

42. Jane Smiley, "Shakespeare in Iceland," in *Shakespeare in the Twentieth Century*, ed. Jonathan Bate, Jill L. Levenson, and Dieter Mehl (Newark: University of Delaware Press, 1996), 53.

43. Bloom, *Shakespeare: The Invention of the Human*, 505.

44. See Stanley Cavell, *A Pitch of Philosophy: Autobiographical Exercises* (Cambridge: Harvard University Press, 1994), 143, and Stanley Cavell, "Thinking of Emerson," in *Emerson's Transcendental Etudes*, 10–19, esp. 13–14.

45. Bloom, *Shakespeare: The Invention of the Human*, 482.

46. Ibid., 503.

47. Ibid., 510–11.

48. Ibid., 511.

49. Ibid., 503–4. Cf. Harold Bloom, ed., introduction, *King Lear*, Major Literary Characters Series (New York: Chelsea House, 1992), 6–7 for an earlier version of this claim upon which Bloom slightly expands in *Shakespeare: The*

Invention of the Human. Those who lament the lack of bibliography and notes in *Shakespeare: The Invention of the Human* can look in the apposite volumes of Bloom's Chelsea House Major Literary Characters Series and *Major Critical Interpretations* for the information they fail to find in *Shakespeare: The Invention of the Human.*

50. Cavell, *Disowning Knowledge,* 80.

51. Cavell, *A Pitch of Philosophy,* 31.

52. Stanley Cavell, "Notes after Austin," *The Yale Review* 76.3 (spring 1987): 313–22, 314–15.

53. See Harold Bloom, *A Map of Misreading* (New York: Oxford University Press, 1975), 32; Cavell, "Notes after Austin," 322.

54. Cavell, "The Philosopher in American Life," in *Emerson's Transcendental Etudes,* 33–58, esp. 37–38.

55. E. Ann Kaplan, review of *Contesting Tears,* by Stanley Cavell, *Film Quarterly* 52.1 (fall 1998): 77–81. Among Shakespeareans this charge recurs more forcibly when Richard Halpern characterizes Cavell's "gestures of intellectual modesty" as "utterly disingenuous." See Richard Halpern, *Shakespeare Among the Moderns* (Ithaca: Cornell University Press, 1997), 107 n. 123.

56. Cavell, *A Pitch of Philosophy,* 187.

57. Cavell, *Disowning Knowledge,* 57–61, 58.

58. Jacob Burckhardt, *The Civilization of the Renaissance in Italy* (New York: Harper and Row, 1958), 1:143.

59. Cavell, *Disowning Knowledge,* 58.

60. For a pertinent quibble over the relative aptness of the terms "discovery" and "invention," see Perry H. Chapman, *Rembrandt's Self-Portraits* (Princeton: Princeton University Press, 1990), 10. Chapman cites from Montaigne, "Of Repentance," as follows: "There is no one who, if he listens to himself, does not discover in himself a pattern all his own." Although it employs the language of discovery rather than that of invention, Montaigne's claim, in turn, evokes Bloom's preoccupation with "self-overhearing." These overlappings and divergences point to a complex tangle of issues that cannot be adequately unraveled in an endnote. However, it is worth noting that the root meaning of "invent"— from the Latin *invenire*—is something very much like "discover," which is a standard definition of that verb. The root meaning is "to come upon."

61. Emerson, "Experience," in *Essays and Poems,* 487.

62. Stanley Cavell, *Contesting Tears: The Hollywood Melodrama of the Unknown Woman* (Chicago: University of Chicago Press, 1996), 212, 219–20.

63. Ibid., 200.

64. For Cavell, Linda Williams is the chief representative of the view that stresses Stella's "obliviousness" to the impression her conduct is making during the episode at the swanky resort. See Linda Williams, " 'Something Else Besides A Mother': *Stella Dallas* and the Maternal Melodrama," in *Home Is Where the Heart Is: Studies in Melodrama and the Woman's Film,* ed. Christine Gledhill (London: British Film Institute Publishing, 1987).

65. Cavell, *Contesting Tears*, 36.

66. Ibid., 212–13

67. See Rhu, "An American Philosopher at the Movies," 115–19.

68. Cavell, *A Pitch of Philosophy*, 29.

69. Søren Kierkegaard, *The Present Age*, trans. Alexander Dru (New York: Harper and Row, 1962), 44–45.

70. Smiley, "Shakespeare in Iceland," in *Shakespeare in the Twentieth Century*, 42–45.

71. Jane Smiley, *A Thousand Acres* (New York: Knopf, 1991), 20.

72. E.g., "Satan does not leave us surprised by sin; rather, we are surprised by Satan because he is as uncanny as the Yahwist's Yahweh, or as Shakespeare's Edmund." From Harold Bloom, *Ruin the Sacred Truths: Poetry and Belief from the Bible to the Present* (Cambridge: Harvard University Press, 1987), 108.

73. Harold Bloom and David Rosenberg, *The Book of J* (New York: Vintage, 1990), 43.

74. Bloom, *The Western Canon*, 4.

75. Harold Bloom, ed., introduction, *Christopher Marlowe*, Major Literary Characters Series (New York: Chelsea House, 1986), 6–7.

76. Stanley Cavell, "Nothing Goes without Saying: Stanley Cavell Reads the Marx Brothers," *London Review of Books* 6 (January 1994): 3–4.

77. Cavell, *Pursuits of Happiness*, 8, 73.

78. Cavell, *A Pitch of Philosophy*, 158.

79. Cavell, *Conditions Handsome and Unhandsome*, 7. See p. 32.

80. E.g., Harold Bloom, *The Anxiety of Influence: A Theory of Poetry*, 2d ed. (New York: Oxford University Press, 1997), 3, 157.

81. Bloom, *How to Read and Why*, 22.

Notes to Chapter 3: From Skepticism to Perfectionism

1. Ralph Waldo Emerson, "History," in *Emerson: Essays and Poems,* ed. Joel Porte, college ed. (New York: Library of America, 1996), 249.

2. Ellen Spolsky, *Satisfying Skepticism: Embodied Knowledge in the Early Modern World* (Oxon, England: Ashgate Press, 2001), 13.

3. Stanley Cavell, *Disowning Knowledge in Seven Plays of Shakespeare,* updated ed. (Cambridge: Cambridge University Press, 2003), 139.

4. Cavell, *Disowning Knowledge,* 166.

5. Stanley Cavell, "Finding as Founding: Taking Steps in Emerson's 'Experience,'" in *Emerson's Transcendental Etudes,* ed. David Justin Hodge (Stanford: Stanford University Press, 2003), 132; Cavell, "The World as Things: Collecting Thoughts on Collecting," in *Philosophy the Day After Tomorrow* (Cambridge: Harvard University Press), 236–80, 275. The discussion of Freud in Cavell's essay on *Now, Voyager* in *Cities of Words: Pedagogical Letters on a Register of the*

Moral Life (Cambridge: Harvard University Press, 2004) focuses upon the idea of the sage or philosopher, and Cavell notes that two of the four essays in which he hears this tone of philosophy in Freud end with this sentence: "If you want to endure life, prepare yourself for death" (242). See also Cavell's essay on *The Awful Truth* in *Pursuits of Happiness: The Hollywood Comedy of Remarriage* (Cambridge: Harvard University Press), 238. There Cavell briefly discusses his use of Montaigne in reading *Othello*. Cavell's emphasis on attitude at this juncture warrants note because it is reminiscent of Emerson's sense of the importance of moods. Their ability to constitute knowledge and create worlds, or what we may call worlds of difference, has telling affinities with Montaigne as does Cavell's stress upon attitude and perspective in this context.

6. Emerson, "Montaigne; or, the Skeptic," "Self-Reliance," in *Essays and Poems*, 697, 259. See Richard R. O'Keefe, "Emerson's 'Montaigne; or, the Skeptic': Biography as Autobiography," *Essays in Literature* 23 (fall 1996): 206–17.

7. Stanley Cavell, *The Claim of Reason: Wittgenstein, Skepticism, Morality, and Tragedy* (New York: Oxford University Press, 1979), 3; Cavell, "The Philosopher in American Life," in *Emerson's Transcendental Etudes*, 45.

8. Stephen Greenblatt, "What Is the History of Literature?," *Critical Inquiry* 23 (spring 1997): 460–81 passim; e.g., 479: "It is the role of the scholar to speak to the dead and to make the dead speak."

9. See David Sedley, introduction, *Sublimity and Skepticism in Montaigne and Milton* (Ann Arbor: University of Michigan Press, 2005).

10. Stanley Cavell, *Conditions Handsome and Unhandsome: The Constitution of Emersonian Perfectionism* (Chicago: University of Chicago Press, 1990), 7.

11. Friedrich Wilhelm Nietzsche, "On the Uses and Disadvantages of History for Life," in *Untimely Meditations,* trans. R. J. Hollingdale (New York: Cambridge University Press, 1983), 59–123, 94. See David Miller, *Dreams of the Burning Child* (Ithaca: Cornell University Press, 2002), 211–13.

12. See Hugo Friedrich, "Opposition to the Stoic School," in *Montaigne,* trans. Dawn Eng (Berkeley: University of California Press, 1991), 169–75.

13. Emerson, "Montaigne; or, the Skeptic," in *Essays and Poems,* 704.

14. Stanley Cavell, "Thinking of Emerson," in *Emerson's Transcendental Etudes,* 11–12.

15. Michel de Montaigne, "Apology for Raymond Sebond," in *The Complete Essays,* trans. Donald M. Frame (Stanford: Stanford University Press, 1958), 363.

16. Emerson, "Prudence," in *Essays and Poems,* 363.

17. Montaigne, "Of Experience," in *The Complete Essays,* 819.

18. Cavell, *Cities of Words,* 425.

19. Cavell, "Finding as Founding," in *Emerson's Transcendental Etudes,* 112.

20. Montaigne, "Of Experience," in *The Complete Essays,* 821.

21. Emerson, "Montaigne; or the Skeptic," in *Essays and Poems,* 708.

22. Ibid., 270.

23. Ibid.

24. Ibid., 264.

25. René Descartes, *Discourse on Method and Meditations on First Philosophy,* ed. David Weissman (New Haven: Yale University Press, 1996), 69. See Gareth Matthews, "Descartes and the Problem of Other Minds," in *Essays on Descartes's Meditations,* ed. Amélie Oksenberg Rorty (Berkeley: University of California Press, 1986), 141–51.

26. Cavell observes that Descartes does not even have access to the argument from analogy as a response to the problem of other minds; for "[a]fter all, the body has essentially nothing to do with the soul" in Cartesian thought (Cavell, *Disowning Knowledge,* 126). However, Cavell does find a version of this argument in *The Merchant of Venice,* when Shylock works through the likeness of certain physical features that Jews share with others on the way to claiming a likeness in their motivation to revenge. See Cavell, *The Claim of Reason,* 478–81.

27. Baldesar Castiglione, *Il libro del cortegiano,* ed. Vittorio Cian (Florence, Italy: Sansoni, 1947), 4.51–70.

28. Plato, *Republic,* trans. G. M. A. Grube (Indianapolis: Hackett, 1974), 238 (592a–b).

29. Cavell, *Conditions Handsome and Unhandsome,* 1–32, 101–26.

30. Greenblatt, "What Is the History of Literature?" *Critical Inquiry* 23 (spring 1997): 460–81 passim; e.g., 479: "It is the role of the scholar to speak to the dead and to make the dead speak," where the representative scholar is Horatio, the limits of whose philosophy Hamlet duly notes.

31. Emerson, "Self-Reliance," in *Essays and Poems,* 259.

32. John Rawls, *A Theory of Justice* (Cambridge: Harvard University Press, 1971), 325.

33. Cavell, "What's the Use of Calling Emerson a Pragmatist?," *Emerson's Transcendental Etudes,* 215–23, 217.

34. On the relation of synchronic to diachronic analysis, a recurrent issue in anthropology that has also gained some currency in Renaissance studies, see Marshall Sahlins, *Islands of History* (Chicago: University of Chicago Press, 1985), 136–56.

35. Erik H. Erikson, *Childhood and Society,* 2d ed. (New York: Norton, 1963), 269–74.

36. See Stanley Cavell, "Knowing and Acknowledging," in *Must We Mean What We Say?* (Cambridge: Cambridge University Press, 1976), 238–66.

37. Ralph Ellison, *Shadow and Act* (New York: Random House, 1964), 152, xii–xiii, 7.

38. Anthony Hecht, *Millions of Strange Shadows* (New York: Atheneum, 1977).

39. All Sidney citations come from *Sir Philip Sidney: Selections,* ed. Katherine Duncan-Jones (Oxford: Oxford University Press, 1989).

With how sad steps, O moon, thou climb'st the skies;
How silently, and with how wan a face.
What, may it be that even in heav'nly place
That busy archer his sharp arrows tries?
Sure, if that long-with-love-acquainted eyes
Can judge of love, thou feel'st a lover's case;
I read it in thy looks; thy languished grace
To me, that feel the like, thy state descries.
Then even of fellowship, O moon, tell me,
Is constant love deemed there but want of wit?
Are beauties there as proud as here they be?
Do they above love to be loved, and yet
Those lovers scorn whom that love doth possess?
Do they call virtue there ungratefulness?

40. Philip Larkin, "Sad Steps," in *High Windows* (New York: Farrar, Straus and Giroux, 1974), 32.

41. Ibid.

42. T. S. Eliot, "East Coker," in *The Complete Poems and Plays, 1909–1950* (New York: Harcourt, Brace and World, 1952), 126.

43. William Shakespeare, *Antony and Cleopatra,* ed. John Wilders, Arden Shakespeare (New York: Routledge, 1995), 4.15.12.

44. David Kalstone, *Sidney's Poetry: Contexts and Interpretations* (New York: Norton, 1970), 117, 118.

45. Sidney, *The Defence of Poesy,* in *Sir Philip Sidney,* 219.

46. Emerson, "History," in *Essays and Poems,* 239.

47. Rawls, *A Theory of Justice,* 325.

48. Emerson, "The American Scholar," in *Essays and Poems,* 67, 68.

49. All citations from the Sonnets come from *Shakespeare's Sonnets,* ed. Katherine Duncan-Jones, Arden Shakespeare (Walton-on-Thames: Thomas Nelson and Sons, 1997).

50. Wallace Stevens, "Esthetique du Mal," stanza 4, in *The Collected Poems of Wallace Stevens* (New York: Knopf, 1954), 316.

51. David Cowart, *Literary Symbiosis: The Reconfigured Text in Twentieth-Century Writing* (Athens: University of Georgia Press, 1993), 175–79, 183–89.

52. Larkin, "Sad Steps," in *High Windows,* 32.

53. Sidney, *The Defence of Poesy,* 228.

54. Cavell, *The Claim of Reason,* 420.

55. Sidney, *The Defence of Poesy,* 212, 249.

56. Sidney, *Astrophil and Stella,* 3.1, 6.1, 15.1–2, 74.1.

57. Castiglione, *Il libro del cortegiano,* 1.9.

58. Ibid., 1.26–28.

59. William Wordsworth, *Poetical Works,* ed. Thomas Hutchinson, new ed., rev. Ernest de Selincourt (London: Oxford University Press, 1904, 1936).

60. Cowart, *Literary Symbiosis,* 185.
61. Stanley Cavell, *Disowning Knowledge,* 240.
62. Castiglione, *Il libro del cortegiano,* 4.73.
63. Plato, *Republic,* 238 (592a–b).

Notes to Chapter 4: From Cyprus to Rushmore

1. Stanley Cavell, *Disowning Knowledge in Seven Plays of Shakespeare,* updated ed. (Cambridge: Cambridge University Press, 2003), 35–36, 126–27.
2. Stanley Cavell, *Pursuits of Happiness: The Hollywood Comedy of Remarriage* (Cambridge: Harvard University Press, 1981), 141–42; Cavell, *Disowning Knowledge,* 219.
3. Jay Cantor, "On Stanley Cavell," *Raritan* 1.1 (summer 1981): 48–67, 65.
4. Cavell, *Pursuits of Happiness,* 142.
5. Stanley Cavell, "Psychoanalysis and Cinema: The Melodrama of the Unknown Woman," in *The Trials of Psychoanalysis,* ed. Francoise Meltzer (Chicago: University of Chicago Press, 1988), 248–89, 235.
6. Cavell, *Disowning Knowledge,* 130.
7. A review of the syllabus and final exam for the spring 1979 version of Humanities 5, Ideas of Man and the World in Western Thought, substantiates this claim. Such materials are available at the Harvard Archive in the Pusey Library at Harvard University.
8. In *Harvard Radcliffe* 361 (Harvard Yearbook Publications, 1997), 70, Cavell writes: "the population of a large Harvard class in the humanities, mostly consisting of undergraduates but with the section persons in attendance, along with graduate students from various departments wishing to collect further images for a kind of teaching their futures might hold in store, and along further with the interspersing of visitors, scholars and others, that a Harvard auditorium draws, constituted as perfect a set of occasions for the public exploration of great philosophical texts of our tradition (eventually including literary texts and film) as I could wish to imagine. I had the feeling that in such a forum, extending through the season of a spring or a fall, what I most had it at heart to say about these works that I love, if articulated clearly and fervently enough, with no withholding, time permitting, of any suggested nuance or complexity at my command, would be fully understood and assessed with intelligence and good will. No comparable experience has had a greater effect on my quest for a sound philosophical prose that I could place conviction in, nor has been more heartening to it."
9. Stanley Cavell, "Finding as Founding: Taking Steps in Emerson's 'Experience,'" in *Emerson's Transcendental Etudes,* ed. David Justin Hodge (Stanford: Stanford University Press, 2003), 137.
10. Cavell, *Pursuits of Happiness,* 150.

11. Given this film's capacity to evoke Shakespearean reflections, George's name also warrants specific notice. Philip Barry, the playwright and, with Donald Ogden Stewart, the scriptwriter, was a student at Harvard in George Pierce Baker's drama program while George Lyman Kittredge presided over the teaching of Shakespeare. Whatever the joke here may be, it is not a gag for the gallery. Such esoterica may gain some furtherance in Tracy Lord's merrily and willfully mistaken greeting of her father, Seth Lord (John Halliday), as "Uncle Willy." However different in stature, both of these actors (Halliday and Roland Young, playing Tracy Lord's uncle, William Tracy) do sport Kittredgian moustaches, as does John Howard as George Kittredge.

12. Stanley Cavell, *The World Viewed: Reflections on the Ontology of Cinema*, enl. ed. (Cambridge: Harvard University Press, 1979),175–77.

13. Stanley Cavell, "The Philosopher in American Life," in *Emerson's Transcendental Etudes*, 33–58, 46–47.

14. Stanley Cavell, "The Thought of Movies," in *Themes out of School: Effects and Causes* (San Francisco: North Point Press, 1984), 3–26, 15.

15. Ralph Waldo Emerson, "The American Scholar," in *Emerson: Essays and Poems*, ed. Joel Porte, college ed. (New York: Library of America, 1996), 62.

16. Stanley Cavell, *Must We Mean What We Say?* (Cambridge: Cambridge University Press, 1976), xxv–xxvii.

17. William Shakespeare, *Hamlet*, ed. Harold Jenkins, Arden Edition (London: Routledge, 1982), 1.5.174–75.

18. Cavell, "The Thought of Movies," in *Themes out of School*, 11.

19. Emerson, "Shakespeare; or, the Poet," in *Essays and Poems*, 718.

20. Cavell, *Pursuits of Happiness*, 73.

21. Ibid., 159.

22. Ibid., 117–18.

23. Thomas L. Dumm, *A Politics of the Ordinary* (New York: New York University Press, 1999), 180–81 n. 1.

24. Cavell, "The Philosopher in American Life," in *Emerson's Transcendental Etudes*, 37–40.

25. Ibid., 53.

26. Cavell, "Finding as Founding," in *Emerson's Transcendental Etudes*, 137.

27. Cavell, *Pursuits of Happiness*, 79.

28. The problem of incest can haunt this sort of connection. Cavell explores this issue most fully in regard to *The Awful Truth*.

29. Stanley Cavell, *The Claim of Reason: Wittgenstein, Skepticism, Morality, and Tragedy* (New York: Oxford University Press, 1979), 111.

30. Cavell, "The Philosopher in American Life," in *Emerson's Transcendental Etudes*, 34.

31. Emerson, "Experience," in *Essays and Poems*, 487.

32. Stanley Cavell, *Contesting Tears: The Hollywood Melodrama of the Unknown Woman* (Chicago: University of Chicago Press, 1996), 22, 220–21.

33. Jacob Burckhardt, *The Civilization of the Renaissance in Italy*, vol. 1 (New York: Harper and Row, 1958), 143. See Emerson, "Experience," in *Essays and Poems*, 487.

34. Cavell, *Disowning Knowledge*, 58.

35. Cavell, "The Thought of Movies," in *Themes Out of School*, 17.

36. Cavell, *Pursuits of Happiness*, 141.

37. Cavell, *The World Viewed*, 22.

38. Michael Wood, "One Mo' Time," *New York Review of Books* 28 (21 January 1982): 29–31, 29.

39. Cavell, *Contesting Tears*, 135.

40. Cavell, *Pursuits of Happiness*, 37–38. See also Stanley Cavell, *Cities of Words: Pedagogical Letters on a Register of the Moral Life* (Cambridge: Harvard University Press, 2004), 81.

41. Giovanna Borradori, "An Apology for Skepticism: Stanley Cavell," in *The American Philosopher: Conversations with Quine, Davidson, Putnam, Nozick, Danto, Rorty, Cavell, MacIntyre, and Kuhn* (Chicago: University of Chicago Press, 1994), 118–36, 126.

42. Cavell, "The Philosopher in American Life," in *Emerson's Transcendental Etudes*, 45.

43. Cavell, *Disowning Knowledge*, 179.

44. Richard Halpern, *Shakespeare Among the Moderns* (Ithaca: Cornell University Press, 1997), 107 n. 123.

45. See Julia Reinhard Lupton and Kenneth Reinhard, *After Oedipus: Shakespeare in Psychoanalysis* (Ithaca: Cornell University Press, 1993), 15–26.

46. Cavell, "*North by Northwest*," in *Themes out of School*, 152–72, 161.

47. Stanley Cavell, "Something out of the Ordinary," *Proceedings and Addresses of the APA* 71.2 (1997): 23–37, 37.

48. Cavell, *Disowning Knowledge*, 179. *Burden* also suggests pregnancy and pertains crucially to what Cavell calls Hamlet's need to let himself be born, to accept his birth by making the claim to existence that only he can deliver.

49. Cavell, "North by Northwest," in *Themes out of School*, 171.

50. See Robert Browning, "Incident of the French Camp," in *Robert Browning: The Poems*, ed. John Pettigrew, vol. 1 (New Haven: Yale University Press, 1981), 355–56. Vv. 37–40 read as follows: "'You're wounded!' 'Nay,' the soldier's pride/Touched to the quick, he said:/'I'm killed, Sire!' And his chief beside,/Smiling the boy fell dead."

51. Pauline Kael, "The Man from Dream City," in *When the Lights Go Down* (New York: Holt, Rinehart, and Winston, 1980), 3–32, 5.

52. Cavell, "The Thought of Movies," in *Themes out of School*, 7.

53. Arnold Davidson, "Beginning Cavell," in *Pursuits of Reason: Essays in Honor of Stanley Cavell*, ed. Ted Cohen, Paul Guyer, and Hilary Putnam (Lubbock, Tex.: Texas Tech University Press, 1993), 230–41, 232.

54. Emerson, "Experience," in *Essays and Poems*, 476.

55. Cavell, "Thinking of Emerson," in *Emerson's Transcendental Etudes*, 12–13.

56. Shakespeare, *Hamlet*,1.2.92–97.

57. See James Wood, "Give All," *The New Republic* (19 January 2001), from which I take this claim about stream-of-consciousness.

58. Saul Bellow, *Herzog* (London: Weidenfeld and Nicolson, 1965), 161–62.

59. Cavell, "Finding as Founding," in *Emerson's Transcendental Etudes*, 137. Stanly Cavell, "Wittgensteinian Event," in *Philosophy the Day after Tomorrow* (Cambridge: Belknap Press of Harvard University Press, 2005), 201, 204.

60. Cavell, *Themes out of School*, 171–72.

61. Cavell, *Pursuits of Happiness*, 159.

62. Cavell, *The World Viewed*, 175–77.

63. Stephen Greenblatt, "What Is the History of Literature?," *Critical Inquiry* 23 (spring 1997): 460–81 passim; e.g., 479: "It is the role of the scholar to speak to the dead and to make the dead speak."

64. Cavell, *Must We Mean What We Say?*, xxv–xxvii.

65. Emerson, "History," in *Essays and Poems*, 249. Cited in *Disowning Knowledge*, 226.

66. Stanley Cavell, *Conditions Handsome and Unhandsome: The Constitution of Emersonian Perfectionism* (Chicago: University of Chicago Press, 1990), 1.

Notes to Chapter 5: Reading Cavell Reading *The Winter's Tale*

1. Stephen Orgel, ed., *The Winter's Tale*, introduction (Oxford: Oxford University Press, 1996), 32–34. All citations from *The Winter's Tale* refer to this edition.

2. David Lee Miller, *Dreams of the Burning Child: Sacrificial Sons and the Father's Witness* (Ithaca: Cornell University Press, 2002), 92–129.

3. Maurice Hunt, *The Winter's Tale: Critical Essays* (New York: Garland, 1995), 50–51.

4. Northrop Frye, *A Natural Perspective: The Development of Shakespearean Comedy and Romance* (New York: Columbia University Press, 1965), ix–xx.

5. T. G. Bishop, *Shakespeare and the Theatre of Wonder* (Cambridge: Cambridge University Press, 1996), 15 and 125–75 passim.

6. Stanley Cavell, *Disowning Knowledge in Seven Plays of Shakespeare*, updated ed. (Cambridge: Cambridge University Press, 2003), 218.

7. Cavell continues his practice of concluding his books with an essay on Shakespeare in his recent collections, *Emerson's Transcendental Etudes*, ed. David Justin Hodge (Stanford: Stanford University Press, 2003) and *Cities of Words: Pedagogical Letters on a Register of the Moral Life* (Cambridge: Harvard University Press, 2004).

8. See Linda Charnes, "Dismember Me: Shakespeare, Paranoia, and the Logic of Mass Culture," *Shakespeare Quarterly* 48.1 (spring 1997): 1–16; and Eric S. Mallin, "'You Kilt My Foddah': Or Arnold, Prince of Denmark," *Shakespeare Quarterly* 50.2 (summer 1999): 127–51. Cavell's essay on *North by Northwest* is reprinted in *Themes out of School: Effects and Causes* (San Francisco: North Point Press, 1984), 152–72.

9. Cavell delivered this lecture at the University of Chicago in the spring of 2002 as part of a year-long course on moral perfectionism. Under the title "Shakespeare and Rohmer: Two Tales of Winter," it appears in Cavell's *Cities of Words*, 421–43.

10. Stanley Cavell, *In Quest of the Ordinary: Lines of Skepticism and Romanticism* (Chicago: University of Chicago Press, 1988), 69–75.

11. Cavell, *Disowning Knowledge*, 193–94.

12. Ibid., 5.

13. Ralph Waldo Emerson, "Self-Reliance," in *Emerson: Essays and Poems*, ed. Joel Porte, college ed. (New York: Library of America, 1996), 269. Ludwig Wittgenstein, *Philosophical Investigations* (New York: Macmillan, 1968), 1.1.

14. See Emerson, "The American Scholar," in *Essays and Poems*, 53–71, 54: "In the degenerate state, when the victim of society, [the scholar] tends to become a mere thinker, or, still worse, the parrot of other men's thinking." Jesus' words come from Matt. 6:7 (KJV).

15. Cavell, *Disowning Knowledge*, 126.

16. Stanley Cavell, *The Claim of Reason: Wittgenstein, Skepticism, Morality, and Tragedy* (New York: Oxford University Press, 1979), 470, 482. This phrase is omitted from the *Othello* essay as it is reprinted in *Disowning Knowledge*.

17. In "'Tongue-Tied Our Queen?': The Deconstruction of Presence in *The Winter's Tale*," in *Shakespeare and the Question of Theory* (New York: Methuen, 1985), 3–18, Howard Felperin plays the devil's advocate (or Descartes's evil genius) and assumes Leontes' point of view. In *Shakespeare and the Theatre of Wonder*, 203 n. 31, T. G. Bishop remarks about Felperin's gambit and the results it produces, "It seems truer to say that the play here reads the critic than vice versa. But this is a danger we all run."

18. See Michel de Montaigne, "On Experience," in *The Essays: A Selection*, ed. M. Screech (Harmondsworth, England: Penguin, 1993), 364–426, 364 n. 6.

19. Cavell, *Disowning Knowledge*, 200.

20. Ibid., 193.

21. Cavell, *The Claim of Reason*, e.g., 420, 442–43.

22. Miller, *Dreams of the Burning Child*, 97.

23. Stanley Cavell, *The World Viewed: Reflections on the Ontology of Film*, enl. ed. (Cambridge: Harvard University Press, 1979), 177.

24. Ibid., 23.

25. Stanley Cavell, *Conditions Handsome and Unhandsome: The Constitution of Emersonian Perfectionism* (Chicago: University of Chicago Press, 1990), 7.

26. Friedrich Wilhelm Nietzsche, *Untimely Meditations* (New York, Cambridge University Press, 1983), 94. See Miller, *Dreams of the Burning Child*, 211–13.

27. D. L. Miller, "Death's Afterword," in *Imagining Death in Spenser and Milton*, ed. Elizabeth Bellamy, Michael Schoenfeldt, and Patrick Cheney (forthcoming).

28. Cavell, *Conditions Handsome and Unhandsome*, 119.

29. Janet Adelman, *Suffocating Mothers: Fantasies of Maternal Origin in Shakespeare's Plays*, Hamlet *to* The Tempest (New York: Routledge, 1992), 230–31, 358–59 n. 83.

30. Cavell, "Shakespeare and Rohmer: Two Tales of Winter," in *Cities of Words*, 441.

31. Plato, *Five Dialogues*, trans. G.M.A. Grube (Indianapolis: Hackett, 1981), 110.

32. Cavell, "Finding as Founding: Taking Steps in Emerson's 'Experience,' " in *Emerson's Transcendental Etudes*, 126.

33. Emerson, "Self-Reliance," in *Essays and Poems*, 270. In "Being Odd, Getting Even," Cavell explores at length the complex matter of Emerson's "citation" of Descartes in "Self-Reliance." See Cavell, in *Emerson's Transcendental Etudes*, 83–109.

34. Emerson, "Self-Reliance," in *Essays and Poems*, 270: "The virtue in most request is conformity. Self-reliance is its aversion."

35. Cavell, "The Philosopher in American Life," in *Emerson's Transcendental Etudes*, 34. See chap. 4 of this book, 120–21.

36. Cavell, *Disowning Knowledge*, 220.

37. Cavell, "Emerson, Coleridge, Kant (Terms as Conditions)," in *Emerson's Transcendental Etudes*, 81.

38. Emerson, "Experience," in *Essays and Poems*, 483: "We thrive by casualties. Our chief experiences have been casual."

39. Felperin, " 'Tongue-Tied Our Queen?" in *Shakespeare and the Question of Theory*, 3–18. See Richard Strier's discussion of this essay in *Resistant Structures: Particularity, Radicalism, and Renaissance Texts* (Berkeley: University of California Press, 1995), 42–45.

40. Cavell, "Emerson, Coleridge, Kant (Terms as Conditions)," in *Emerson's Transcendental Etudes*, 82.

41. Walter Lim, "Knowledge and Belief in *The Winter's Tale*," SEL 41.2 (spring 2001): 317–34, 332 n. 4.

42. See Frye, *A Natural Perspective*, 116–17 for a pertinent passage.

43. Orgel, ed., William Shakespeare, *The Winter's Tale* (2.1.121 n.), 124.

44. Robert N. Watson, *Shakespeare and the Hazards of Ambition* (Cambridge: Harvard University Press, 1984), 255.

45. Cavell, *The Claim of Reason*, 481.

46. Inga-Stina Ewbank, "The Triumph of Time in *The Winter's Tale*," *Review of English Literature* 5 (1964): 83–100.

47. Emerson, "Experience," in *Essays and Poems*, 473.

48. See James Conant, "Nietzsche's Perfectionism," in *Nietzsche's Postmoralism: Essays on Nietzsche's Prelude to Philosophy's Future*, ed. Richard Schacht (New York: Cambridge University Press, 2001); and David Mikics, *The Romance of Individualism in Emerson and Nietzsche* (Athens, Ohio: Ohio University Press, 2003).

49. Emerson, "History," in *Essays and Poems*, 239. Cited in Cavell, *Pursuits of Happiness*, 5.

50. Marian Keane, *The Lady Eve*, produced by Paul Jones, written and directed by Preston Sturges, (Criterion Collection, 2001).

51. Cavell, *Contesting Tears*, 24.

52. Cavell, *Pursuits of Happiness*, 19.

53. Ibid., 31.

54. Ibid., 57.

55. See Naomi Scheman, "Missing Mothers/Desiring Daughters: Framing the Sight of Women," in *Engenderings: Constructions of Knowledge, Authority, and Privilege* (New York: Routledge, 1993), 126–52.

56. Maria DiBattista, *Fast-Talking Dames* (New Haven: Yale University Press, 2001), 24.

57. Ibid., 305.

58. Ibid., 300, 308.

59. Emerson, "Self-Reliance," in *Essays and Poems*, 262.

60. Ibid., 263.

61. DiBattista, *Fast-Talking Dames*, 87.

62. Ibid., 305.

63. Cavell, *Pursuits of Happiness*, 101.

64. Kelly Dean Jolley, "Wittgenstein and *Seinfeld* on the Commonplace," in *Seinfeld and Philosophy: A Book About Everything and Nothing*, ed. William Irwin (Chicago: Open Court, 2000), 115.

65. Emerson, "Experience," in *Essays and Poems*, 487.

66. Preston Sturges, *Five Screenplays by Preston Sturges*, ed. Brian Henderson (Berkeley: University of California Press, 1985), 426. I have silently altered punctuation and spelling in citations from this script to conform with the principles of punctuation and spelling in this book.

67. Sturges, *Five Screenplays*, 509.

68. See Scheman, "Missing Mothers/Desiring Daughters," in *Engenderings*, 149.

69. E. Ann Kaplan, review of *Contesting Tears*, by Stanley Cavell, *Film Quarterly* 52.1 (fall 1998): 77–81, 80.

70. See E. Ann Kaplan, "The Case of the Missing Mother," *Heresies* 16 (1983): 81–85.

71. Cavell, *Pursuits of Happiness*, 239. See Martin Luther, "The Pagan Servitude of the Church," in *Martin Luther: Selections from His Writings*, ed. John Dillenberger (Garden City, N.Y.: Anchor, 1961), 249–359, 303. Notably Cavell

cites this sentence from Luther in an early discussion of romanticism, an interest that will later coincide with his Emersonian perspective on remarriage comedy. See Stanley Cavell, *Must We Mean What We Say?* (Cambridge: Cambridge University Press, 1976), 229.

72. Cavell, "Aversive Thinking: Emersonian Representations in Heidegger and Nietzsche," in *Emerson's Transcendental Etudes*, 159.

73. Sturges, *Five Screenplays*, 419.

74. Walker Percy, *The Moviegoer* (New York: Knopf, 1961), 235. See the end of the next chapter for further discussion of this moment.

75. Of course, like all language, and perhaps even more so, this silence is subject to interpretation. Cf. Northrop Frye, "Shakespeare's Romances: *The Winter's Tale.*" *Northrop Frye on Shakespeare.* Ed. Robert Sandler (New Haven: Yale University Press, 1986) 154–70, 169: "In several comedies of Shakespeare, including this one [*The Winter's Tale*] and *The Tempest*, the action gets so hard to believe that a central character summons the rest of the cast into—I suppose— the green room afterward, where, it is promised, all the difficulties will be cleared away. Here it looks as though the green room session will be quite prolonged."

Notes to Chapter 6: Cavell's Rome

1. Stanley Cavell, "Emerson's Constitutional Amending," in *Emerson's Transcendental Etudes,* ed. David Justin Hodge (Stanford: Stanford University Press, 2003), 192–214, 207.

2. Stanley Cavell, "Responses," in *Contending with Stanley Cavell,* ed. Russell Goodman (Oxford: Oxford University Press, 2005), 157–76, 171.

3. Stanley Cavell, "What's the Use of Calling Emerson a Pragmatist?," in *Emerson's Transcendental Etudes,* 215–23.

4. Russell Goodman, "Cavell and American Philosophy," in *Contending with Stanley Cavell,* 100–117; John Albrecht, "What's the Use of Reading Emerson Pragmatically? The Example of William James" *Nineteenth-Century Prose* 30.1–2 (spring and fall 2003): 388–432.

5. Stanley Cavell, *Senses of Walden,* exp. ed. (San Francisco: North Point, 1981), 126.

6. Charles Taylor, *Philosophical Arguments* (Cambridge: Harvard University Press, 1995), 1–19.

7. In this regard see William Day, "*Moonstruck,* or How to Ruin Everything," *Philosophy and Literature* 19.2 (1995): 292–307, a reading along lines laid out by Emerson and Cavell. The Nicolas Cage character's passionate and persuasive acceptance of the fact that love ruins everything amounts to a compelling response to Tina Turner's question. Indeed one could argue that Turner and Ronny Cammareri (Cage) know the same thing about love and the heart, but

from different sides. There is also no insurmountable reason that they couldn't change sides.

8. Ralph Waldo Emerson, "Experience," "Self-Reliance," in *Emerson: Essays and Poems,* ed. Joel Porte, college ed. (New York: Library of America, 1996), 489, 269.

9. Lars Engle, *Shakespearean Pragmatism: Market of His Time* (Chicago: University of Chicago Press, 1993), 224.

10. Stanely Cavell, *Disowning Knowledge in Seven Plays of Shakespeare,* updated ed. (Cambridge: Cambridge University Press, 2003), 68.

11. Engle, *Shakespearean Pragmatism,* 223.

12. William Shakespeare, *Antony and Cleopatra,* ed. John Wilders, Arden Edition (New York: Routledge, 1995). All citations from *Antony and Cleopatra* refer to this edition.

13. Stanley Cavell, *Pursuits of Happiness: The Hollywood Comedy of Remarriage* (Cambridge: Harvard University Press, 1981) 272–73.

14. Cavell, *Disowning Knowledge,* 25.

15. Emerson, "Give All to Love," in *Essays and Poems,* 1123.

16. Cavell, *Disowning Knowledge,* 30.

17. Stanley Cavell, *Themes out of School: Effects and Causes* (San Francisco: North Point Press, 1984), 171.

18. On Cleopatra as a "paradoxical stoic" and Shakespeare's source for this view in Horace's ode, see Charles and Michelle Martindale, *Shakespeare and the Uses of Antiquity* (London: Routledge, 1990), 186–89.

19. Lawrence F. Rhu, "An American Philosopher at the Movies," *Double-Take* (spring 2001): 115–19.

20. Cavell, *Themes out of School,* 54.

21. Emerson, "Montaigne; or, the Skeptic," in *Essays and Poems,* 700.

22. Stanley Cavell, *The Claim of Reason: Wittgenstein, Skepticism, Morality, and Tragedy* (New York: Oxford University Press, 1979), 478.

23. Richard Rorty, *Truth and Progress* (New York: Cambridge University Press, 1998), 46–47.

24. Cavell, *Claim of Reason,* 111. Like Part 4, in which the *Othello* essay appears, this section of *Claim of Reason,* "The Normal and the Natural," does not appear in Cavell's dissertation, "The Claim to Rationality," which forms the major portion of *The Claim of Reason.* Thus, they probably both derive from the same later period of the writing, when Cavell was turning to Emerson and American movies, and continuing to write about Shakespeare.

25. Stanley Cavell, *Contesting Tears: The Hollywood Melodrama of the Unknown Woman* (Chicago: University of Chicago Press, 1996), 110.

26. Toril Moi, *What Is a Woman? and Other Essays* (Oxford; New York: Oxford University Press, 1999); Also see Moi, "From Femininity to Finitude: Freud, Lacan and Feminism, Again" *Signs: Journal of Women in Culture and Society* 29, no. 3 (spring 2004): 841–78, and Cavell's response to Rorty in Goodman, *Contending with Stanley Cavell.*

27. Cavell, "Being Odd, Getting Even (Descartes, Emerson, Poe)," in *Emerson's Transcendental Etudes,* 83–109, 86.

28. Erich Auerbach, *Mimesis: The Representation of Reality in Western Literature* (Princeton: Princeton University Press, 1953), 311.

29. Alasdair MacIntyre, "Epistemological Crises, Dramatic Narrative, and the Philosophy of Science," *The Monist* 60 (1977): 453–72; Charles Taylor, "Explanation and Practical Reason," *Philosophical Arguments,* 34–60.

30. Lars Engle, "*Measure for Measure* and Modernity: The Problem of the Skeptic's Authority," in *Shakespeare and Modernity: Early Modern to Millennium,* ed. Hugh Grady (New York: Routledge, 2000), 85–104, 88–89.

31. Ellen Spolsky, *Satisfying Skepticism: Embodied Knowledge in the Early Modern World* (Oxon, England: Ashgate Press, 2001), 13.

32. West cites this passage to just this effect. See Cornel West, *The American Evasion of Philosophy: A Genealogy of Pragmatism* (Madison, Wis.: University of Wisconsin Press, 1989), 243 n. 4.

33. Cavell, *Claim of Reason,* 20–25; idem, *Pursuits of Happiness,* 180–82; idem, *Contesting Tears,* 147.

34. Cavell, *Disowning Knowledge,* 167.

35. Ibid., 144, 156, 163.

36. Sir Philip Sidney, "The Defence of Poesy," in *Sir Philip Sidney,* ed. Katherine Duncan-Jones (Oxford: Oxford University Press, 1989), 228.

37. Emerson, "Montaigne; or, the Skeptic, in *Essays and Poems* 690–707, 691.

38. Cavell, *Disowning Knowledge,* 81.

39. Stanley Cavell, *This New yet Unapproachable America: Lectures after Emerson and Wittgenstein* (Albuquerque, N. Mex.: Living Batch, 1989), 114.

40. Barbara Packer, "Turning to Emerson," *Common Knowledge* 5.2 (fall 1996): 51–60, 59.

41. Engle, *Shakespearean Pragmatism,* 10. As Engle indicates the bracketed word is "struck" in the original, for which he provides "stuck" as a sensible alternative.

42. Emerson, "Self-Reliance," in *Essays and Poems,* 272, 268–69. I am grateful to Steven Affeldt for initially drawing my attention to these passages.

43. Cavell, *Disowning Knowledge,* 4.

44. Engle, *Shakespearean Pragmatism,* 12.

45. William Shakespeare, *The Tragedy of Coriolanus,* ed. R. B. Parker (Oxford: Oxford University Press, 1998).

46. Cavell, *Disowning Knowledge,* 98.

47. Michael Bristol, *Big-Time Shakespeare* (London; New York: Routledge, 1996), 198–99.

48. Stanley Cavell, *The World Viewed: Reflections on the Ontology of Film,* enl. ed. (Cambridge: Harvard University Press, 1979), 75.

49. William Rothman and Marian Keane, *Reading Cavell's* The World Viewed: *A Philosophical Perspective on Film* (Detroit: Wayne State University Press, 2000), 141.

50. The most recent versions of these writings appear in *Philosophy the Day after Tomorrow* (Cambridge: Belknap Press of Harvard University Press, 2005), 7–27, 61–110.

51. I am grateful to Robert Gooding-Williams for sharing with me a draft of his essay, "Aesthetics and Receptivity: Kant, Nietzsche, Cavell, and Astaire," which is to be published in *The Claim to Community: Essays on Stanley Cavell and Political Theory,* ed. Thomas Dumm and Andrew Norris (Stanford: Stanford University Press, 2006).

52. Gooding-Williams, "Aesthetics and Receptivity," in *Stanley Cavell and Political Theory,* 19.

53. Ibid., 24–25.

54. Stanley Cavell, *Cities of Words: Pedagogical Letters on a Register of the Moral Life* (Cambridge: Harvard University Press, 2004), 11–12.

55. Emerson, "Friendship," in *Essays and Poems,* 341–54, 351.

56. Michael Bristol, *Shakespeare's America, America's Shakespeare* (London; New York: Routledge, 1990), 196.

57. Stanley Cavell, *Conditions Handsome and Unhandsome: The Constitution of Emersonian Perfectionism* (Chicago: University of Chicago Press, 1990), 1; Thomas Dumm, *A Politics of the Ordinary* (New York: New York University Press, 1999), passim; Stephen Mulhall, *Stanley Cavell: Philosophy's Recounting of the Ordinary* (Oxford: Clarendon Press, 1994), 72. Dumm's book, in many ways, follows Cavell to demonstrate the usefulness of Emerson's thought for democratic political theory and thus sharply disagrees with the account of Emerson by John Wikse, Dumm's former mentor, an account very much in the spirit of Bristol's reading of Emerson and Cavell. See John Wikse, *About Possession: The Self as Private Property* (University Park: Pennsylvania State University Press, 1977). Hans von Rautenfeld's recent essays are a further contribution to this recuperation of Emerson for democratic political thought. See "Thinking for Thousands: Emerson's Theory of Political Representation in the Public Sphere," *American Journal of Political Science,* 41.1 (January 2005): 184–97; and "Charitable Interpretations: Emerson, Rawls, and Cavell on the Use of Public Reason," *Political Theory* 32.1 (February 2004): 61–84.

58. Cavell, "The Thought of Movies," in *Themes out of School,* 3–26, 22–23.

59. Friedrich Wilhelm Nietzsche, *Untimely Meditations,* trans. R. J. Hollingdale (Cambridge: Cambridge University Press, 1983), 135.

60. "City of words" is the phrase near the end of book 9 of Plato's *Republic* that Cavell adapts for his recent book's title, *Cities of Words.* See "Emerson's Constitutional Amending: Reading 'Fate,'" in *Emerson's Transcendental Etudes,* 206, for Cavell's invocation of this phrase with regard to the relevance of Emerson's philosophy to the politics of race and the issue of abolition in particular.

61. Cavell, *Emerson's Transcendental Etudes,* 194.

62. Cavell, *This New yet Unapproachable America,* 8.

63. Cavell, *The World Viewed,* x–xii.

64. Lawrence Buell, *Emerson* (Cambridge: Belknap Press of Harvard University Press, 2003); Stephen Mulhall, review of *Emerson's Transcendental Etudes,* ed. David Justin Hodge, *Times Literary Supplement,* 21 May 2004.

65. Emerson, "Self-Reliance," in *Essays and Poems,* 271.

66. Edward Rothstein, "Can Movies Teach Moral Philosophy?," review of *Cities of Words,* by Stanley Cavell, *The New York Times,* 29 May 2004, B9.

67. Emerson, "Self-Reliance," in *Essays and Poems,* 279.

68. Emerson, "Fate," in *Essays and Poems,* 769–94, 779.

69. Cavell, *Pursuits of Happiness,* 15.

70. Walker Percy, *The Moviegoer* (New York: Knopf, 1961), 235.

INDEX

Adam's Rib. See Cukor, George
Adelman, Janet, 9, 11, 137, 149, 190, 196
Affeldt, Steven, 204, 237n42
Agee, James, 199
Albercht, James, 173, 235n4
Alpers, Paul, 63
Aristotle, 181
Arnold, Matthew, "Dover Beach," 132
Astaire, Fred, 197–206, 207
    "By Myself," 199, 203
    "A Shine on Your Shoes," 199–200,
        203–4, 209
Auden, W. H., "The Shield of Achilles,"
    15
Auerbach, Eric, *Mimesis*, 188
Aurelius, Marcus, 19
Austin, J. L., 3, 42, 49, 60, 74–75, 78–79,
    87, 114, 138, 167
Awful Truth, The. See McCarey, Leo

Bacon, Sir Francis, 33–34, 194
Baker, George Pierce, 229n11
Band Wagon, The. See Minnelli, Vincente
Barry, Philip, 229n11
Beauvoir, Simone de, 212n26
Bellow, Saul, *Herzog*, 130–31
Berger, Henry, 216n42; *Making Trifles of
    Terrors*, 5
Bergman, Ingrid, 10
Berlin, Irving, 61
Bernstein, Charles, 32

Bible, 162
    Deuteronomy, 18
    Ephesians, 51
    Ezekiel, 50
    1 Corinthians, 155
    Genesis, 54, 120, 144, 152–55, 161–69
    Isaiah, 50, 52
    James, 156
    Jeremiah, 50
    Job, 156, 189, 196
    Matthew, 232n14
    2 Samuel, 80
Bishop, Elizabeth, 125
Bishop, T. G., *Shakespeare and the Theatre of
    Wonder*, 137, 232n17
Bloom, Harold, 49–50, 60–67, 71–76,
    79–82, 204
    The Anxiety of Influence, 81
    The Book of J, 80
    How to Read and Why, 65–67, 82
    Introduction to *Christopher Marlowe*, 80
    A Map of Misreading, 49, 74
    Poetics of Influence, 60, 71
    Ruin the Sacred Truths, 67, 80
    Shakespeare: The Invention of the Human,
        64–65, 67, 73, 76
    The Western Canon, 60, 66–68, 80
Boleyn, Ann, 161
Borradori, Giovanna, 124
Boyer, Charles, 10
Bradley, A. C., *Shakespearean Tragedy*, 190

Brando, Marlon, 41
Bringing Up Baby. See Hawks, Howard
Bristol, Michael
   Big-Time Shakespeare, 197
   Shakespeare's America, America's Shakespeare, 203
Browning, Robert, "Incident of the French Camp," 128
Bruckman, Clyde, *The General*, 13–14; 178
Bruster, Douglas, 219n79
Buell, Lawrence, *Emerson*, 206
Burckhardt, Jacob, *The Civilization of the Renaissance in Italy*, 75, 120

Cage, Nicolas, 235n7
Camus, Albert, 33
Cantor, Jay, 32, 105
Capra, Frank, 30, 44, 53
   It Happened One Night, 29, 46, 52–54, 116, 118, 166, 207–8
   Mr. Smith Goes to Washington, 205
Carroll, Leo G., 121
Carter, President Jimmy, 71
Carter, Stephen, 57
Cartesian skepticism, 84–86; 89–93, 105, 141–43, 187–88
Castiglione, Baldassare, *Il libro del cortegiano*, 84, 94, 100, 103–4
Cato the Younger, 182
Cavell, Stanley
   "Aversive Thinking," 1–2
   "The Avoidance of Love," 4–6, 17–18, 25, 33–34, 38, 48–49, 61, 64–65, 74–76, 120, 124, 138, 176, 183, 193, 200, 211n4
   "Being Odd, Getting Even," 44, 185–86, 233n33
   Cities of Words, 10, 44, 174, 211n7, 225n5
   The Claim of Reason, 32, 58–59, 102, 105, 138, 157, 160, 166, 174, 191–92, 198, 233n45
   "The Claim to Rationality," 236n24
   Conditions Handsome and Unhandsome, 67–71, 82, 88, 94, 97, 99, 161, 211n7

Contesting Tears, 10–12, 17–19, 34–37, 51, 65, 76–77, 162, 174, 183–84
Disowning Knowledge in Seven Plays of Shakespeare, 6, 24, 64–65, 84–87, 138, 140, 174, 211n4, 218n72
"Emerson, Coleridge, Kant," 153, 233n37 and n40
"Emerson's Constitutional Amending," 193–94, 204, 235n1
Emerson's Transcendental Etudes, 174
"Finding as Founding," 87–88, 90–91, 186, 193, 225n5
"Hamlet's Burden of Proof," 125–27, 230n48
"Hope Against Hope," 221n16
"The Importance of Importance," 57–58, 106–9, 112–17, 128–29, 133–34
In Quest of the Ordinary, 20, 138
"Knowing and Acknowledging," 8, 226n36
"Macbeth Appalled," 7–12, 104
"More of *The World Viewed*, 134
Must We Mean What We Say?, 31, 78, 108, 111, 138, 211n1
"Naughty Orators," 11–12
"North by Northwest," 118–35, 138
"Notes After Austin," 49–50, 74
"Nothing Goes without Saying," 224n76
"The Philosopher in American Life," 11–12, 62, 114–15, 152
Philosophy the Day After Tomorrow, 225n5
A Pitch of Philosophy, 58, 63, 81
"Praise as Identification," 48, 202
"Psychoanalysis and Cinema," 228n5
Pursuits of Happiness, 3, 26–30, 42, 45, 51–55, 57, 105–18, 144–45, 162–70, 174, 225n5
"Recounting Gains, Showing Loses," 136–46, 152
The Senses of Walden, 50–52, 205
"Skepticism as Iconoclasm," 48, 65
"Something Out of the Ordinary," 199, 230n47
Themes Out of School, 4, 13, 181

"Thinking of Emerson," 31–32, 129–30, 173

"The Thought of Movies," 31, 60–61, 110–12

"Two Tales of Winter," 4, 13, 148–51

"What's the Use of Calling Emerson a Pragmatist?" 172–73, 185

"The World as Things," 225n5

The World Viewed, 121, 145, 198, 205

Cervantes, Miguel de, *Don Quixote*, 23, 45

Chapman, Perry H., *Rembrandt's Self-Portraits*, 223n60

Charnes, Linda, 175, 232n8

Christian conservatives, 56–57

Cicero, *Academica*, 84

Colbert, Claudette, 29, 52–54, 118

Coleridge, Samuel Taylor, 129

Conant, James, 222n29, 234n48

Conte d'hiver. See Rohmer, Eric

Cooper, Merian C., and Schoedsack, Ernest, *King Kong*, 200

Cotton, Joseph, 12

Cowart, David, *Literary Symbiosis*, 100–1, 103

Cukor, George

    Adam's Rib, 18, 27

    Gaslight, 5, 10–12, 14–15

    The Philadelphia Story, 2–4, 27, 57–58, 106–17, 120–21, 124, 127–9, 133–34; 143–44, 205

Daniell, Henry, 112

Davidson, Arnold, "Beginning Cavell," 230n53

    The Senses of Stanley Cavell, 63

Davis, Bette, 17, 35–38

Day, William, 235n7

de Lauretis, Teresa, 37

Denby, David

    Great Books, 43, 48–49, 52–53, 58–59, 221n21

Derrida, Jacques, 49

Descartes, René, 33–34, 43–44, 76, 83–86, 89–93, 126–27, 138, 141, 143, 151, 159, 185, 187

    Meditations on First Philosophy, 13, 93, 108

DiBattista, Maria, *Fast-Talking Dames*, 163–66, 168, 214n46

Dumm, Thomas L.

    A Politics of the Ordinary, 231n23, 238n57

    Stanley Cavell and Political Theory, 238n51

Dunne, Irene, 117

Einstein, Albert, *The Universe as I See It*, 46

Eldridge, Richard, *Stanley Cavell*, 211n6

Eliot, T. S., "East Coker," 98

Elizabeth I, 161

Ellison, Ralph Waldo, 104

    Shadow and Act, 96

Emerson, Ralph Waldo, 7, 12, 30–32, 47, 50–51, 60–61, 67, 72, 76, 78, 83, 87–93, 95, 106, 110–15, 138, 164–68, 172–75, 183, 192–94, 197, 203, 212n19, 213n26 and n37, 225n5, 237n24, 238n57

    "The American Scholar," 21–22, 37, 42, 69, 82, 110, 232n14, 233n33

    "Circles," 174

    Emersonian perfectionism, 3, 67–71, 161, 179–80

    "Experience," 21, 38, 76, 83, 87, 90, 120, 129, 151, 153, 160, 186–89, 214n42

    "Fate," 10, 172, 194, 203–5

    "Friendship," 202

    "Give All to Love," 178–79

    "History," 9, 61, 66, 89, 99, 104, 135, 147

    "Montaigne; or, the Skeptic," 69, 89–90, 92

    "Prudence," 90–91

    "Self-Reliance," 1–2, 66, 70, 92, 95, 140, 150–52, 159–60, 166

    "Shakespeare; or, The Poet," 8, 66, 112

Empiricus, Sextus, *Outlines of Pyrrhonism*, 84

Empson, William, 138

Engle, Lars, *Shakespearean Pragmatism*, 173, 175–78, 180, 187–90, 219n75

Erasmus, Desiderius, 142; *Praise of Folly*, 31

INDEX

Erikson, Erik, 49, 101; *Childhood and Society*, 95

Fall of Man, 76, 119–20, 153–55
Faulkner, William, *Sound and the Fury, The*, 130
Felperin, Howard, 153, 232n17
Fischer, Michael
    Stanley Cavell and Literary Skepticism, 211n6, 212n18, 216n9, 219n75
Fish, Stanley
    Professional Correctness, 63
    "Why We Can't All Just Get Along," 56
Fitzgerald, F. Scott, *The Great Gatsby*, 63
Flaubert, Gustave, *Madame Bovary*, 23, 45
Fleming, Richard, *The Senses of Stanley Cavell*, 212n10, 220n6
Florio, John, 182
Follow the Fleet. See Sandrich, Mark
Fonda, Henry, 145, 167
Forster, E. M., *A Passage to India*, 21
Freud, Sigmund, 49, 125, 138, 168–69, 183–85, 225n5
    Three Essays on Sexuality, 108
Friedrich, Hugo, *Montaigne*, 225n12
Frost, Robert, 180, 186; "The Gift Outright," 7
Frye, Northrop, 27–28, 61, 106–7, 112
    A Natural Perspective, 137, 154, 138, 154
    Northrop Frye on Shakespeare, 235n75
    The Secular Scripture, 107

Gable, Clark, 29, 52–54, 118
Galileo, 34
Garber, Marjorie, 9, 11
Gaslight. See Cukor, George
Geertz, Clifford, 219n71
General, The. See Bruckman, Clyde *and* Keaton, Buster
Giamatti, Bart, 63
Goethe, Johann Wolfgang von, 90
Goodman, Russell, 173, 235n4
    Contending with Cavell, 173, 211n6, 236n26
Gould, Timothy, *Hearing Things*, 63, 211n6

Grant, Cary, 27–28, 55, 109–10, 114, 117, 119, 128–29, 131, 143–44
Greenblatt, Stephen, 6, 88, 95, 134–35
    Marvelous Possessions, 54
    Shakespearean Negotiations, 8–9, 11
Grube, G. M. A., 226n28, 233n31

Hall, Ronald, *The Human Embrace*, 216n48
Halliday, John, 229n11
Halpern, Richard, *Shakespeare Among the Moderns*, 6, 125, 223n55
Harvard Radcliffe, 228n8
Hawks, Howard
    Bringing Up Baby, 114, 117, 128
    His Girl Friday, 27–28, 191, 205
Hecht, Anthony, 84
    "A Birthday Poem," 96
    "The Dover Bitch," 132
    "Going the Rounds," 96–97, 103
    Millions of Strange Shadows, 96
Hegel, George Wilhelm Friedrich, 69, 91, 131, 175
Heidegger, Martin, 12, 33, 173, 178, 193–94
    Being and Time, 34
Heilbrun, Carolyn, 55; *Writing a Women's Life*, 27
Henreid, Paul, 17
Henry VIII, 55, 105, 134, 161
Hepburn, Katharine, 19, 109, 117, 128, 143–44
His Girl Friday. See Hawks, Howard
Hitchcock, Alfred, *North By Northwest*, 118–33
Hobbes, Thomas, 28–29
Hoffmann, E. T. A., 184
Hollander, John, 32, 220n2
Horace (Quintus Horatius Flaccus), 176–77, 180–82, 186
Howard, John, 109
Hume, David, 58, 127, 138
Hunt, Maurice, 137

Ibsen, Henrik, 76

James I, 161
Jameson, Frederic, *The Political Unconscious*, 219n73

Johnson, President Lyndon B., 65, 132
Johnson, Dr. Samuel, 17
Joughin, John, *Philosophical Shakespeares*, 6
Joyce, James, *Ulysses*, 130

Kael, Pauline, 230n51
Kalstone, David, *Sidney's Poetry*, 99
Kant, Immanuel, 18, 21, 30, 32, 42, 58,
    72, 81, 116, 127, 129, 149, 166,
    173, 193, 202, 207–8
    Foundations of the Metaphysics of Morals,
    52
Kaplan, Ann, 39–40, 168, 214n46, 223n55
Kaufmann, Stanley, 21
Kazan, Elia, *Panic in the Streets*, 44
Keane, Marian, 15–16, 161–62, 198
Keaton, Buster, *The General*, 13–14, 178
Kenny, Anthony, 32
Kierkegaard, Søren, 18, 20, 33, 41–43, 45
    Concluding Unscientific Postscript, 22
    Fear and Trembling, 22, 217n47
    The Present Age, 78–79
King Kong. See Cooper, Merian C. and
    Schoedsack, Ernest B.
Kittredge, George Lyman, 219n79,
    229n11
Kleist, Heinrich von, *The Marquise von
    O——*, 149
Klevan, Andrew, *Disclosure of the Everyday*,
    214n45
Kugel, James, *The God of Old*, 218n60

Landau, Martin, 119
Larkin, Philip
    "Continuing to Live," 184–85
    "Sad Steps," 84, 97–104, 181, 186
Lim, Walter, 154
Locke, John, 33–34
    Second Treatise of Government, 28–29,
    58–59, 219n81
Lowell, Robert, 132
Lupton, Julia Reinhard, *After Oedipus*,
    230n45
Luther, Martin, 55, 105, 134, 156, 176,
    181
    "The Pagan Servitude of the Church,"
    38–39, 116, 169, 234n71

Machiavelli, Niccolò, 176
MacIntyre, Alasdair, 188
Mack, Maynard, 65
Mallin, Eric S., 232n8
Marlowe, Christopher, 73, 80
Marsden, George, 57
Martindale, Charles and Michelle, *Shake-
    speare and the Uses of Antiquity*,
    236n18
Marx, Groucho, 61, 80
Mason, James, 119
Matthews, Gareth, 226n25
Matthiessen, F. O., 87
McCarey, Leo, *The Awful Truth*, 61, 117,
    225n5
Merleau-Ponty, Maurice, 33
Mikics, David, 234n48
Miller, David
    "Death's Afterword," 147
    Dreams of the Burning Child, 6, 137, 139,
    144, 225n11
Milton, John, 51–52, 80, 162
    The Doctrine and Discipline of Divorce, 10,
    15, 29, 53–54, 57–59, 108, 116,
    162
    Of Education, 52–53
    Paradise Lost, 53, 55–57
Minnelli, Vincente, *The Band Wagon*, 197–
    204, 207–9
Modleski, Tania, 6
Moi, Toril, 184, 212–13n26
Montaigne, Michel de, 2, 9, 69, 83, 85–86,
    187, 192
    "Apology for Raymond Sebond," 56–
    57, 84, 90
    "Of the Cannibals," 86
    "Of Cruelty," 176, 180, 182
    "Of the Education of Children," 53
    "Of Experience," 86–87, 89–92, 142
    "Of the Power of the Imagination," 86
    "Of Repentance," 223n60
    "Of Some Verses of Virgil," 86
    "To Philosophize Is to Learn How to
    Die," 87
Mothersill, Mary, 32
Mr. Smith Goes to Washington. See Capra,
    Frank

Mulhall, Stephen, 206
  Stanley Cavell: Philosophy's Recounting of the Ordinary, 211n6, 219n81, 238n57
Mullaney, Steven, 8
Myerowitz, Rael, 75

New Yorker, 48
New York Magazine, 52
Nietzsche, Friedrich, 33, 67, 78, 88–89, 99, 138, 161, 193, 207
  The Birth of Tragedy, 75–76, 120–21
  "On the Advantages and Disadvantages of History for Life," 225n11
  "Schopenhauer as Educator," 68–70
  Untimely Meditations, 147
Night at the Opera, A. See Wood, Sam
Night Before the Wedding, The (German title for *A Philadelphia Story*), 116
Norris, Andrew, *Stanley Cavell and Political Theory*, 238n51
North by Northwest. See Hitchcock, Alfred
Now, Voyager. See Rapper, Irving

O'Connor, Flannery, *Wise Blood*, 16
Oliver, Kelly, 206
Olivier, Laurence, 64
ordinary language philosophy, 3, 8–9, 42, 49, 60, 78, 87, 106, 114, 120, 135, 167, 184, 192, 201
Orgel, Stephen, 6, 136–37, 139, 155
Orwell, George, 98
Ovid, 103

Packer, Barbara, 193–94
Pagels, Elaine, *Adam, Eve, and the Serpent*, 162, 169
Panic in the Streets. See Kazan, Elia
Pascal, Blaise, 131, 150, 183; *Pensées*, 118
Paul, Saint, 51, 155
Payne, Michael, *The Senses of Stanley Cavell*, 212n10, 220n6
Percy, Walker, 2
  "From Facts to Fiction," 216n11
  The Last Gentleman, 19
  Letter to Stanley Kauffmann, 21
  "The Man on the Train," 216n16

The Moviegoer, 3, 5, 14–15, 19–23, 29, 32–34, 37, 39–48, 171, 208–9
  "Stoicism in the South," 214n57, 216n25
Petrarch, Francesco, 98–99, 103
Philadelphia Story, The. See Cukor, George. *See also The Night Before the Wedding* and *Scandalous Marriage*
Phillips, Adam, 38
Plato, 68–69, 83–84, 89, 96, 98, 108, 135, 147
  Phaedo, 150–51
  Republic, 94–95
  Symposium, 104
Plutarch, 180
Potter, Harry, 145

Rapper, Irving, *Now, Voyager*, 17, 34–38, 191
Rautenfeld, Hans von, 238n57
Rawls, John, *A Theory of Justice*, 68–70, 94–95, 99, 193
Reinhard, Kenneth, *After Oedipus*, 230n45
Renoir, Jean, *Rules of the Game*, 205
Rhu, Lawrence F.
  "An American Philosopher at the Movies," 216n31, 220n10, 224n67, 236n19
  The Genesis of Tasso's Narrative Theory, 217n51
Richardson, Ralph, 64, 73
Rodin Auguste, *The Thinker*, 114
Rohmer, Eric, *Conte d'hiver*, 138, 148–51
  The Marquise von O—, 149
Rorty, Richard, 189, 192–94
  Contingency, Irony, and Solidarity, 185–87
  Truth and Progress, 7, 183–86, 212n19
Rosenberg, David, *The Book of J*, 224n73
Rothman, William, 22, 198, 205
Rules of the Game. See Renoir, Jean
Ruskin, John, 98
Russell, Rosalind, 28

Sahlins, Marshall, *Islands of History*, 226n34
Saint, Eva Marie, 119
Sandrich, Mark, *Follow the Fleet*, 203
Santayana, George, 137

Sartre, Jean-Paul, *Nausea*, 21
Scandalous Marriage (Portuguese title for *A Philadelphia Story*), 116
Scheman, Naomi, 164, 168
Schoedsack, Ernest B., *King Kong*, 200
Sedley, David, 88, 92
Seinfeld, 166
Shakespeare, William
    Antony and Cleopatra, 81, 172–82, 188, 190, 195, 227n43
    As You Like It, 28
    Coriolanus, 86–87, 92, 190–91, 196–97
    Hamlet, 32, 80, 111, 114, 121–30, 132, 134–35, 137–38, 190, 197, 226n30
    Henry IV, 64
    King Lear, 4–6, 8, 17–18, 25, 48, 61–62, 65, 71–75, 82, 106, 108, 113, 115, 122–23, 133–34, 144
    Love's Labors Lost, 32
    Macbeth, 5, 7–12, 104, 175, 195–96
    The Merchant of Venice, 28, 164, 183, 226n26; *A Midsummer Night's Dream*, 28, 106, 112, 164
    Much Ado About Nothing, 142
    Othello, 3–4, 84–86, 90, 105–10, 112, 134, 138, 140–41, 157, 166, 174, 183, 193, 195, 197, 205
    Sonnet *53*, 96, 177
    Sonnet *151*, 96–97
    The Tempest, 106, 111, 146
    The Winter's Tale, 4, 6, 13, 28, 81, 85, 88, 106, 108, 112, 133, 136–63, 176, 183
Shakespearean tragedy, 5, 12–13, 25, 33, 79, 83, 85–86, 105, 108, 141, 186, 188–90, 192, 195
Shaw, George Bernard, 66
Shawcross, John T., *John Milton*, 219n74
Shine, Cathleen, 71
Shklar, Judith, 70; *Pursuits of Reason*, 222n37 and n38
Shumway, David, 214n46, 219n79
Sidney, Sir Philip, 94, 96
    Astrophil and Stella, 84, 97–103, 181, 186
    The Defence of Poesy, 99, 102, 191, 195
Smiley, Jane
    "Shakespeare in Iceland," 71, 79

A Thousand Acres, 65, 71–72, 79–80, 82
Socrates, 34, 73, 94, 104, 150, 167, 182
Spenser, Edmund, *Faerie Queene*, 151
Spolsky, Ellen, *Satisfying Skepticism*, 85, 189, 196
Stanwyck, Barbara, 17, 38, 77, 145, 164, 167
Stella Dallas. See Vidor, King
Stevens, Wallace
    "Esthétique du Mal," 100
    "The Sense of the Sleight-of-Hand Man," 20
Stevenson, Diane, 212n15
Stewart, Donald Ogden, 229n11
Stewart, Garret, 212n14
Stewart, James, 115, 144
stoicism, 5, 17–19, 37, 41, 180–82
Strier, Richard, *Resistant Structures*, 233n39
Sturges, Preston, *The Lady Eve*, 54, 118, 138–39, 144, 161–70

Tasso, Torquato, 90–91
Tate, Nahum, 71
Tayler, Edward, 48
Taylor, Charles
    The Ethics of Authenticity or *The Malaise of Modernity*, 33; *Philosophical Arguments*, 173, 237n29
Tillich, Paul, *The Courage to Be*, 214n48
Thoreau, Henry David, 2, 8, 12, 17, 32, 35, 41, 52, 76, 78, 87, 102, 110, 124, 138, 167, 173, 178
    Walden, 50–51, 66, 114–15
Tolson, Jay, *Pilgrim in the Ruin*, 40, 214n55, 215n63
Tolstoy, Leo, *War and Peace*, 46
Toulmin, Stephen, 187–88, 219n75
Tracy, Spencer, 18
Traub, Valerie, 137
Turner, Tina, 175

Updike, John, 203

Vermeule, Emily, 221n27
Vidor, King, *Stella Dallas*, 17, 61, 65, 76–77, 79, 82, 120, 206–7
Vietnam, 16, 65, 71, 132

Vigo, Jean, *L'Atalante*, 134
Virgil (Publius Vergilius Maro), 176

Watson, Robert N., *Shakespeare and the Hazards of Ambition*, 156
West, Cornel, 189–90, 204–5
   The American Evasion of Philosophy, 237n32
Wheeler, Richard, 5
Whittey, Dame May, 14
Wikse, John, *About Possession*, 238n57
Williams, Linda, *Home Is Where the Heart Is*, 223n64
Wittgenstein, Ludwig, 3, 8, 12, 33, 42, 81, 87, 114, 116–17, 138, 173

   Philosophical Investigations, 60, 140, 166
Wood, James, 231n57
Wood, Michael, 123
Wood, Sam, *A Night at the Opera*, 61, 81
Wordsworth, William, 6, 59, 103, 138, 158
Wyatt, Sir Thomas, 98

Young, Roland, 229n11

Žižek, Slavoj, *Enjoy Your Sympton! Jacques Lacan in Hollywood and Out*, 35–36, 42